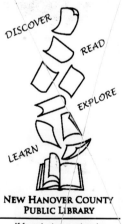

Crash Lane News

CrashLaneNews.com

authorHOUSE®

AuthorHouse™
1663 Liberty Drive
Bloomington, IN 47403
www.authorhouse.com
Phone: 1-800-839-8640

Published by AuthorHouse 01/30/2015

ISBN: 978-1-4969-0831-5 (sc)
ISBN: 978-1-4969-0830-8 (hc)
ISBN: 978-1-4969-0832-2 (e)

Library of Congress Control Number: 2014913186

Contents

1

A Traveler Should Know
Who Controls the News

A traveler should know the government of the country he or she is traveling in and how the companies that lobbied that government into office want it to function. The government will try to protect its supporters and lobbyists. This can include passing laws that will protect those supporters while amending laws that might threaten them. The news releases from the public relations office in the government may offer a limited version of what occurred to protect the government and its friends.

There is an entire public relations operation controlling the amount of news being released by each company and government. Most government news releases do not focus on the bad but on new programs and technologies that promise improvements. It is the private news industry that has the ability to sometimes build a story when the government fails to release information. This can lead to investigations of an incident by an oversight committee or other kind of inspection through the inspector general.

The president of the United States and the U.S. Congress control the news significantly when it comes to foreign policy issues and issues surrounding everyday life in America. Large corporations that lobby the government will also convey information in a news release, which influences the news even more than the government. Companies can alter the truth of safety news that goes out to the public.

This is where *Crash Lane News* comes in. It is an alternative source of accident news. If you are driving and realize your lane on the interstate or street is stopped, you can wait it out or try to get out while you can. Many drivers do not want to wait for someone else's accident to get investigated and cleaned up, and so they change out of the crash lane. *Crash Lane News* covers issues the regular media swerve around as they make no effort to discover the real story.

There is a level of false reporting that exists due to the major news media controlling what is reported. False reporting protects the existing government from becoming irrelevant. False reporting protects businesses from becoming safety and security violators. As false reporting controls the news media, false reporting controls the world.

A traveler should know that news releases can sometimes mislead the public into thinking things are getting safer. In the category of "color of law" violations, this could represent a "failure to keep from harm" violation on the part of the government if a report ends up causing injury and death because the public believed something to be safe. Another issue is the fact that manipulation of safety data released by governments and companies may cover up the reality of dangers.

One example is the traffic violations and accidents caused by commercial truck drivers. Many members of the public have fears regarding the safety of trucks on the highway. The Federal Motor Carriers Security Administration (FMCSA) is a Department of Transportation program. The FMCSA is designed to control and release safety data to the public, hoping to increase awareness of unsafe driving issues related to commercial motor vehicles. Trucking companies have had their safety information posted online on the FMCSA website for a few years, and the data are presented as showing a reduction in accidents and fatalities.

With all the good the government and large companies appear to be doing with the FMCSA, there is an issue of why things get reported and released to the public the way they do. Unfortunately, the strategy of focusing on the trucking side means that safety at the warehouse and the responsibility shipping and receiving companies bear in the violations and accidents are not mentioned by the FMCSA. There are other causes to the accidents and violations than what is mentioned by the FMCSA. Currently, the commercial trucking industry is broken down by the FMCSA with a focus on the physical act of trucking not being safe, forgetting to mention the problems of management. The company rating is as close as the FMCSA gets to the trucking companies' involvement, but it does not mention management to be the cause of the poor ratings. The data the FMCSA presents are on a violation's citation. They leave out the example of an accident being caused by the weather or management. Even though there is this company rating, the FMCSA shows the accident to have only been caused by the driver, being that they do not rate the dispatchers and the trucking companies' supervisors.

The death rate is also something the regular news does not really focus on. The number of trucking issues is also relatively small compared to the death rate from health problems, violent crime, property crime, and disasters. Yet this FMCSA website goes into detail on accidents and violations. It can cause confusion as to what is most important. With the example of the FMCSA, the government seems to be suggesting that traffic violations and accidents are more important and more in need of detailed examination than healthcare, violent crime, property crime, and disasters.

Most of the public would appreciate a government website that rates healthcare with a focus on increasing the quality and length of life. Most of the public would also like to know the details of violent crime and property crime areas and other circumstances. The public would like to know where the color-of-law-violating law enforcement officers are so they can avoid becoming a victim of misconduct. Most of the public would like to know more about how to prevent damage from a disaster and ways to avoid a disaster. Most of the public does not get this information through the news media in any simple form.

News about the government is spread out and very limited at times. Some of the government agencies that provide information to the public include the Department of Health, the Food and Drug Administration (FDA), the Department of Homeland Security (DHS), the Department of Justice, the Federal Bureau of Investigation (FBI), and the Department of Defense.

This book contains some lessons learned from traveling in the weather as well, including interviews with personnel from the National Oceanic Atmospheric Administration (NOAA), also known as the National Weather Service. NOAA is a part of the Department of Commerce, which also has some information available to the public online. Note that one of the issues presented about FMCSA is that some of the causes of accidents are never made public. There are many violations publicized in which the driver did something wrong, but when you take a step back, there may be other issues on the management end of a driver's company that resulted in accidents. Other accidents may result from the absence of an updated law enforcement system.

Most law enforcement agencies work with weather information, and are the first eyewitnesses as to what kind of accidents occur as a result of the weather. Unfortunately, it is also a challenge for law enforcement to keep the public safe by not being everywhere in a storm system. Another continuing problem is law enforcement and the Department of Transportation's lack of road closures during severe weather. The solution is that the public needs the government to be available at the right time, helping to prevent accidents. Many times, this issue does not come back as a failure of law enforcement to keep a traveler from a harmful situation, so the strategy to make the needed changes does not get funded or become an updated part of how things are done. For the most part, the public is more informed than ever by law enforcement and NOAA, but questions remain.

The graphic of the blooming into disaster meter on the front cover is a good example of some of the issues that affect travelers that may go unnoticed by the news agencies because of the political issues or the ability of a challenged investigative reporter. The managers of news agencies sometimes make decisions to limit reporting that would tarnish local area businesses and provoke lawsuits. Some things that affect everyone do go unreported—for example, issues with healthcare. Large industries can sometimes limit and silence a news story, which is another important thing to be aware of.

According to the FMCSA, most accidents are caused by unsafe driving. But when the same logic is applied to other vehicles and types of travel, the reality of how the weather is a danger sometimes is forgotten. The interviews and the discussions with NOAA summarize some suggestions for travelers that may add to their knowledge of how to be safe.

The attempt to make a news report based on the weather information available through NOAA is a continuing theme in this book. The information about the weather and how to learn more about it is one of the more important areas of focus. Travelers should know that news agencies are going to have a weather reporter as well as a weather page that can help them know about hazardous conditions when traveling. Also note that there is a great deal of information on government websites that is worth searching out. Ways to find that information and learn from it are included in this book.

Unfortunately, there are some things that are not as transparent and not available on the Internet and to the public as a result of a lack of government accountability and oversight. Some of those are issues for an inspector general to deal with; in other cases, the authorities employ a strategy of learning what hazards exist for a location in order to keep them from becoming an issue. It's worth remembering that often what is available to the public is what has been reported in the news media. A traveler should watch the news, because it offers a point of view on which issues the news agency has chosen to focus on.

Some of the information made public by the government regarding travel may not include the entire story. Many in the United States feel as though their freedom to travel has become restricted as a result of violations to their constitutional rights. One example is that there are many safety violations that can be handed down by law enforcement. The public did not vote directly on these laws, but their representatives did, which is the basis for an interesting discussion of how freedom and democracy can be defined. It is not the intention of this book to badmouth the government that is in place now or in the future, just to make clear that there are many opinions about traveling and the issues of why things are the way they are. Another example is how some of the larger and better-financed groups can end up working with the government in a way that benefits them more. This is also something to be aware of, because it can affect which news is reported.

The reason behind a particular news story is not always obvious. Some decisions are made behind the scenes that determine how the public receives the news. Politics is sometimes a motivation for a story about an issue, and a news agency will not always reveal what political concerns are a factor in the way a news report is created and planned. There is a complex maze of available information that can help a traveler learn about an area, but remember, the level of transparency can vary.

Crash Lane News shares information about some areas through real-world experience and professional discussions of security and safety. The topics of organizational security and management focus on ways to manage security that travelers can supply to their own needs to make a plan on how to be safe and secure. Many travelers rely on businesses to plan their trip but should know the security management strategies these companies rely on. A traveler can build a substantial list of areas to remember and plan to visit on a trip. After reading this book, travelers will have advice they can use to be more safe and secure.

This book was written in the United States of America, and it is for U.S. citizens who travel. A reader should keep an open mind when reading this book, knowing that it may contain some errors and some information that is out of date. The main intention is to discuss serious issues at a simplified and understandable level. Travel safely.

Property of *Crash Lane News*

2

Meaning and Language

The translation of the title *Crash Lane News* into different languages results in some variations and loses some of the original meaning. Many of the foreign names that follow do translate back to *Crash Lane News*. In some languages, though, the words are changed or modified to, for example, *Accident Lane News* or *Crash Road News* or *Accident Road News*. The meaning may get lost along the way.

Some languages do not have a direct translation for *crash* and *lane*. It's interesting that a language would not have a word for *lane* even though most countries do have some multilane roads. When there are a limited number of roads, the lack of lanes can cause delays when there is no traffic control. A road without multiple lanes is not always a bad thing, as long as there is a way to be safe and secure. For example, some remote or rural areas may have a single-lane road. Most states in the United States have multilane roads, and there is one single language being used, so it's easy to communicate when there is an accident in a lane.

Travelers should understand that language varies over time, and some phrases are going to be misunderstood or totally confusing. A traveler should also know that languages vary, and being able to describe things accurately or learn about safety situations beforehand by knowing the language is an important addition to a safety plan. Being able to communicate to others while traveling about hazards that may affect a route ahead has a major impact on whether a trip will be safe.

The word *news* in the title *Crash Lane News* is also meaningful, part of my attempt to write about how to be safe with a catchy title that makes it clear there will be news coverage of crashes. The *lane* part is supposed to mean that many travelers have been in the crash lane. Travelers usually see the crash up ahead and get delayed. Travelers may also unfortunately end up being involved in the crash itself. This book is an attempt to give a traveler advice on how not to become involved in a crash. The main objective is to express the importance of watching the weather and traffic density when a trip is routed. Know that transportation accidents are caused by severe weather.

As a result of this awareness, travelers will learn from the existing public crash statistics, know more about what is available to help them drive safely, and avoid any involvement in a crash in the future.

One of the main pieces of advice suggested by the title *Crash Lane News* is that when travelers have more options and information from the news about where they are, it can help them to plan for their trip to be as safe as possible. For example, a traveler who knows what to do and what kind of unsafe driving conditions are out there can make a plan to avoid them ahead of time. The Department of Motor Vehicles and law enforcement do not always mention all the different violations in a neat list greatest to least. Other than some public information available through the National Highway Traffic Safety Administration, the government is not that transparent and does not show regular updates in real time about what it enforces.

What has been posted by the FMCSA regarding ratings has been considered by them to be transparent. When some government departments do mention the accident rates and other information like violations, as the National Highway Traffic Safety Administration does, the traveling public can learn about them and know what to avoid. Other suggestions and many examples of information are included in this book. Also the opinion on how transportation is being managed is included along with some failures and suggested solutions.

There are other reasons why these title words were chosen. One was that many news agencies share stories or seem to print the exact same story on the front page. This is interesting for travelers to know about in that there will be some variations in the way the story is covered. The local news in the region may have some strategies designed to hold on to advertisers. Newspapers want people to read and be their customers, so certain things may end up getting reported on more. Sometimes important stories do not get put out there.

Thanks to the Internet, there are more ways available to get helpful news, including friends on social media and looking up the different websites of news agencies around the world. You'll need the right language to help you describe an area. Even in the United States, there are some variations in the words used to describe traffic, the weather, and other safety issues. The language is mostly English, but there are also street and city names that are from the Bible. In addition there are street and city names used in the United States originating from foreign languages like Czech, Dutch (Netherlands), French (France), German (Germany), Italian (Italy), Native American, Polish (Poland), Spanish (Spain, Mexico, Central and South America), and many other languages. Some local and state regions may have variations of American English for street signs that can be confusing. The English language is complex, and that's apparent when looking at travel directions in the United States. Communication is vital to a traveler, and without it there are unsafe hazards.

Note that there are hundreds of different languages in the world, and not all are publicly mentioned in the news. In the US major metro areas, there are hundreds of different languages spoken. Knowing where a language is spoken in the United States can give a traveler a useful language map. Most areas and routes in the United States are considered English speaking.

3

Introduction to CrashLaneNews.com

CrashLaneNews.com is the advertising and promotional website for the book, and it includes a detailed introduction to the book's content. This chapter shares specific sections that were online as of January 2014.

A website makes a book more interactive for readers. Maps and spreadsheets can be made available to download for free, and readers can find updates on issues discussed in the book that change after the book is printed. They can also make suggestions for editing and for adding ideas for future stories as well as submit their own reports. You can suggest additions to the website by contacting crashlanenews777@gmail.com. Just read the book and then send a request with your own story about how to travel safe, and a page will be added online at *crashlanenews.com*.

Note that websites have become one of the leading ways to advertise among most businesses. Social media is also a cheap way to spread the word, and you may be able to link up with more people because of the ease of use.

Crash Lane News

This section is available online at http://www.crashlanenews.com/Home. html.

Crash Lane News is a self-help book. Travelers who are new or experienced in how to travel safely and securely can include this book in their plans. A traveler can make a comprehensive security plan using current safety and security data referenced directly from the government. This plan is for drivers, passengers, bicyclists, pedestrians, and those using other methods of travel.

Anyone who wants to travel more safely should purchase and read this self-help book. The objectives and content are based on current federal, state, and local public safety laws. There are also some professional suggestions about personal security procedures for a trip. The book's main focus is on how to travel safely while taking advantage of current examples of safety data. These travel suggestions can help a traveler avoid accidents, and there are also prevention plans to instruct readers on how to avoid driving violations, prevent violent crime, and avoid financial loss from property crime.

A sample safety objective is knowing a location's risk level, possible threats, and traffic information. This information touches on many areas of security and safety, and can be valuable in finding out what to expect while on a trip. A detailed risk assessment as outlined in this book can help you avoid traveling to or around dangerous areas. Additional safety information and a traveler's code of ethics are offered to make your trip more safe and secure.

Crash Lane News also includes tips on preparedness for, prevention of, response to, and recovery from a number of different disasters. Travelers can be exposed to all four seasons of weather and should have a plan for dealing with the disasters weather can cause. Travelers should make a goal of reading this book and using its information for their own travel security plan.

The objective of the comprehensive security plan will be to enable a traveler to build on his or her own safety and understanding. This understanding will be increased by considering examples of possible threats and strategizing ways to prevent accidents. A review of accident statistics and data released by federal government agencies for public viewing is included, covering cars, trucks, pedestrians, motorcycles, and bicyclists.

The comprehensive security plan also includes budget information. The government's security budget and security objectives should be known to all travelers. For example, the DHS is mentioned so that travelers will know how the government's security budget can affect their own life and trip. The government's budgeted safety and security plan affects a traveler's own safety and security, and government objectives should be a foundation in a traveler's own comprehensive plan. Travelers who are planning their own personal budgets should know there is also a government budget in place and proportion their own budget to the risk and threat. A smart budget can manage security effectively.

There are many helpful plans in this book that are currently the subject of discussion at the college and professional level. The information in *Crash Lane News* can be applied to real-life situations and make a difference in safety, leading to a better-planned trip.

About Writing *Crash Lane News*

This section is available online at http://www.crashlanenews.com/About. html.

The book *Crash Lane News* is based on college papers related to a degree in Organizational Security and Management. This is a bachelor of science degree from the University of Phoenix Online. The papers were later edited to focus on how organizational security and management topics can become a traveler's security plan. There is a difference between travel security and organizational security, and this book builds a connecting route between the two sides.

New sections added for the book include information from the National Highway Traffic Safety Administration (NHTSA), Federal Emergency Management Agency (FEMA), Federal Motor Carriers Safety Administration (FMCSA), Department of Transportation (DOT), and many more government agencies. Accident, violation, and disaster rates have been included. A plan to prevent and control these rates along with updated information is included as well.

Crash Lane News combines security strategies and plans to benefit a traveler. This can bring awareness and improve safety for the reader and others around him or her on a trip. A full explanation of travel tips and strategies will be covered in *Crash Lane News*. Some of the graphics, including the vehicle, disaster, and other meters, were developed by the *Crash Lane News* website development team. The graphics are a reflection of some of the issues and scenarios mentioned in the book. The graphics are intended to promote the need to travel safely and securely.

This book is being self-published. It is also being edited, electronically copyrighted, and made available as an e-book through AuthorHouse. AuthorHouse has 60,000 titles. Its website address is *http://www. authorhouse.com*, and its online bookstore is at *http://bookstore. authorhouse.com/*. The contact for information about the book or website is crashlanenews777@gmail.com.

Vehicle Inspection

This section is available online at http://www.crashlanenews.com/Vehicle-Inspection.html.

Every driver should have a vehicle-inspection plan and checklist. Permits, licenses, and proof of insurance should be checked prior to departure. The status of a route's condition should also be checked for existing threats. The local weather can be checked through local news stations and websites like *www.noaa.gov*. Also, check the *www.fema.gov* website to know if there is a disaster area near the route or that the route will pass through. There should be inspections or research into an area's traffic density before a trip. Traffic-alert websites and mobile applications can give a driver more to expect and be aware of.

Vehicle inspections should be conducted daily and can be listed in a log book. Some additional information to log includes a vehicle's mileage, hours, location, service schedule, and accident history. A vehicle's maintenance and performance can help to summarize the current operating status. Inspections should check for maintenance faults and mechanical failure. Inspections can prevent a maintenance issue that results in a broken-down vehicle.

A safety plan can keep your trip from being threatened when your vehicle becomes a target. The plan should use inspections to identify signs of sabotage that can disrupt the safety of the vehicle and cargo or have an impact on the trip. The possibility exists that a vehicle might be tampered with in order to cause a later accident. Something to do before every trip is a walk-around inspection of a vehicle. An external vehicle inspection can focus on the vehicle's lights, including headlights and warning flashers. Another important step is to check the tires for low air pressure or damage that would require replacement to prevent tire failure while driving.

After an external inspection is complete, an in-vehicle inspection of the vehicle's performance should be conducted. A brake check can be done on almost every type of vehicle. While en route, an inspection can be done every two hours or at every rest stop. Travelers should make a list of external and internal things to check before and during a trip for their own personal preferences and what they think is the most important. *Crash Lane News* recommends following the regulations of what is required on a vehicle according to the local, state, and federal law.

Travelers' Rights

This section is available online at http://www.crashlanenews.com/Travelers-Rights.html.

Travelers' rights are include the U.S. Constitution, state constitutions, county law, city law, and local law. U.S. citizens' rights come directly from the U.S. Constitution. One list of a U.S. citizen's travel rights is the protection from "color of law" violations. A section of the book *Crash Lane News* covers a discussion of "color of law" violations.

Misconduct can make travelers uneasy and suspicious of the government, but there are agencies that conduct internal investigations. The FBI lists the areas of misconduct it investigates. The FBI investigates misconduct and "color of law" violations including excessive force, sexual assaults, false arrest, fabrication of evidence, deprivation of property, and failure to keep from harm. A traveler can make a plan on how to avoid being a victim of "color of law" violations.

Travel Behavior

This section is available online at http://www.crashlanenews.com/Travel-Behavior.html.

Crash Lane News recommends that a traveler should have a plan to be safe and secure for each type of vehicle. A behavior and management plan for travelers can prevent threats, attacks, and panic, as well as potential injury from these three issues. Those traveling by car, truck, bus, bicycle, train, airline, or on foot can develop their own preparedness plans. Preparation can be useful for avoiding accidents and disasters. The behavior of a traveler should also be part of the preparedness plan, starting before the trip and continuing on after the trip is over.

Good behavior that will keep a traveler prepared includes insurance for some of the different disasters that could occur as a result of the weather, natural disasters, and manmade disasters. Developing and acquiring supplies and materials is also a part of preparation. Preparation and planning should allow for the best possible management of a disaster. An individual's ability to manage and control himself or herself when near and in the middle of a disaster will allow for maximum success.

Behavior is usually not something the average person thinks to survey before going on a trip, but it can affect the decisions that guide travelers through difficult routes and dangerous events. A person's behavior is an automatic reaction in almost every situation, and when there is some additional knowledge, that reaction can be more thorough as to what kind of preparedness is possible. When travelers are conscious and aware of their own behavior and the behavior of those around them, that behavior can be modified to increase productivity in some areas. Travelers can be more aware of how they act and use that knowledge to find the safest way to travel.

The traveling strategy described in *Crash Lane News* is that the ability of travelers to watch themselves is going to protect them more. Travelers will know more about their surroundings, and that will affect them as individuals. The use of existing government laws can improve a traveler's own security and safety. An awareness of what is going on allows a traveler be more open, adding improvements to every trip. A traveler should make a list of behaviors that may cause an unsafe situation. Examples of such behaviors are in red boxes on the web page at *www.crashlanenews.com/Dashboard.html*. A traveler should plan to avoid things on his or her own unsafe-behavior list.

Vehicle Meter

This section is available online at http://www.crashlanenews.com/Travel-Behavior.html.

If you will be traveling as a driver or a passenger in cars, trucks, buses, and unknown vehicles, look into the statistics on fatalities and injuries in the country you will be journeying in. The National Highway Traffic Safety Administration, www.NHTSA.gov, has released its data to raise public awareness of these statistics. The NHTSA website has information available to the public that can be useful when applied to their trip. A traveler can study statistics to choose the safest way to travel, be aware of the risk of certain types of travel, and have more of a reason to be cautious while on a trip.

NHTSA's statement on its 2002 to 2011 fact sheet mentions where the information that makes up those statistics came from. The fact sheet states:

> This overview fact sheet contains statistics on motor vehicle fatalities based on data from the Fatality Analysis Reporting System (FARS). FARS is a census of fatal crashes in the 50 States, the District of Columbia, and Puerto Rico (although Puerto Rico is not included in U.S. totals). Crash and injury statistics are based on data from the National Automotive Sampling System General Estimates System (GES). GES is a probability-based sample of police-reported crashes, from 60 locations across the country, from which estimates of national totals for injury and property-damage-only crashes are derived.

The NHTSA describes fatalities and injuries in accidents from different forms of travel to include pedacyclists, pedestrians, cars, pickups, commercial vehicles, and motorcycles. This all relates to travel behavior and other aspects of knowing what accident information exists about different types of travel on the road. Note the NHTSA states that driving under adverse weather conditions is a problem and one example is an interactive they have available about the winter weather online, http://www.safercar.gov/WinterDrivingTips.

Health

This page is available online at http://www.crashlanenews.com/Driver-Health.html.

Crash Lane News has researched, tested, and developed an easy list of ways to prevent unsafe driving, decrease driver impairment, increase driver awareness, inspect vehicle maintenance, monitor and increase driver health, and protect a driver's crash and violation record. Drivers have weaknesses that can ruin their trip, and a plan to evaluate, mitigate, and prevent these is outlined in this book. The following is a summary of what is in the book and explains the graphic of the crash meter on the CrashLaneNews.com home page. The descriptions here are also based on government safety websites that cover many safety suggestions.

MPH

MPH is at the bottom of the meter to represent that safety issues like the ones mentioned can occur while driving. When traveling by car and similar forms of transportation, regular concerns can become more life-threatening. MPH also represents that a trip is not something that exists on a piece of paper. For example, a travel itinerary does have the dates and locations of a trip, but what about everything else? A trip exists over multiple locations, distances, and times, and moves through obstacles. Travelers have to do research for their own safety beyond a single itinerary. This research requires details, history, theory, statistics, weather reports, and additional information that can be found in *Crash Lane News.*

Unsafe Driving

The icon of the truck tipping over symbolizes unsafe driving. The symbol can also represent unsafe conditions in other forms of travel, including taking the train, flying, walking, motorcycling, and bicycling. There are many forms of travel that can become unsafe. Unsafe driving includes a long list of violations: speeding, failure to use a seat belt, failure to follow a traffic-control device, reckless driving, driving while under the influence of alcohol/drugs, and more. This meter can bring awareness to unsafe driving.

Driver Impairment

The icon of the bottle symbolizes a driver's impairment from controlled substances, alcohol, and illegal drugs. There is mention by the NHTSA that alcohol is a cause of some vehicle crashes. Not drinking while driving is a way to prevent this safety issue. Many accident studies mention the rate of drunk drivers. A traveler should know that drunk driving is something that is not accepted and is enforced by law. There are additional ways a driver can be impaired, through prescription medications and illegal drug use. A traveler should know the risk of operating a motor vehicle while impaired.

Driver Awareness

The icon of the cloud with ZZZ symbolizes the importance of a driver being awake and aware. This refers to a driver's ability to drive rested. A rested driver or passenger is able to travel safely and pay more attention to the traffic and hazards. A driver or passenger who is awake will be able to avoid accidents. Being awake will also give travelers the opportunity to learn and remember additional safety concerns. Drowsy drivers can be a threat to themselves, and drowsy driving through bad weather conditions or a disaster can cause an accident or violation to occur. One simple suggestion is to pull over and take a break at a rest area or other safe place off the road.

Vehicle Maintenance

The icon of the screwdriver and wrench represents a driver's vehicle maintenance record. Vehicle inspections are a large part of being able to drive safely. Some routine maintenance can prevent crashes. Oil changes, for example, keep the engine moving and prevents a stalled vehicle on a busy interstate. Brake checks can improve stopping distance, and light checks can prevent failed brake lights or turn signals.

Driver Health

The icon of the man jumping rope represents a driver's fitness. A driver's physical health can cause safety concerns on a trip. Examples include cardiovascular issues, such as heart attacks; cholesterol levels; diagnosed diseases like HIV, hepatitis, rashes, and cancers; breathing problems, such as asthma; vision capabilities, perhaps caused by incorrect eyeglass prescriptions or no vision tests; and mental health, including hallucinations and attention deficit disorder. A traveler with a health concern should speak to his or her doctor or nurse about how to improve health problems before a trip. Travelers should consider whether their own health is going to cause driving and traveling problems on their trip. A plan to deal with an issue ahead of time can prevent an accident.

Accident Record

The icon of the crash symbol represents vehicles crashing while on a trip, whether into other vehicles or stationary objects like the curb, lane dividers, and parked traffic. The number of crashes and types of crashes can explain what kind of driver a person is, and this driving record is usually monitored by insurance companies and the state Department of Motor Vehicles. The type and amount of crashes lead to someone being considered safe or unsafe. The data the government collects about accidents can also become part of a traveler's plan on how to drive and choose a particular way to travel.

Security

This page is available online at http://www.crashlanenews.com/Travel-Security.html.

Crash Lane News includes a plan travelers can use for their own physical security, personal security, and information security. These areas of security can be necessary to complete a trip. They can also be helpful while traveling in the event a threat occurs. An individual's awareness of the government's DHS mission can be part of his or her own travel plan. Homeland Security uses physical, personal, and information security to protect many areas of the United States. A traveler who knows how to follow the government's current travel procedures in advance will be more likely to have a safe and incident-free trip.

A traveler should also know that both security agencies and organizations he or she may be a customer of when on a trip enforce the law. This is done to protect employees, property, and the traveling public. Individuals traveling should also consider the physical security of some businesses they are a customer of as part of their own plan and for their own trip's safety. The ability to follow a travel plan while also making the current area's security a priority will decrease the risk of becoming part of a possible incident.

A traveler's security plan should also follow a predetermined outline of a budget. This is good to have in order to know what type of security is available and in what location it is used. When in an area where businesses have a low budget for security or no security, try to either invest in some temporarily or make a simple security plan, which is better than nothing. Travelers constantly on the move may become caught off guard if they are not paying attention to security procedures during every trip. Be aware of the hourly, daily, weekly, monthly, and yearly importance of following security procedures. Anticipating security procedures can also help to prevent travel delays and keep a trip from being terminated and canceled should an incident develop.

Travelers should also make a list of areas they need secured before going on a trip and then plan some route security. The goal of all this is to have a trip that avoids areas in which security might be threatened.

Dashboard

Check out the dashboard on the *Crash Lane News* site at *www.crashlanenews. com/Dashboard.html*. There are tables containing data about crashes and unsafe driving violations for commercial motor carriers. You can click to enlarge the image or to download a free Excel spreadsheet file that you can sort and save. Feel free to add your own company, a competitor, and your car into the table and find your rank among over two hundred commercial motor carriers. This is a good example of what travelers can make for themselves by gathering information about other possible risks in addition to the ones mentioned.

These spreadsheets communicate some of the current safety and security issues in the transportation industry. The information is from the FMCSA and the Department of Transportation. The data is from the FMCSA accidents and violations about commercial motor carriers in the United States from 2010 to 2012, from www.fmcsa.dot.gov.

The fifteen red boxes on the dashboard page are labeled with unsafe driving violations given to commercial drivers and represent the data mentioned in the charts. These should be part of a traveler's awareness, allowing them to prevent from doing, saving themselves from getting a ticket from traffic enforcement and avoiding preventable accidents.

1. **Failure to obey a traffic control device.**
2. **Speeding.**
3. **Reckless Driving**
4. **Failing to use seat belt.**
5. Improper lane change.
6. Improper passing.
7. Unlawfully parking or leaving a vehicle in roadway.
8. Lane restriction violation.
9. Failing to use hazard warning flashers.
10. Driving under the influence.
11. Failure to yield right of way.
12. Scheduling run to necessary speeding.
13. Driving a motor vehicle while texting.
14. Using a handheld mobile telephone.
15. Failure to stop at a railroad crossing.

These 15 unsafe driving violations are just a sample of the many violations that are listed by the FMCSA that cause accidents. The majority of traffic enforcement focuses on these first 15 but there are many more that include maintenance violations, for example, inoperable lights. These accidents later result in the Department of Transportation and law enforcement distributing citations for violations like speeding with the strategy that it will reduce accidents.

A traveler should be aware of these violations while working with a commercial motor carrier and when traveling with other forms of transportation. Be aware that these are stated by law enforcement, the Department of Transportation, and the FMCSA to be the main cause of most accidents. Traffic enforcement is likely to target drivers that do these 15 things, all of which are preventable.

Since these are mentioned directly about commercial vehicles from the FMCSA, pay attention to these violations when around the area of those vehicles. One reason is these vehicles are being watched closely as of 2014. Even if not traveling in one, it is possible the area is being watched for the same violations. Awareness of these violations can give some ability to change a driving behavior and travel safe. This suggestion can help secure any form of transportation at the driver's level. Both accident and violation trends are described in detail, and a traveler should continue reading to learn some in-depth coverage of what is current now and what will likely occur in the future. Some trends are from the weather, companies' accidents, and violations. The following will add an extensive amount of information about how a company is ranked by the FMCSA as well as other points of view about accidents and violations.

A driver of commercial motor vehicles as well as travelers of personal cars and other forms of transportation should know the patterns of crashes are linked to certain times of the year. The time of year consists of the different seasons of weather. These weather conditions contribute to crashes most of all. When the weather is the cause of accidents and is compared to the above examples of the most common 15 unsafe driving violations, the two seem to be important issues. The problem is that it is legal to drive in severe weather and then when there are accidents a unsafe driving violation may end up getting written instead of noting that it was only because of the severe weather.

This is an interesting point and one of the main reasons *Crash Lane News* decided to write the book and have the website. The weather has not been factored into the FMCSA explanation of the safety rating system. The table below has data from 2010 to 2012 combined and divided by month. The commercial motor carriers are in the order of their total crashes for that time period. The company Swift is at the beginning on the list of companies because it has the most crashes. This does not mean that Swift is the most unsafe but that it has the most trucks for one company on the road that end up in an accident, which is later listed by the FMCSA. The order descends from Swift on this table.

The examples of how the FMCSA rating system is being aimless originates with the simple idea that there is a greatest to least amount of crashes per company that the FMCSA has listed. But even with this list, the FMCSA does not make that comparison easily viewable and list easy to understand. The FMCSA website is really confusing and this book is trying to explain the most important parts. In addition, there is also a greatest to least of unsafe driving violations similar to the 15 mentioned above. Both crashes and violations when listed greatest to least differ dramatically between commercial carriers. The FMCSA system claims to be transparent, while not showing the descending list of crashes per company, being later compared to a list of the unsafe driving violations. In *Crash Lane News'* opinion, not including more of a broad view is proving there is aimlessness in the FMCSA's presentation of data. A wider and broader view can really put things into perspective actually proving the companies are safer than ever, considering the circumstances of the U.S. government and company managers continually forcing drivers into weather disasters. This may sound confusing, but it means that the same companies that crash at a certain rate do not receive unsafe violations at the same rate. This difference is a big issue when both types of data are used to rate a company. Some companies get more violations simply because the state they are in is enforcing traffic more strictly. Many critics have not once mentioned the accumulation of the FMCSA data to be inconsistent between the crashes and violations.

The carrier-based ratings are stated by the FMCSA to be the most transparent ever. These ratings do not provide enough detailed comparisons to be accurate. They also are limited in their point of view. The FMCSA is aimless because it lacks the alternate points of view, including those of the commercial drivers. There is still a lot being left out to include the fact that the weather causes accidents.

Hundreds of additional suggestions can be made by anyone briefly looking at the FMCSA's data based from their own experience driving. These would also explain why the ratings may not be that transparent and accurate. The larger issues of the weather not being mentioned in the rating system is definitely a big failure by the FMCSA to make the rating system comprehensive. Without the mention of the weather affecting crashes that end up affecting a company's safety rating shows an aimlessness, but also for some reason the weather is an unnoticeable cause of accidents by the FMCSA. Usually, if law enforcement is out to give a ticket the conditions can also be used against the driver with the argument that he or she was speeding in an unsafe condition. But this is limited because of the counter argument stating that the road was open according to the Department of Transportation in the state and according to law enforcement. This is difficult when put into words, but this issue really affects the entire transportation system and those that rely on it.

Some of the critics of the FMCSA rating program do not mention "the weather is not really mentioned by the FMCSA." The critics have not included the weather as being the cause of some of these crashes in their argument enough. That argument is really one of the strongest points that can be made as to what is lacking, and as to how there are inconsistencies in the way the system rates a company.

The solution is for a review of the following points about the rating system and weather problems. Readers if interested or affected by these realities should contact their representative in Congress to communicate the solution of editing the FMCSA rating system to include the weather as the cause of some accidents. It is possible the response will be the weather is already considered the cause when a unsafe ticket is not written. But the problem is that the accident is still being counted if law enforcement is present and reports it, which later affects the companies' rating.

In addition, mention to your representative that the weather is also able to be predicted by the National Weather Service/NOAA. The Department of Transportation and Law enforcement have the ability to close the roads when weather is severe, but do not sometimes. This annually results in many crashes occurring during the winter season. The message is simple: severe weather is annually occurring and so are the crashes caused by it. These data are not emphasized enough by the FMCSA, and the FMCSA rating system is not comprehensive as a result. That is a failure by the Department of Transportation, the FMCSA rating system, and local, state, and federal law enforcement to protect the public from harm. The failure to close roads and have a more accurate rating system should be a reminder to elected officials.

The winter season and the months leading in and out of winter have a higher amount of crashes compared to the other times of the year. The month of January has 7 of the highest crash totals per carrier out of the 13 largest carriers with the most accidents in the United States. There are many other observations that can be made, all going back to the weather. Each individual traveler could probably add their own input into how the current rating and traffic enforcement system could be updated and included in a message to their representative in Congress. These solutions can add to the overall discussion about how to travel safely and make it more of a reality than the current system. Below is a list of the total crashes per month for all the companies totaled. This simplified list is the most important point of the book. It leads into the concern about the weather but is also not mentioned anywhere by the FMCSA. Note, the months of the greatest enforcement of unsafe driving violations compared to this list of crash month totals is very different. The point is the different pattern of enforcement is not following the seasonal weather issues at all. This aimless strategy by FMCSA, the Department of Transportation, and law enforcement is important to know as a traveler going out during winter, while also traveling when the weather is mild when tickets end up being given out more. The solution is to focus on driving safe year round to avoid an accident and a unsafe violation. Then, focus on the list above as when the most crashes occur, to take extra time for a trip during a month high on the list, and to drive with caution during a month high on the list.

1. **January**
2. **December**
3. **February**
4. **November**
5. **October**
6. **March**

7. September
8. May
9. April
10. June
11. August
12. July

CRASH MONTH TOTAL PER COMPANY 2010 - 2012. Each company is listed in the order of greatest to least off the crash totals. Proof of seasonal weather causing accidents is clear with the month totals. Each month decends from out of winter. Winer has more crashes than the rest of the other seasons for the year. This is becuase the roads are left open by the Department of Transportation in each state during lowered visibility resulting from forcasted thunderstorms, blizzards, fog, and icy roads. The grey highlighted boxes denote the largest crash month for each company. This data is from www.fmcsa.dot.gov	TOTALS PER MONTH	SWIFT TRANSPORTATION COMPANY LLC DOT # 54283	UNITED PARCEL SERVICE DOT # 21800	WERNER ENTERPRISES INC DOT # 53467	SCHNEIDER NATIONAL CARRIERS INC DOT # 264184	PENSKE TRUCK LEASING CO LP DOT # 327574	FEDEX FREIGHT INC DOT # 239039	J.B. HUNT TRANSPORT INC DOT # 80806	RYDER TRUCK RENTAL INC DOT # 16130	C.R. ENGLAND INC DOT # 28406	CON-WAY FREIGHT INC DOT # 241829	US XPRESS INC DOT # 303024
January	2091	221	163	99	89	84	77	68	52	58	71	83
December	1978	147	168	93	89	67	66	75	52	82	53	64
February	1805	69	124	90	79	77	75	61	52	67	52	49
November	1760	163	135	98	71	62	58	63	57	53	48	66
October	1652	129	120	116	74	75	65	61	46	39	54	37
March	1617	133	132	77	78	56	64	48	64	44	49	44
September	1551	131	124	90	75	61	50	59	60	47	56	34
May	1518	116	107	57	63	69	65	61	62	45	56	41
April	1466	101	98	69	62	72	59	50	57	40	34	39
June	1452	94	93	60	61	96	63	43	64	37	36	40
August	1373	139	122	56	92	39	37	48	37	49	32	40
July	1162	82	88	70	47	68	38	38	43	31	36	25
2010-2012 TOTALS	19425	1525	1474	975	880	826	717	675	646	592	577	562
THE TOTALS TO THE RIGHT ARE INSPECTIONS WHERE UNSAFE DRIVING VIOLATIONS WERE GIVEN		3870	1046	2355	1934	316	754	1225	280	1569	604	1775

CRASH LANE NEWS

CRASH MONTH TOTAL PER COMPANY 2010 - 2012. Each company is listed in the order of greatest to least off the MONTH crash totals. This information is from www.fmcsa.dot.gov	FEDERAL EXPRESS CORPORATION DOT # 86876	NEW PRIME INC. DOT # 3706	YRC INC DOT # 71821	OLD DOMINION FREIGHT LINE INC DOT#90849	WESTERN EXPRESS INC DOT#511412	ESTES EXPRESS LINES DOT # 121018	CRETE CARRIER CORPORATION DOT#73705	WAL-MART TRANSPORTATION LLC	CRST EXPEDITED INC DOT # 53773	AVERITT EXPRESS INC DOT # 36684
January	60	55	50	42	40	38	61	28	28	22
December	37	51	52	43	35	42	29	40	40	29
February	50	49	50	40	42	42	37	31	31	30
November	42	51	41	45	30	34	36	27	29	24
October	45	55	34	33	39	21	31	44	27	26
March	38	33	42	36	37	40	22	32	35	28
September	44	46	39	27	39	40	25	26	27	29
May	37	37	37	34	27	33	33	26	27	24
April	32	45	51	44	29	40	39	18	25	27
June	34	33	47	32	37	30	24	26	29	24
August	44	34	24	27	33	25	27	22	27	36
July	34	24	21	32	35	15	21	22	17	17
2010-2012 TOTALS	497	513	488	435	423	400	385	342	342	316
TOTAL INSPECTIONS WHERE VIOLATIONS WERE GIVEN	219	1219	850	547	1011	556	1045	406	1045	506

Design of Crashes by Month Table is Property of *Crash Lane News*. All Rights Reserved ©

CRASH MONTH TOTAL PER COMPANY 2010 - 2012. Each company is listed in the order of greatest to least off the MONTH crash totals. This information is from www.fmcsa.dot.gov	LANDSTAR RANGER INC DOT #241572	KNIGHT TRANSPORTATION INC DOT #428823	USA TRUCK INC DOT #213754	CELADON TRUCKING SERVICE INC DOT # 261902	SAIA MOTOR FREIGHT LINE LLC DOT #29124	ABF FREIGHT SYSTEM INCORPORATED DOT # 82866	MARTEN TRANSPORT LTD DOT #74432	USF HOLLAND INC DOT # 75806	COVENANT TRANSPORT INC DOT # 273818	CENTRAL REFRIDGERATED SERVICE DOT # 21331
January	27	26	23	22	23	18	25	28	28	23
December	22	38	28	30	37	16	26	33	33	29
February	30	17	24	30	24	39	28	30	31	18
November	23	22	23	24	20	24	21	20	18	25
October	25	29	14	21	22	25	24	21	14	23
March	24	35	33	23	15	28	19	18	20	18
September	25	23	23	21	21	17	25	22	17	10
May	30	19	26	25	19	17	21	15	19	12
April	25	20	23	12	22	22	10	18	16	13
June	29	24	18	22	17	23	10	11	13	16
August	22	20	18	13	26	18	24	8	15	20
July	14	16	13	20	9	16	11	14	10	10
2010-2012 TOTALS	296	289	266	263	255	263	244	238	234	217
TOTAL INSPECTIONS WHERE VIOLATIONS WERE GIVEN	1075	939	627	854	383	341	778	580	607	599

Design of Crashes by Month Table is Property of *Crash Lane News*. All Rights Reserved ©

CRASH MONTH TOTAL PER COMPANY 2010 - 2012. Each company is listed in the order of greatest to least off the MONTH crash totals. This information is from www.fmcsa.dot.gov	QUALITY CARRIER INC DOT # 76600	STEVENS TRANSPORT INC DOT # 79466	P.A.M. TRANSPORT DOT #179752	DART TRANSIT COMPANY DOT # 75525	SUPER SERVICE LLC DOT # 1972877	ROEHL TRANSPORT INC DOT # 74481	TRANSAM TRUCKING INC DOT # 315503	FFE TRANSPORTATION SERVICES INC DOT	GREYHOUND LINES INC DOT # 44110	PASCHALL TRUCK LINES INC DOT # 105234
January	22	18	17	23	19	19	9	10	11	16
December	24	21	9	17	16	14	18	12	9	6
February	16	13	18	11	15	17	14	14	13	18
November	18	13	16	18	13	7	14	13	9	7
October	18	18	16	9	8	13	8	9	1	17
March	12	9	16	13	14	16	9	10	7	5
September	11	16	4	8	9	6	8	10	12	11
May	21	11	20	15	6	13	10	12	11	9
April	11	11	13	14	12	10	13	13	8	11
June	10	14	17	12	18	12	13	8	12	8
August	10	15	14	7	6	7	8	11	16	9
July	11	6	4	7	8	13	10	9	17	8
2010-2012 TOTALS	184	165	164	154	144	147	134	131	126	125
TOTAL INSPECTIONS WHERE VIOLATIONS WERE GIVEN	598	412	428	542	541	359	414	411	196	513

Design of Crashes by Month Table is Property of *Crash Lane News*. All Rights Reserved ©

CRASH MONTH TOTAL PER COMPANY 2010 - 2012. Each company is listed in the order of greatest to least off the MONTH crash totals. This information is from www.fmcsa.dot.gov	MERCER TRUCK LINES CO INC DOT # 154712	INTERSTATE DISTRIBUTOR CO DOT# 8273	KLLM TRANSPORT SERVICES LLC DOT # 154237	CRST MALONE INC DOT # 105790	RUAN TRANSPORT CORPORATION DOT #55787	GORDON TRUCKING INC DOT # 190991	TRANSPORT CORPORATION OF AMERICA INC DOT# 183949	MVT SERVICES LLC (MESILLA VALLEY TRANSPORTATION) DOT #270179	SOUTHERN REFRIDGERATED TRANSPORT INC DOT # 276010	ARNOLD TRANSPORTATION SERVICES INC DOT #148974
January	17	9	13	15	18	13	10	13	10	13
December	10	16	15	8	17	8	13	10	17	7
February	15	14	11	13	9	12	13	15	7	7
November	11	10	12	16	11	10	11	13	12	9
October	9	9	9	9	10	7	10	7	9	15
March	9	7	11	10	10	13	7	5	3	5
September	3	8	10	5	7	12	11	10	6	9
May	9	7	7	10	6	6	11	3	8	7
April	10	7	12	6	8	11	11	12	10	5
June	8	6	8	10	13	7	7	11	6	5
August	10	16	5	3	7	5	5	3	2	3
July	8	10	6	11	8	9	4	10	13	3
2010-2012 TOTALS	119	119	119	116	124	113	113	112	103	88
TOTAL INSPECTIONS WHERE VIOLATIONS WERE GIVEN	509	330	423	511	232	310	380	469	320	189

Design of Crashes by Month Table is Property of *Crash Lane News*. All Rights Reserved ©

CRASH MONTH TOTAL PER COMPANY 2010 - 2012. Each company is listed in the order of greatest to least off the MONTH crash totals. This information is from www.fmcsa.dot.gov	RUAN LOGISTICS CORPORATION DOT # 149350	MAVERICK TRANSPORTATION LLC DOT # 178538	ATLAS VAN LINES INC DOT # 125550	BOYD BROS TRANSPORTATION INC DOT # 92321	JOHN CHRISTNER TRUCKING INC DOT # 273897	TANGO TRANSPORT LLC DOT # 459762	COWAN SYSTEMS LLC DOT # 548880	MAY TRUCKING COMPANY DOT # 94081	PENSKE LOGISTICS LLC DOT # 268015	INSERT YOUR COMPETITOR	INSERT YOUR VEHICLE	INSERT A COMPANY THAT WORKS WITH YOUR COMPANY
January	11	7	6	8	5	8	6	7	6			
December	6	10	4	1	6	7	11	8	12			
February	8	6	7	8	11	8	8	7	9			
November	5	9	10	12	6	3	8	6	5			
October	9	2	5	6	4	4	4	9	9			
March	5	7	5	7	9	12	6	5	5			
September	6	3	3	5	6	7	2	4	6			
May	8	13	5	7	7	2	7	5	2			
April	9	4	5	6	4	7	5	2	4			
June	6	7	11	8	1	5	7	7	9			
August	3	3	3	5	6	5	4	5	3			
July	7	5	11	2	8	5	4	7	1			
2010-2012 TOTALS	83	76	75	75	73	73	72	72	71			
TOTAL INSPECTIONS WHERE VIOLATIONS WERE GIVEN	214	252	483	131	306	188	179	181	158			

CRASH LANE NEWS

Design of Crashes by Month Table is Property of *Crash Lane News*. All Rights Reserved ©

Below is the Ratings Table. The commercial motor carriers are sorted from greatest to least based on crash totals. The FMCSA has been using a rating system said to have been created to increase safety and transparency. The ratings are listed in the order they are presented on the FMCSA website:

1. Unsafe Driving
2. Fatigued Driving
3. Driver Fitness
4. Controlled Substances and Alcohol
5. Vehicle Maintenance
6. Cargo-Related (*not public*)
7. Crash-Related (*not public*)

In many areas in the government, a public rating system regarding a company like this would be considered a public display of favoritism and illegal. This favoritism has also not been an issue of argument against the current FMCSA ratings. Normally favoritism is avoided by the government to be as public as it is now with this rating. It is strange it is not brought up enough about the rating system by some of the bigger companies that have the ability to have a more powerful voice about the current problems. Favoritism by the U.S. government is something that should be mentioned when summarizing some issues a traveler should know. Many times, like in this example it is unnoticeable, similar to the weather. With this favoritism and public rating there has been an entirely different commercial trucking industry in the past few years.

A traveler in the trucking industry and one just learning about it should know the current rating system has not been accepted by all commercial carriers. One reason is that the ratings have hurt profits because no one wants to hire and use a company that has a low rating. That has been argued by many about the rating system, but not in the format of favoritism for some reason.

The drivers for a company that have an unsafe FMCSA rating should be aware of the fact they may be scrutinized and targeted by law enforcement while on the interstate or where they patrol, and targeted more at commercial inspection stations. This targeting means they will be inspected based on the company's rating. Further violations end up getting added to the driver's record and the company based on that fact alone. Most of these inspections at a weigh station are not unsafe driving violations but a maintenance violation. Many have mentioned they have been cited for stains or things they have no control over since the company's mechanics had approved the vehicle was ready to go. As a result, there have been some lawsuits as well as lobbying of members of Congress to confront the FMCSA.

Many commercial carriers use Kenworth, Freightliner, Peterbilt, or International commercial trucks. In the commercial industry the driver many times will be away from the company's regular mechanics when in need of repairs. The inspection at a certain truck shop may vary in quality and also be a big difference across all the 50 states. The point of mentioning this is there is no public rating of these companies' vehicles or the maintenance shops working on them added to the existing FMCSA rating system. All of these different things add up even if it is the cause of only one ticket. This also affects the safety on the road in that the drivers out working end up ticketed and eventually lose their ability to drive. Some companies do not want drivers that have been ticketed and have points on their driving record. Many companies are aware of the fact there are some inaccuracies in the rating system and what is happening, but are literally forced to terminate drivers that have points; they are also forced to not hire drivers because they do not want something to later occur and look like they hired someone unsafe. This is one of the more critical things about the commercial carriers but it also shows that things may not really be made safer if they later hire someone with no experience after an experienced driver was fired.

There has also been a message placed at the bottom of all the ratings in 2013, mentioning that the rating system should not be used to discriminate against a company. This was temporary. Unfortunately, many believe this may not be enough to compensate for losses to everyone running a business. Many big companies have been forced to sell and reduce their size, terminating employees. The message to not discriminate based on the rating does not replace a driver's record that becomes bombarded with tickets because he or she worked for a company with a low unsafe rating. With all these important points, there is not much being announced to improve transparency. Most of the FMCSA changes are very small. What is predicted to change in the future will not be including the company's and driver's point of view.

Going back to the spreadsheet: Another thing to consider is the size of the fleet, being the amount of vehicles, and the miles traveled, which can help to sort which companies have the highest crash rates per the least amount of miles. This can be done by downloading this spreadsheet and sorting the size of a fleet and the number of miles from greatest to least. Fleets that have a large number of miles may have a higher number of crashes because they are doing more driving, and the FMCSA may have added this fact into the ratings without really describing the details. The mileage may raise some questions as to the accuracy of this rating system. Note that with a spreadsheet, there are many ways to sort the data made public by the FMCSA but it tends to be limited. The availability of this data can contribute to different points of view and explanations of the issues of safety in the commercial industry. Some believe it has made things safer. But, if there are still accidents there must be something missing like the weather, the favoritism leading to more tickets, no ratings for truck manufacturers, and no ratings for maintenance shops. The FMCSA rating system has been in place for a few years now, and it failed. The proof is there are still some accidents that occur and the cause is not transparent. Another solution can be suggested and put in place through legislation and elected official intervention.

Company Ratings 2010 - 2012. The order of the companies are listed to the order of their crash totals from greatest to least. All information is from www.fmcsa.dot.gov	SWIFT TRANSPORTATION COMPANY LLC DOT # 54283	UNITED PARCEL SERVICE DOT # 21800	WERNER ENTERPRISES INC DOT # 53467	SCHNEIDER NATIONAL CARRIERS INC DOT # 264184
UNSAFE DRIVING	40.2	4.3	45	26
FATIGUED DRIVING	41.7	8.7	12	9
DRIVER FITNESS	63.9	30	44.6	39.9
CONTROLLED SUBSTANCES AND ALCHOHOL	20.4	NO VIOLATIONS	12	4
VEHICLE MAINTENANCE	53.2	15.4	55	60.4
CARGO RELATED	NOT PUBLIC	NOT PUBLIC	NOT PUBLIC	NOT PUBLIC
CRASH RELATED	NOT PUBLIC	NOT PUBLIC	NOT PUBLIC	NOT PUBLIC
POWER UNITS	15212	97371	7201	10503
MILES TRAVELED	1658727633	2407710000	855180000	1102597163
DRIVERS	14300	91065	10338	11899
COMPANY ADDRESS STATE	Arizona	Georgia	Nebraska	Wisconsin

Grey Hightighted Boxes Denote a carrier exceeds the FMCSA intervention threshold relative to its safety event grouping based upon roadside data.	PENSKE TRUCK LEASING CO LP DOT # 327574	FEDEX FREIGHT INC DOT # 239039	J.B. HUNT TRANSPORT INC DOT # 80806	RYDER TRUCK RENTAL INC DOT # 16130
UNSAFE DRIVING	4.3	1.8	13	0
FATIGUED DRIVING	29.3	16	38.9	34.9
DRIVER FITNESS	68.4	26.2	31.9	37.7
CONTROLLED SUBSTANCES AND ALCHOHOL	0	15.3	8.1	NO VIOLATIONS
VEHICLE MAINTENANCE	3.8	43	44.1	14.2
CARGO RELATED	NOT PUBLIC	NOT PUBLIC	NOT PUBLIC	NOT PUBLIC
CRASH RELATED	NOT PUBLIC	NOT PUBLIC	NOT PUBLIC	NOT PUBLIC
POWER UNITS	29644	14703	10512	106053
MILES TRAVELED	13176970	1005719674	766066548	549416327
DRIVERS	7312	18820	10096	488
COMPANY ADDRESS STATE	Pennsylvania	Arkansas	Arkansas	Florida

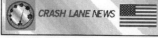

Information in public domain from *www.fmcsa.dot.gov*. Gray boxes indicate that the carrier exceeds the FMCSA intervention threshold relative to its safety-event grouping based upon roadside data, and/or has been cited for one or more serious violations in the past twelve months during an investigation. Such carriers may be prioritized for an intervention action and roadside inspection. (Special note from *Crash Lane News:* many companies received additional tickets as a result of this rating system alone and not for unsafe driving as a result of FMCSA inaccurate ratings.) These ratings are lacking in transparency and do not take into account the reality of the weather causing crashes. A spreadsheet with this information and more is available to download for free at *www.crashlanenews.com*. Design of Ratings Table is property *of Crash Lane News*. All Rights Reserved ©.

Company Ratings 2010 - 2012. The order of the companies are listed to the order of their crash totals from greatest to least. All information is from www.fmcsa.dot.gov	C.R. ENGLAND INC DOT # 28406	CON-WAY FREIGHT INC DOT # 241829	US XPRESS INC DOT # 303024	FEDERAL EXPRESS CORPORATION DOT # 86876
UNSAFE DRIVING	88.1	2.4	60.1	1
FATIGUED DRIVING	11.7	23.4	45.7	9.9
DRIVER FITNESS	75.3	25.1	40.4	43.8
CONTROLLED SUBSTANCES AND ALCHOHOL	6.1	0.2	14.8	NO VIOLATIONS
VEHICLE MAINTENANCE	40.5	22.5	51.7	18.7
CARGO RELATED	NOT PUBLIC	NOT PUBLIC	NOT PUBLIC	NOT PUBLIC
CRASH RELATED	NOT PUBLIC	NOT PUBLIC	NOT PUBLIC	NOT PUBLIC
POWER UNITS	4303	9304	6072	30964
MILES TRAVELED	488292627	655636676	631620000	854210962
DRIVERS	5890	14103	7484	59018
COMPANY ADDRESS STATE	Utah	Michigan	Tennessee	Tennessee

Grey Hightighted Boxes Denote a carrier exceeds the FMCSA intervention threshold relative to its safety event grouping based upon roadside data.	NEW PRIME INC. DOT # 3706	YRC INC DOT # 71821	OLD DOMINION FREIGHT LINE INC DOT#90849	WESTERN EXPRESS INC DOT#511412
UNSAFE DRIVING	46.1	4.9	6.1	86.4
FATIGUED DRIVING	26.1	27.8	29.8	63.5
DRIVER FITNESS	63.5	28.2	33.5	92.8
CONTROLLED SUBSTANCES AND ALCHOHOL	26.5	0	NO VIOLATIONS	56
VEHICLE MAINTENANCE	38.1	74.5	40.4	65.8
CARGO RELATED	NOT PUBLIC	NOT PUBLIC	NOT PUBLIC	NOT PUBLIC
CRASH RELATED	NOT PUBLIC	NOT PUBLIC	NOT PUBLIC	NOT PUBLIC
POWER UNITS	4392	8766	6065	2450
MILES TRAVELED	551138340	570511922	425205659	305524848
DRIVERS	5272	14279	6978	2450
COMPANY ADDRESS STATE	Missouri	Kansas	North Carolina	Tennessee

Company Ratings 2010 - 2012. The order of the companies are listed to the order of their crash totals from greatest to least. All information is from www.fmcsa.dot.gov	ESTES EXPRESS LINES DOT # 121018	CRETE CARRIER CORPORATION DOT#73705	WAL-MART TRANSPORTATIO N LLC DOT#63585	CRST EXPEDITED INC DOT # 53773
UNSAFE DRIVING	11.1	24	1.2	**94.4**
FATIGUED DRIVING	32.1	28.8	0.3	32.5
DRIVER FITNESS	21.5	21.9	7.8	52.6
CONTROLLED SUBSTANCES AND ALCHOHOL	0	2	0.5	14
VEHICLE MAINTENANCE	60.4	42.4	5	29.6
CARGO RELATED	NOT PUBLIC	NOT PUBLIC	NOT PUBLIC	NOT PUBLIC
CRASH RELATED	NOT PUBLIC	NOT PUBLIC	NOT PUBLIC	NOT PUBLIC
POWER UNITS	5812	?	6142	1931
MILES TRAVELED	388028264	?	703082807	299805738
DRIVERS	5795	?	7366	3979
COMPANY ADDRESS STATE	Tennessee	Nebraska	Arkansas	Iowa

Grey Hightighted Boxes Denote a carrier exceeds the FMCSA intervention threshold relative to its safety event grouping based upon roadside data.	AVERITT EXPRESS INC DOT # 36684	LANDSTAR RANGER INC DOT # 241572	KNIGHT TRANSPORTATIO N INC DOT # 428823	USA TRUCK INC DOT #213754
UNSAFE DRIVING	14.2	22.2	49.3	48.1
FATIGUED DRIVING	55.9	55.1	25.1	**62.3**
DRIVER FITNESS	23.6	27.1	71	54.8
CONTROLLED SUBSTANCES AND ALCHOHOL	2.7	0	36	24
VEHICLE MAINTENANCE	44.9	57.9	52.2	66.6
CARGO RELATED	NOT PUBLIC	NOT PUBLIC	NOT PUBLIC	NOT PUBLIC
CRASH RELATED	NOT PUBLIC	NOT PUBLIC	NOT PUBLIC	NOT PUBLIC
POWER UNITS	3888	5103	3644	2368
MILES TRAVELED	363395102	515167442	380000000	235195802
DRIVERS	4609	5596	3704	2508
COMPANY ADDRESS STATE	Tennesse	Florida	Arizona	Arkansas

Company Ratings 2010 - 2012. The order of the companies are listed to the order of their crash totals from greatest to least. All information is from www.fmcsa.dot.gov	CELADON TRUCKING SERVICE INC DOT # 261902	SAIA MOTOR FREIGHT LINE LLC DOT # 29124	ABF FREIGHT SYSTEM INCORPORATED DOT # 82866	MARTEN TRANSPORT LTD DOT # 74432
UNSAFE DRIVING	50.2	11.2	4.7	63.9
FATIGUED DRIVING	35.9	20.2	21.7	11.2
DRIVER FITNESS	80.1	36.4	23.9	72.4
CONTROLLED SUBSTANCES AND ALCHOHOL	3.8	NO VIOLATIONS	1.1	28.5
VEHICLE MAINTENANCE	48.1	59.6	47.7	26.2
CARGO RELATED	NOT PUBLIC	NOT PUBLIC	NOT PUBLIC	NOT PUBLIC
CRASH RELATED	NOT PUBLIC	NOT PUBLIC	NOT PUBLIC	NOT PUBLIC
POWER UNITS	3810	3626	3816	2430
MILES TRAVELED	297248000	293815030	340178334	246922519
DRIVERS	2650	4181	6730	2684
COMPANY ADDRESS STATE	Indiana	Georgia	Arkansas	Wisconsin

Grey Hightighted Boxes Denote a carrier exceeds the FMCSA intervention threshold relative to its safety event grouping based upon roadside data.	USF HOLLAND INC DOT # 75806	COVENANT TRANSPORT INC DOT # 273818	CENTRAL REFRIDGERATED SERVICE DOT # 21331	QUALITY CARRIER INC DOT # 76600
UNSAFE DRIVING	16.6	44.3	63.5	31
FATIGUED DRIVING	26.5	28.2	16.7	41.9
DRIVER FITNESS	13.3	47.2	38.4	49.8
CONTROLLED SUBSTANCES AND ALCHOHOL	INCONCLUSIVE	5.7	32	INCONCLUSIVE
VEHICLE MAINTENANCE	58.1	35.8	34.1	59.8
CARGO RELATED	NOT PUBLIC	NOT PUBLIC	NOT PUBLIC	NOT PUBLIC
CRASH RELATED	NOT PUBLIC	NOT PUBLIC	NOT PUBLIC	NOT PUBLIC
POWER UNITS	3910	1675	1799	3424
MILES TRAVELED	275820320	259538070	218574996	285000000
DRIVERS	5239	3000	2138	3360
COMPANY ADDRESS STATE	Michigan	Tenneessee	Utah	Florida

Design of Ratings Table is Property of *Crash Lane News*. All Rights Reserved ©

Company Ratings 2010 - 2012. The order of the companies are listed to the order of their crash totals from greatest to least. All information is from www.fmcsa.dot.gov	STEVENS TRANSPORT INC DOT # 79466	P.A.M. TRANSPORT DOT #179752	DART TRANSIT COMPANY DOT # 75525	SUPER SERVICE LLC DOT # 1972877
UNSAFE DRIVING	36.4	**60.4**	32	**85.2**
FATIGUED DRIVING	47.3	45.5	30.3	43.8
DRIVER FITNESS	56.3	58.4	42.2	60.4
CONTROLLED SUBSTANCES AND ALCHOHOL	7.6	44	11.5	INCONCLUSIVE
VEHICLE MAINTENANCE	42.8	68.2	**83.5**	**75.6**
CARGO RELATED	NOT PUBLIC	NOT PUBLIC	NOT PUBLIC	NOT PUBLIC
CRASH RELATED	NOT PUBLIC	NOT PUBLIC	NOT PUBLIC	NOT PUBLIC
POWER UNITS	1950	1789	2500	1275
MILES TRAVELED	219855639	214933327	255079165	165928172
DRIVERS	2577	2158	2422	1303
COMPANY ADDRESS STATE	Texas	Arkansas	Minnesota	Kentucky

Grey Hightighted Boxes Denote a carrier exceeds the FMCSA intervention threshold relative to its safety event grouping based upon roadside data.	ROEHL TRANSPORT INC DOT # 74481	TRANSAM TRUCKING INC DOT # 315503	FFE TRANSPORTATION SERVICES INC DOT #109745	GREYHOUND LINES INC DOT # 44110
UNSAFE DRIVING	18.5	**72.8**	38.2	30.7
FATIGUED DRIVING	30.6	**57.3**	41	37.5
DRIVER FITNESS	19.8	61.7	**85.9**	47
CONTROLLED SUBSTANCES AND ALCHOHOL	INCONCLUSIVE	5.2	34	NO VIOLATIONS
VEHICLE MAINTENANCE	32.5	69.9	69.1	22.1
CARGO RELATED	NOT PUBLIC	NOT PUBLIC	NOT PUBLIC	NOT PUBLIC
CRASH RELATED	NOT PUBLIC	NOT PUBLIC	NOT PUBLIC	NOT PUBLIC
POWER UNITS	2054	1117	1543	1420
MILES TRAVELED	192500231	130289608	170341285	138237133
DRIVERS	2160	1182	1782	2720
COMPANY ADDRESS STATE	Wisconsin	Kansas	Texas	Texas

Company Ratings 2010 - 2012. The order of the companies are listed to the order of their crash totals from greatest to least. All information is from www.fmcsa.dot.gov	PASCHALL TRUCK LINES INC DOT # 105234	MERCER TRUCK LINES CO INC DOT # 154712	INTERSTATE DISTRIBUTOR CO DOT# 8273	KLLM TRANSPORT SERVICES LLC DOT # 154237
UNSAFE DRIVING	70.9	50	16	54.9
FATIGUED DRIVING	64	69	44.2	53.6
DRIVER FITNESS	57.4	24.3	30.3	53.3
CONTROLLED SUBSTANCES AND ALCHOHOL	28	0	INCONCLUSIVE	1.3
VEHICLE MAINTENANCE	65.6	53.1	31.5	62.8
CARGO RELATED	NOT PUBLIC	NOT PUBLIC	NOT PUBLIC	NOT PUBLIC
CRASH RELATED	NOT PUBLIC	NOT PUBLIC	NOT PUBLIC	NOT PUBLIC
POWER UNITS	1138	2072	1905	1420
MILES TRAVELED	168946471	186129473	183464246	154676098
DRIVERS	1138	2311	1681	1428
COMPANY ADDRESS STATE	Kentucky	Kentucky	Washington	Mississippi
Grey Hightighted Boxes Denote a carrier exceeds the FMCSA intervention threshold relative to its safety event grouping based upon roadside data.	CRST MALONE INC DOT # 105790	RUAN TRANSPORT CORPORATION DOT # 55787	GORDON TRUCKING INC DOT # 190991	TRANSPORT CORPORATION OF AMERICA INC DOT # 183949
UNSAFE DRIVING	90.1	14.1	20.9	33.1
FATIGUED DRIVING	86.8	26	30.9	38.4
DRIVER FITNESS	70.5	14.6	23.4	57.2
CONTROLLED SUBSTANCES AND ALCHOHOL	13.4	NO VIOLATIONS	INCONCLUSIVE	INCONCLUSIVE
VEHICLE MAINTENANCE	77.6	18.2	21.5	48.9
CARGO RELATED	NOT PUBLIC	NOT PUBLIC	NOT PUBLIC	NOT PUBLIC
CRASH RELATED	NOT PUBLIC	NOT PUBLIC	NOT PUBLIC	NOT PUBLIC
POWER UNITS	1495	1672	1933	1872
MILES TRAVELED	148804930	155235108	191753670	190432740
DRIVERS	1495	2445	1983	2173
COMPANY ADDRESS STATE	Alabama	Iowa	Washington	Minnesota

Grey Hightighted Boxes Denote a carrier exceeds the FMCSA intervention threshold relative to its safety event grouping based upon roadside data.	MVT SERVICES LLC (MESILLA VALLEY TRANSPORTATION) DOT # 270179	SOUTHERN REFRIDGERATED TRANSPORT INC DOT # 276010	ARNOLD TRANSPORTATION SERVICES INC DOT # 148974	RUAN LOGISTICS CORPORATION DOT # 149350
UNSAFE DRIVING	80.4	67.9	34.5	28.3
FATIGUED DRIVING	87.2	50.7	66.4	41.7
DRIVER FITNESS	60.2	44.2	67.1	37.2
CONTROLLED SUBSTANCES AND ALCHOHOL	57.1	20	21.1	2.9
VEHICLE MAINTENANCE	43.3	28.4	51.2	27
CARGO RELATED	NOT PUBLIC	NOT PUBLIC	NOT PUBLIC	NOT PUBLIC
CRASH RELATED	NOT PUBLIC	NOT PUBLIC	NOT PUBLIC	NOT PUBLIC
POWER UNITS	1175	1001	969	1486
MILES TRAVELED	164125189	119812341	113282100	108055107
DRIVERS	1420	1012	950	1583
COMPANY ADDRESS STATE	New Mexico	Arkansas	Florida	Iowa
Company Ratings 2010 - 2012. The order of the companies are listed to the order of their crash totals from greatest to least. All information is from www.fmcsa.dot.gov	MAVERICK TRANSPORTATION LLC DOT # 178538	ATLAS VAN LINES INC DOT # 125550	BOYD BROS TRANSPORTATION INC DOT # 92321	JOHN CHRISTNER TRUCKING INC DOT # 273897
UNSAFE DRIVING	31.6	87	11.7	60.3
FATIGUED DRIVING	16.8	78.2	71.9	60.7
DRIVER FITNESS	20.8	78	32	80.7
CONTROLLED SUBSTANCES AND ALCHOHOL	1.7	70.2	NO VIOLATION	0.5
VEHICLE MAINTENANCE	28.3	76.7	39.5	51.8
CARGO RELATED	NOT PUBLIC	NOT PUBLIC	NOT PUBLIC	NOT PUBLIC
CRASH RELATED	NOT PUBLIC	NOT PUBLIC	NOT PUBLIC	NOT PUBLIC
POWER UNITS	1321	3818	841	870
MILES TRAVELED	116740003	95122217	76100000	130646700
DRIVERS	1414	2875	665	870
COMPANY ADDRESS STATE	Arkansas	Indiana	Alabama	Oklahoma

Grey Hightighted Boxes Denote a carrier exceeds the FMCSA intervention threshold relative to its safety event grouping based upon roadside data.	TANGO TRANSPORT LLC DOT # 459762	COWAN SYSTEMS LLC DOT # 548880	MAY TRUCKING COMPANY DOT # 94081	PENSKE LOGISTICS LLC DOT # 268015
UNSAFE DRIVING	72.7	26.5	28.9	9.8
FATIGUED DRIVING	41.1	55.6	3.6	20.2
DRIVER FITNESS	15.9	11.7	42	38.2
CONTROLLED SUBSTANCES AND ALCHOHOL	42.3	2.3	23	NO VIOLATIONS
VEHICLE MAINTENANCE	39.1	75.3	37.7	35.9
CARGO RELATED	NOT PUBLIC	NOT PUBLIC	NOT PUBLIC	NOT PUBLIC
CRASH RELATED	NOT PUBLIC	NOT PUBLIC	NOT PUBLIC	NOT PUBLIC
POWER UNITS	786	1395	998	1264
MILES TRAVELED	68865000	105000000	86450000	136488702
DRIVERS	816	1400	1093	2572
COMPANY ADDRESS STATE	Louisiana	Mary Land	Oregon	Pennsylvania

CRASH LANE NEWS

*These FMCSA ratings show the United States government's point of view about Commercial Carriers. Public **"safety"** ratings such as these, have been considered as favoritism, proof of a failure to protect the public from harm from the weather, excessive, and fabrications. The **"safety"** ratings are described to improve transparency over the industry but also appear limited in range, and filled with aimlessness.

Note, there are many other areas within the Commercial Industry not being publicly rated for **"safety."** They include the Warehouses or Distribution Centers where freight is manufactured, shipped, and received. Areas not rated publicly for safety by the FMCSA and United States government as of 2015 include the 50 State's governments and emergency services statewide, and their Counties, and Cities. There is also no official United States government safety rating for Interstates, Highways, Roads, Streets, Drives, Parkways, Rest Areas, Truck Stops (Citgo, Chevron, Exxon, Kangaroo, Petro, Pilot, Shell, Flying J, Love's, TA, BP, Conoco, Valero, Sunoco, Wilco-Hess, Sinclair), Mechanic/Maintenance Shops, and there are other areas a Commercial Vehicle travels which are unrated by the government. There are some areas that could be **"safer."** The existing accidents and violations that the FMCSA presents in its safety snapshot of Commercial Carriers is not a fraction of the Commercial Industry. The industry relies on Commercial Carriers and Drivers, but they are the only area being rated in a false way.

THIS IS FOR YOUR OWN USE. USE THIS TABLE TO BUILD EXISTING KNOWLEDGE OF A SPECIFIC AREA/ROUTE TRAVELED.	ADD A COMPETITOR HERE	ADD A COMPANY THAT WORKS WITH YOUR COMPANY HERE	ADD YOUR VEHICLE HERE
UNSAFE DRIVING			
FATIGUED DRIVING			
DRIVER FITNESS			
CONTROLLED SUBSTANCES AND ALCHOHOL			
VEHICLE MAINTENANCE			
CARGO RELATED			
CRASH RELATED			
POWER UNITS			
MILES TRAVELED			
DRIVERS			
COMPANY ADDRESS STATE			
IT IS RECOMMENDED TO USE THE FMCSA RATINGS, EVEN THOUGH IT IS NOT COMPREHENSIVE LEAVING OUT THE WEATHER AS THE CAUSE.	ADD A COMPETITOR HERE	ADD A COMPANY THAT WORKS WITH YOUR COMPANY HERE	ADD YOUR VEHICLE HERE
UNSAFE DRIVING			
FATIGUED DRIVING			
DRIVER FITNESS			
CONTROLLED SUBSTANCES AND ALCHOHOL			
VEHICLE MAINTENANCE			
CARGO RELATED			
CRASH RELATED			
POWER UNITS			
MILES TRAVELED			
DRIVERS			
COMPANY ADDRESS STATE			

Below is the *Crash Lane News* Crash Table that can be viewed in larger form or downloaded from www.crashlanenews.com/Dashboard.html. Note that it may take twenty seconds to view or download. This table includes over two hundred of the biggest and most well-known motor carriers and what their crash rate is per state for 2010–2012. It is recommended to download it and opening it in Microsoft Excel. For your convenience add your own company or one not listed. See how it compares and ranks these companies. Each company is listed from greatest to least across the top based on their crash totals. The state with the most crashes, Texas, is listed greatest to least. The Crash Table is sorted with the company having the most crashes, Swift. Review all tables of information and their explanation in the following. Then review the tables again while remembering the fact the ratings did not include the weather as the cause of any of the accidents, and that only the commercial driver is blamed to cause each. This review should also note that the entire system put in place as of 2014 to rate companies does not use the causes of the accidents enough. The causes are studied to a certain point which is why certain violations are focused on like speeding. But other obvious areas such as the weather seemed to go unnoticed, which is a failure when making a public rating system. FEMA has been a federal agency in part because the weather can cause a disaster. The use of FEMA's data proving that the weather is a disaster to be used to help rate companies is also another thing not mentioned.

A simple summary of the most crash states based on the Crash Table below greatest to least. Note, the FMCSA does not mention they rate each state as being the possible cause for accidents but they have mentioned they sometimes look at trends. When hearing that the FMCSA do sometimes look at state data and knowing the below list has been this way for many years it is a real concern to the traveling public as to how accurate the Department of Transportation, traffic enforcement, and FMCSA data and mission are. There are some states with a considerable amount of crashes compared to others. Hawaii and Washington D.C. are not included in this list and would rank very low if they were. The state with the largest total of crashes out of all others for the companies listed is Texas. The least is Alaska. The explanation of this order is based on the population density of the state driving vehicles, amount of interstate lanes, the amount of street lanes, forcing drivers into severe weather, forcing drivers into disasters, and many more, to include the 15 unsafe driving violations that traffic enforcement focuses on for unsafe drivers.

1. Texas
2. California
3. Ohio
4. Indiana
5. Illinois
6. Pennsylvania

7. Georgia	22. Wisconsin	37. Connecticut
8. Missouri	23. South Carolina	38. Minnesota
9. Tennessee	24. Vermont	39. Montana
10. New Jersey	25. Wyoming	40. Nevada
11. Virginia	26. Iowa	41. Idaho
12. North Carolina	27. Kansas	42. Maine
13. New York	28. Colorado	43. North Dakota
14. Kentucky	29. Oregon	44. South Dakota
15. Michigan	30. Washington	45. Delaware
16. Florida	31. West Virginia	46. New Hampshire
17. Arizona	32. Mississippi	47. Vermont
18. Louisiana	33. Massachusetts	48. Rhode Island
19. Alabama	34. Maryland	49. Alaska
20. Oklahoma	35. New Mexico	
21. Arkansas	36. Nebraska	

This list is a summary of the states with the most crashes given unsafe driving violations, later posted at FMCSA. The pattern of crashes does not mean these states are more dangerous to travel in. But, these totals show there are crashes and there is an attempt by that state to give out tickets when they occur. The state with the highest amount of crashes will never be known because some are not reported, and/or placed on the FMCSA website. For all these reasons, the FMCSA's rating system is filled with misdirection. The problem areas are also not identified on their website like the above, proving their current system is aimless. It is impossible to rate a company accurately on safety and not include the fact that there are some areas in the United States more likely to have an accident. The solution is to know the above list as the FMCSA's point of view only. It should be remembered as only their point of view, and a very limited one. The main suggestion is to adjust the driving for the trip to have more caution in the states towards the top of the list. Also use more caution when driving or as a passenger in the states toward the top of the list. This tip should be used by Commercial Carriers and their Drivers, and is guaranteed to work as well as the FMCSA data can also be considered accurate. Be realistic, but also put in the extra time, and use the right strategy, to prevent future accidents. Drive in a defensive way to avoid an accident.

STATE CRASH TOTALS 2010 - 2012 LEFT TO RIGHT GREATEST TO LEAST TOTAL CRASHES. BELOW STATE ORDER ARE OFF STATE CRASH TOTALS.	TOTALS	SWIFT TRANSPORTATION COMPANY LLC DOT # 54283	UNITED PARCEL SERVICE DOT # 21800	WERNER ENTERPRISES INC DOT # 53467	SCHNEIDER NATIONAL CARRIERS INC DOT # 264184	PENSKE TRUCK LEASING CO LP DOT # 327574	FEDEX FREIGHT INC DOT # 239039	J.B. HUNT TRANSPORT INC DOT # 80806
Texas	1823	170	115	89	94	39	63	75
California	1144	102	150	28	71	52	41	58
Ohio	1099	55	103	57	65	59	39	37
Indiana	973	58	78	69	44	4	40	40
Illinois	949	55	74	42	54	26	48	64
Pennsylvania	799	49	69	50	45	41	18	35
Georgia	729	55	53	38	21	27	14	29
Missouri	694	62	48	47	26	16	33	25
Tennessee	672	49	44	33	35	2	22	29
New Jersey	610	23	58	17	16	114	17	24
Virginia	599	45	37	26	40	18	24	19
North Carolina	576	38	31	19	23	1	28	11
New York	572	44	52	24	27	37	17	23
Kentucky	563	36	46	38	35	3	17	14
Michigan	531	32	43	31	26	45	22	21
Florida	510	27	47	33	15	41	15	13
Arizona	471	70	22	13	9	47	17	7
Louisiana	423	27	34	15	15	24	13	9
Alabama	381	34	15	27	16	3	13	20
Oklahoma	373	26	12	26	18	6	21	14
Arkansas	357	22	15	14	23	7	14	12
Wisconsin	342	13	33	28	26	16	11	12
South Carolina	340	22	21	14	15	30	12	4
Utah	289	46	23	19	7	3	13	3
Wyoming	283	31	7	17	8	0	16	3
Iowa	279	23	29	19	13	3	5	5
Kansas	253	27	25	10	4	2	17	6
Colorado	252	33	12	10	7	5	16	1
Oregon	224	27	24	9	10	0	13	6
Washington	220	39	13	6	4	10	5	9
West Virginia	219	23	13	10	8	6	18	9
Mississippi	216	23	16	12	7	5	6	3

CRASH LANE NEWS

Crash Table information from the public domain found at *www.fmcsa.dot.gov*. There is no method to the madness of citations for unsafe violations to random commercial motor-vehicle drivers. The number of violations is excessive and aimless when looking at the order of crashes per violations. There is no pattern and the totals differ. The ratings of commercial motor carriers by the FMCSA are not comprehensible, without the weather as the cause of accidents. When looking at the inconsistency of the ticket distribution and what is considered the cause of the accident the blame is only on the driver. In summary, the most important point is that the ratings do not mention anything about the weather being a safety factor. The design of the Crash Table is property of *Crash Lane News*. All Rights Reserved ©.

STATE CRASH TOTALS 2010 - 2012 LLEFTO RIGHT GREATEST TO LEAST TOTAL CRASHES. BELOW STATE ORDER ARE OFF STATE CRASH TOTALS.	TOTALS	SWIFT TRANSPORTATION COMPANY LLC DOT # 54283	UNITED PARCEL SERVICE DOT # 21800	WERNER ENTERPRISES INC DOT # 53467	SCHNEIDER NATIONAL CARRIERS INC DOT # 264184	PENSKE TRUCK LEASING CO LP DOT # 327574	FEDEX FREIGHT INC DOT # 239039	J.B. HUNT TRANSPORT INC DOT # 80806
Massachusetts	205	9	28	5	4	30	2	3
Maryland	190	10	31	6	10	4	6	10
New Mexico	170	32	2	8	1	8	11	3
Nebraska	168	8	4	12	3	5	3	2
Connecticut	163	10	6	6	12	18	7	4
Minnesota	154	9	8	15	8	0	6	6
Montana	139	14	1	9	1	57	0	1
Nevada	111	16	4	8	6	0	0	1
Idaho	111	13	2	4	1	2	6	0
Maine	63	2	9	1	2	4	0	2
North Dakota	43	4	4	4	2	0	1	0
South Dakota	41	5	1	5	0	1	2	0
Delaware	41	3	3	1	0	4	0	3
New Hampshire	31	1	4	1	2	0	4	0
Vermont	18	0	4	0	1	0	1	0
Rhode Island	11	3	1	0	0	1	0	0
Alaska	1	0	0	0	0	0	0	0
TOTAL CRASHES PER CARRIER	19452	1525	1474	975	880	826	717	675
TOTAL INSPECTIONS WHERE VIOLATIONS WERE GIVEN	40094	3870	1046	2355	1934	316	754	1225

The design of the Crash Table is property of *Crash Lane News*. All Rights Reserved ©

STATE CRASH TOTALS 2010 - 2012 GREATEST TO LEAST TOTAL CRASHES.	RYDER TRUCK RENTAL INC DOT # 16130	C.R. ENGLAND INC DOT # 28406	CON-WAY FREIGHT INC DOT # 241829	US XPRESS INC DOT # 303024	FEDERAL EXPRESS CORPORATION DOT # 86876	NEW PRIME INC. DOT # 3706	YRC INC (YELLOW) DOT # 71821
Texas	37	43	49	36	48	36	32
California	37	42	32	21	63	22	18
Ohio	56	24	43	48	9	23	39
Indiana	1	28	44	37	25	23	33
Illinois	26	35	38	29	18	25	22
Pennsylvania	38	14	29	24	21	27	29
Georgia	15	3	15	27	28	12	13
Missouri	13	23	25	18	18	31	18
Tennessee	0	9	25	17	15	24	19
New Jersey	88	4	4	17	12	16	9
Virginia	5	12	15	20	15	27	7
North Carolina	26	13	25	22	9	10	23
New York	62	8	13	14	17	15	16
Kentucky	0	11	15	16	15	13	10
Michigan	33	8	25	13	21	10	13
Florida	28	3	7	15	26	10	17
Arizona	10	23	5	7	10	15	16
Louisiana	11	12	15	18	10	6	4
Alabama	0	6	13	21	7	7	8
Oklahoma	9	15	11	12	2	12	7
Arkansas	5	9	8	13	12	16	9
Wisconsin	13	18	11	6	7	4	5
South Carolina	14	7	3	26	5	3	15
Utah	10	28	5	3	8	13	9
Wyoming	2	37	1	11	3	14	6
Iowa	3	18	11	5	3	8	7
Kansas	0	9	7	5	7	6	6
Colorado	1	25	4	3	5	9	12
Oregon	0	11	8	1	4	2	3
Washington	6	9	5	1	9	2	6
West Virginia	3	5	5	9	1	7	7
Mississippi	2	3	4	5	0	4	7

STATE CRASH TOTALS 2010 - 2012 GREATEST TO LEAST TOTAL CRASHES.	RYDER TRUCK RENTAL INC DOT # 16130	C.R. ENGLAND INC DOT # 28406	CON-WAY FREIGHT INC DOT # 241829	US XPRESS INC DOT # 303024	FEDERAL EXPRESS CORPORATION DOT # 86876	NEW PRIME INC. DOT # 3706	YRC INC (YELLOW) DOT # 71821
Massachusetts	57	1	8	1	8	6	7
Maryland	0	1	1	7	10	8	5
New Mexico	1	7	4	4	0	5	4
Nebraska	4	20	4	6	4	11	6
Connecticut	12	2	8	9	2	11	2
Minnesota	1	4	14	3	3	0	4
Montana	0	7	3	2	3	1	0
Nevada	0	8	3	3	1	6	8
Idaho	1	13	0	1	3	0	3
Maine	10	1	1	1	2	9	2
North Dakota	0	9	2	2	2	0	0
South Dakota	0	4	5	0	0	1	0
Delaware	3	0	0	0	1	1	1
New Hampshire	1	0	3	1	3	1	0
Vermont	1	0	1	2	0	1	1
Rhode Island	1	0	0	0	1	0	0
Alaska	0	0	0	0	1	0	0
TOTAL CRASHES PER CARRIER	646	592	577	562	496	523	488
TOTAL INSPECTIONS WHERE VIOLATIONS WERE GIVEN	280	1569	604	1775	219	1219	850

The design of the Crash Table is property of *Crash Lane News*. All Rights Reserved ©

STATE CRASH TOTALS 2010 - 2012 GREATEST TO LEAST TOTAL CRASHES.	OLD DOMINION FREIGHT LINE INC DOT#90849	WESTERN EXPRESS INC DOT#511412	ESTES EXPRESS LINES DOT # 121018	CRETE CARRIER CORPORATION DOT#73705	WAL-MART TRANSPORTATION LLC DOT#63585	CRST EXPEDITED INC DOT # 53773	AVERITT EXPRESS INC DOT # 36684
Texas	43	16	31	25	48	37	50
California	14	15	1	3	24	10	0
Ohio	19	13	26	16	9	12	6
Indiana	24	12	18	21	21	13	0
Illinois	21	9	18	30	11	23	0
Pennsylvania	20	25	25	21	9	12	3
Georgia	23	17	26	31	16	9	35
Missouri	14	12	17	19	13	13	2
Tennessee	13	22	14	19	6	8	36
New Jersey	18	34	9	9	2	9	2
Virginia	13	40	34	6	9	9	10
North Carolina	29	14	30	14	14	4	31
New York	17	30	10	14	10	5	0
Kentucky	9	16	21	15	8	8	23
Michigan	13	2	11	7	8	5	3
Florida	7	7	18	4	19	10	14
Arizona	8	2	0	5	9	19	1
Louisiana	4	6	10	7	6	5	18
Alabama	6	17	10	5	4	5	25
Oklahoma	6	10	6	10	12	10	4
Arkansas	7	2	5	9	10	9	2
Wisconsin	6	1	8	6	4	3	4
South Carolina	9	8	9	8	2	1	6
Utah	9	3	1	1	7	6	0
Wyoming	9	5	1	7	1	17	0
Iowa	6	7	4	8	4	11	8
Kansas	15	1	5	13	5	7	0
Colorado	4	5	0	6	7	10	0
Oregon	3	0	0	0	6	4	0
Washington	1	0	0	0	7	5	0
West Virginia	3	9	4	2	1	5	5
Mississippi	9	3	4	4	3	0	16

The design of the Crash Table is property of *Crash Lane News*. All Rights Reserved ©

STATE CRASH TOTALS 2010 - 2012 GREATEST TO LEAST TOTAL CRASHES.	OLD DOMINION FREIGHT LINE INC DOT#90849	WESTERN EXPRESS INC DOT#511412	ESTES EXPRESS LINES DOT # 121018	CRETE CARRIER CORPORATION DOT#73705	WAL-MART TRANSPORTATION LLC DOT#63585	CRST EXPEDITED INC DOT # 53773	AVERITT EXPRESS INC DOT # 36684
Massachusetts	3	8	5	1	1	1	0
Maryland	3	15	6	5	4	1	1
New Mexico	0	2	0	1	3	10	0
Nebraska	2	2	0	14	3	10	0
Connecticut	6	9	5	4	1	3	1
Minnesota	6	3	2	0	1	2	0
Montana	4	1	0	1	3	2	0
Nevada	0	1	1	2	1	1	0
Idaho	3	2	0	4	2	5	10
Maine	0	9	1	1	3	0	0
North Dakota	2	0	0	1	0	2	0
South Dakota	2	0	0	4	0	1	0
Delaware	0	5	2	0	3	0	0
New Hampshire	0	3	2	1	2	0	0
Vermont	1	0	0	1	0	0	0
Rhode Island	1	0	0	0	0	0	0
Alaska	0	0	0	0	0	0	0
TOTAL CRASHES PER CARRIER	435	423	400	385	342	342	316
TOTAL INSPECTIONS WHERE VIOLATIONS WERE GIVEN	547	1011	556	1045	406	1045	506

STATE CRASH TOTALS 2010 - 2012 GREATEST TO LEAST TOTAL CRASHES.	LANDSTAR RANGER INC DOT # 241572	KNIGHT TRANSPORTATION INC DOT # 428823	USA TRUCK INC DOT #213754	CELADON TRUCKING SERVICE INC DOT # 261902	SAIA MOTOR FREIGHT LINE LLC DOT # 29124	ABF FREIGHT SYSTEM INCORPORATED DOT # 82866
Texas	46	33	26	49	42	18
California	15	46	7	5	21	8
Ohio	12	13	22	14	5	13
Indiana	14	16	17	21	7	21
Illinois	10	6	11	18	9	7
Pennsylvania	7	7	22	4	0	14
Georgia	11	4	13	10	12	19
Missouri	7	3	7	8	6	19
Tennessee	12	5	12	8	8	13
New Jersey	2	2	8	3	0	4
Virginia	15	4	15	11	1	5
North Carolina	3	2	14	14	10	3
New York	10	4	2	6	0	6
Kentucky	7	1	15	10	13	5
Michigan	9	2	9	6	8	0
Florida	17	7	1	3	12	4
Arizona	9	21	4	3	9	17
Louisiana	10	5	6	10	22	1
Alabama	6	3	2	6	4	7
Oklahoma	5	2	1	5	11	3
Arkansas	5	1	11	9	4	2
Wisconsin	2	3	2	1	3	5
South Carolina	3	3	10	6	2	1
Utah	4	9	1	2	3	9
Wyoming	3	7	1	2	1	11
Iowa	2	0	1	5	1	1
Kansas	1	5	3	1	4	6
Colorado	6	8	1	2	6	0
Oregon	1	10	2	0	6	3
Washington	3	16	1	0	7	7
West Virginia	6	2	4	4	0	5
Mississippi	8	3	1	3	8	5

STATE CRASH TOTALS 2010 - 2012 GREATEST TO LEAST TOTAL CRASHES.	LANDSTAR RANGER INC DOT # 241572	KNIGHT TRANSPORTATION INC DOT # 428823	USA TRUCK INC DOT #213754	CELADON TRUCKING SERVICE INC DOT # 261902	SAIA MOTOR FREIGHT LINE LLC DOT # 29124	ABF FREIGHT SYSTEM INCORPORATED DOT # 82866
Massachusetts	0	0	2	1	0	2
Maryland	0	3	5	3	0	4
New Mexico	9	2	1	1	3	3
Nebraska	1	0	0	2	1	0
Connecticut	0	1	3	1	0	4
Minnesota	0	5	0	2	2	0
Montana	4	2	0	0	0	0
Nevada	4	14	0	0	3	2
Idaho	3	4	0	0	1	4
Maine	1	0	1	0	0	0
North Dakota	0	2	0	1	0	0
South Dakota	1	2	0	1	0	1
Delaware	2	1	1	0	0	0
New Hampshire	0	0	0	0	0	1
Vermont	0	0	0	1	0	0
Rhode Island	0	0	1	1	0	0
Alaska	0	0	0	0	0	0
TOTAL CRASHES PER CARRIER	296	289	266	263	255	263
TOTAL INSPECTIONS WHERE VIOLATIONS WERE GIVEN	1075	939	627	854	383	341

STATE CRASH TOTALS 2010 - 2012 GREATEST TO LEAST TOTAL CRASHES.	MARTEN TRANSPORT LTD DOT # 74432	USF HOLLAND INC DOT # 75806	COVENANT TRANSPORT INC DOT # 273818	CENTRAL REFRIDGERATED SERVICE DOT # 21331	QUALITY CARRIER INC DOT # 76600	STEVENS TRANSPORT INC DOT # 79466	P.A.M. TRANSPORT DOT #179752
Texas	15	0	20	13	25	30	41
California	21	0	14	5	5	11	1
Ohio	12	41	14	12	14	4	14
Indiana	23	27	12	2	7	9	11
Illinois	21	31	15	15	8	9	5
Pennsylvania	13	2	5	5	11	5	2
Georgia	12	9	7	12	7	2	11
Missouri	12	10	9	10	6	6	3
Tennessee	11	18	13	9	6	6	10
New Jersey	3	0	1	2	6	6	3
Virginia	8	0	6	8	5	13	2
North Carolina	4	10	6	12	4	2	2
New York	10	0	5	3	12	2	2
Kentucky	7	13	10	7	9	0	9
Michigan	5	31	1	1	7	0	10
Florida	7	0	10	4	2	6	2
Arizona	8	0	9	3	2	11	2
Louisiana	2	0	4	1	15	1	7
Alabama	4	7	5	2	5	3	1
Oklahoma	3	0	3	3	0	5	6
Arkansas	4	0	2	1	3	6	13
Wisconsin	1	15	3	5	4	2	0
South Carolina	1	7	3	8	3	1	1
Utah	4	0	3	11	0	2	0
Wyoming	3	0	9	10	0	3	0
Iowa	4	4	5	7	1	1	0
Kansas	2	4	3	3	1	3	0
Colorado	4	0	1	5	0	7	0
Oregon	2	0	1	7	2	1	0
Washington	0	0	5	5	2	0	0
West Virginia	4	7	4	3	1	0	2
Mississippi	2	0	3	2	3	1	0

STATE CRASH TOTALS 2010 - 2012 GREATEST TO LEAST TOTAL CRASHES.	MARTEN TRANSPORT LTD DOT # 74432	USF HOLLAND INC DOT # 75806	COVENANT TRANSPORT INC DOT # 273818	CENTRAL REFRIDGERATED SERVICE DOT # 21331	QUALITY CARRIER INC DOT # 76600	STEVENS TRANSPORT INC DOT # 79466	P.A.M. TRANSPORT DOT #179752
Massachusetts	0	0	0	0	1	1	1
Maryland	1	0	2	0	2	0	0
New Mexico	2	0	6	0	1	6	0
Nebraska	0	1	3	10	0	0	2
Connecticut	0	0	2	0	2	0	0
Minnesota	5	1	1	2	0	0	0
Montana	0	0	5	3	0	0	0
Nevada	4	0	1	0	1	0	0
Idaho	0	0	0	6	0	0	1
Maine	0	0	0	0	0	0	0
North Dakota	0	0	2	0	0	0	0
South Dakota	0	0	0	0	0	0	0
Delaware	0	0	1	0	1	0	0
New Hampshire	0	0	0	0	0	0	0
Vermont	0	0	0	0	0	0	0
Rhode Island	0	0	0	0	0	0	0
Alaska	0	0	0	0	0	0	0
TOTAL CRASHES PER CARRIER	244	238	234	217	184	165	164
TOTAL INSPECTIONS WHERE VIOLATIONS WERE GIVEN	778	580	607	599	598	412	428

The design of the Crash Table is property of *Crash Lane News*. All Rights Reserved ©

STATE CRASH TOTALS 2010 - 2012 GREATEST TO LEAST TOTAL CRASHES.	DART TRANSIT COMPANY DOT # 75525	SUPER SERVICE LLC DOT # 1972877	ROEHL TRANSPORT INC DOT # 74481	TRANSAM TRUCKING INC DOT # 315503	FFE TRANSPORTATION SERVICES INC DOT #109745	GREYHOUND LINES INC DOT # 44110	PASCHALL TRUCK LINES INC DOT # 105234
Texas	27	4	2	14	31	11	21
California	2	0	0	1	4	16	2
Ohio	5	21	13	12	1	2	13
Indiana	14	10	17	8	4	3	5
Illinois	5	6	13	8	3	4	5
Pennsylvania	5	7	7	5	8	9	3
Georgia	8	5	5	4	5	3	6
Missouri	10	7	5	14	4	1	8
Tennessee	2	5	8	2	6	2	13
New Jersey	3	4	3	4	3	21	1
Virginia	4	8	6	1	3	6	3
North Carolina	0	6	2	7	1	8	6
New York	3	9	4	0	1	3	0
Kentucky	3	17	9	2	4	2	5
Michigan	1	5	4	4	3	4	1
Florida	2	8	2	2	4	4	4
Arizona	0	2	1	1	3	2	0
Louisiana	3	0	0	4	2	1	4
Alabama	4	2	2	1	1	2	2
Oklahoma	4	1	1	7	5	3	0
Arkansas	5	1	3	8	6	0	4
Wisconsin	14	0	15	0	4	2	4
South Carolina	5	5	4	1	2	3	7
Utah	0	0	0	0	4	0	0
Wyoming	0	0	2	1	2	0	1
Iowa	9	2	1	5	1	0	1
Kansas	2	0	1	9	2	0	0
Colorado	0	0	0	5	3	3	0
Oregon	0	0	1	0	3	1	0
Washington	0	1	0	0	0	0	0
West Virginia	0	4	3	0	0	0	1
Mississippi	0	2	0	2	1	0	4

The design of the Crash Table is property of *Crash Lane News*. All Rights Reserved ©

STATE CRASH TOTALS 2010 - 2012 GREATEST TO LEAST TOTAL CRASHES.	DART TRANSIT COMPANY DOT # 75525	SUPER SERVICE LLC DOT # 1972877	ROEHL TRANSPORT INC DOT # 74481	TRANSAM TRUCKING INC DOT # 315503	FFE TRANSPORTATION SERVICES INC DOT #109745	GREYHOUND LINES INC DOT # 44110	PASCHALL TRUCK LINES INC DOT # 105234
Massachusetts	0	1	1	0	2	1	0
Maryland	2	1	0	0	0	3	1
New Mexico	0	0	0	0	2	1	0
Nebraska	0	0	3	1	0	0	0
Connecticut	1	0	0	0	0	1	0
Minnesota	10	0	5	1	0	0	0
Montana	0	0	0	0	2	0	0
Nevada	0	0	0	0	0	0	0
Idaho	0	0	1	0	0	2	0
Maine	0	0	1	0	0	0	0
North Dakota	0	0	0	0	1	0	0
South Dakota	1	0	0	0	0	0	0
Delaware	0	0	1	0	0	0	0
New Hampshire	0	0	1	0	0	0	0
Vermont	0	0	0	0	0	2	0
Rhode Island	0	0	0	0	0	0	0
Alaska	0	0	0	0	0	0	0
TOTAL CRASHES PER CARRIER	154	144	147	134	131	126	125
TOTAL INSPECTIONS WHERE VIOLATIONS WERE GIVEN	542	541	359	414	411	196	513

STATE CRASH TOTALS 2010 - 2012 GREATEST TO LEAST TOTAL CRASHES.	MERCER TRUCK LINES CO INC DOT # 154712	INTERSTATE DISTRIBUTOR CO DOT# 8273	KLLM TRANSPORT SERVICES LLC DOT # 154237	CRST MALONE INC DOT # 105790	RUAN TRANSPORT CORPORATION DOT # 55787	GORDON TRUCKING INC DOT # 190991	TRANSPORT CORPORATION OF AMERICA INC DOT # 183949
Texas	7	5	24	6	10	0	6
California	5	33	6	0	26	25	5
Ohio	11	4	5	9	2	1	13
Indiana	10	3	5	12	9	3	13
Illinois	1	5	5	7	4	3	11
Pennsylvania	1	0	1	2	4	1	8
Georgia	2	3	4	6	1	0	2
Missouri	6	3	3	3	2	1	3
Tennessee	9	3	4	7	1	1	3
New Jersey	1	2	1	1	2	0	2
Virginia	3	1	2	2	2	0	2
North Carolina	4	0	4	4	2	0	0
New York	4	0	2	0	6	0	1
Kentucky	9	1	4	6	2	0	2
Michigan	2	1	1	3	2	2	6
Florida	2	0	1	1	1	2	1
Arizona	0	3	3	3	8	1	2
Louisiana	0	1	5	0	1	0	1
Alabama	5	0	3	7	3	0	6
Oklahoma	4	2	2	5	4	0	5
Arkansas	2	1	5	5	0	0	3
Wisconsin	2	0	0	0	5	2	3
South Carolina	3	1	7	4	0	0	1
Utah	3	4	0	0	0	5	0
Wyoming	3	4	1	0	0	5	0
Iowa	1	1	1	2	4	3	2
Kansas	2	2	3	1	1	2	2
Colorado	2	2	2	2	2	2	0
Oregon	2	13	1	0	2	24	0
Washington	1	10	0	1	1	16	0
West Virginia	1	0	1	3	2	0	0
Mississippi	2	0	11	3	0	0	0

STATE CRASH TOTALS 2010 - 2012 GREATEST TO LEAST TOTAL CRASHES.	MERCER TRUCK LINES CO INC DOT # 154712	INTERSTATE DISTRIBUTOR CO DOT# 8273	KLLM TRANSPORT SERVICES LLC DOT # 154237	CRST MALONE INC DOT # 105790	RUAN TRANSPORT CORPORATION DOT # 55787	GORDON TRUCKING INC DOT # 190991	TRANSPORT CORPORATION OF AMERICA INC DOT # 183949
Massachusetts	0	0	0	0	0	0	0
Maryland	1	0	0	0	1	0	0
New Mexico	1	3	0	1	2	2	0
Nebraska	3	0	0	4	0	1	2
Connecticut	1	0	0	0	0	0	2
Minnesota	1	1	0	1	10	1	4
Montana	1	1	2	2	0	2	1
Nevada	1	2	0	0	0	5	0
Idaho	0	4	0	0	0	3	0
Maine	0	0	0	0	0	0	0
North Dakota	0	0	0	1	0	0	0
South Dakota	0	0	0	2	0	0	1
Delaware	0	0	0	0	1	0	0
New Hampshire	0	0	0	0	0	0	0
Vermont	0	0	0	0	1	0	0
Rhode Island	0	0	0	0	0	0	0
Alaska	0	0	0	0	0	0	0
TOTAL CRASHES PER CARRIER	119	119	119	116	124	113	113
TOTAL INSPECTIONS WHERE VIOLATIONS WERE GIVEN	509	330	423	511	232	310	380

STATE CRASH TOTALS 2010 - 2012 GREATEST TO LEAST TOTAL CRASHES.	MVT SERVICES LLC (MESILLA VALLEY TRANSPORTATION) DOT # 270179	SOUTHERN REFRIDGERATED TRANSPORT INC DOT # 276010	ARNOLD TRANSPORTATION SERVICES INC DOT # 148974	RUAN LOGISTICS CORPORATION DOT # 149350	MAVERICK TRANSPORTATION LLC DOT # 178538	ATLAS VAN LINES INC DOT # 125550	BOYD BROS TRANSPORTATION INC DOT # 92321
Texas	33	24	16	4	4	2	4
California	7	4	0	12	0	5	0
Ohio	3	0	6	0	9	2	1
Indiana	3	6	2	2	5	3	6
Illinois	5	1	1	4	5	3	4
Pennsylvania	2	0	6	6	5	3	4
Georgia	1	3	8	1	3	4	1
Missouri	1	1	1	3	4	5	3
Tennessee	8	2	4	1	5	2	2
New Jersey	2	1	4	3	1	3	0
Virginia	1	6	4	1	4	3	1
North Carolina	0	2	7	1	7	3	6
New York	0	2	5	1	2	1	0
Kentucky	4	3	0	2	5	0	4
Michigan	0	1	0	1	0	2	0
Florida	1	3	4	2	0	5	4
Arizona	3	1	0	12	0	2	0
Louisiana	2	9	1	1	3	1	8
Alabama	2	2	1	1	0	2	12
Oklahoma	5	6	2	0	2	1	3
Arkansas	4	5	3	0	3	0	0
Wisconsin	2	1	1	2	2	0	0
South Carolina	1	1	2	0	0	2	1
Utah	0	4	0	0	0	1	0
Wyoming	4	2	0	1	0	0	0
Iowa	0	1	0	6	2	2	0
Kansas	1	0	0	3	1	1	1
Colorado	3	1	0	1	0	2	0
Oregon	0	0	0	0	0	1	0
Washington	0	2	0	0	0	2	0
West Virginia	0	2	3	1	1	0	0
Mississippi	2	2	2	0	0	1	4

STATE CRASH TOTALS 2010 - 2012 GREATEST TO LEAST TOTAL CRASHES.	MVT SERVICES LLC (MESILLA VALLEY TRANSPORTATION) DOT # 270179	SOUTHERN REFRIDGERATED TRANSPORT INC DOT # 276010	ARNOLD TRANSPORTATION SERVICES INC DOT # 148974	RUAN LOGISTICS CORPORATION DOT # 149350	MAVERICK TRANSPORTATION LLC DOT # 178538	ATLAS VAN LINES INC DOT # 125550	BOYD BROS TRANSPORTATION INC DOT # 92321
Massachusetts	0	0	1	0	0	2	0
Maryland	1	0	3	0	1	2	2
New Mexico	7	1	0	3	1	1	0
Nebraska	3	2	0	1	0	0	2
Connecticut	0	0	1	0	1	0	1
Minnesota	0	0	0	3	0	2	1
Montana	0	1	0	0	0	1	0
Nevada	0	0	0	1	0	0	0
Idaho	1	1	0	1	0	1	0
Maine	0	0	0	0	0	0	0
North Dakota	0	0	0	1	0	0	0
South Dakota	0	0	0	0	0	0	0
Delaware	0	0	0	1	0	1	0
New Hampshire	0	0	0	0	0	0	0
Vermont	0	0	0	0	0	0	0
Rhode Island	0	0	0	0	0	1	0
Alaska	0	0	0	0	0	0	0
TOTAL CRASHES PER CARRIER	112	103	88	83	76	75	75
TOTAL INSPECTIONS WHERE VIOLATIONS WERE GIVEN	469	320	189	214	252	483	131

The design of the Crash Table is property of *Crash Lane News*. All Rights Reserved ©

STATE CRASH TOTALS 2010 - 2012 GREATEST TO LEAST TOTAL CRASHES.	JOHN CHRISTNER TRUCKING INC DOT # 273897	TANGO TRANSPORT LLC DOT # 459762	COWAN SYSTEMS LLC DOT # 548880	MAY TRUCKING COMPANY DOT # 94081	PENSKE LOGISTICS LLC DOT # 268015	ADD A COMPETITOR HERE	ADD A COMPANY THAT WORKS WITH YOUR	ADD YOUR VEHICLE HERE
Texas	11	17	4	0	2			
California	8	0	0	12	8			
Ohio	1	0	8	2	7			
Indiana	1	1	6	0	2			
Illinois	1	1	3	5	3			
Pennsylvania	0	0	5	3	3			
Georgia	0	7	6	2	3			
Missouri	2	2	0	1	2			
Tennessee	2	3	2	2	1			
New Jersey	0	0	2	1	3			
Virginia	1	1	7	1	2			
North Carolina	1	1	1	1	1			
New York	0	0	3	0	8			
Kentucky	0	1	3	0	0			
Michigan	0	0	0	0	7			
Florida	3	0	1	0	2			
Arizona	7	0	0	2	2			
Louisiana	3	18	1	0	1			
Alabama	1	3	1	1	0			
Oklahoma	9	2	0	1	3			
Arkansas	2	13	0	0	0			
Wisconsin	0	0	0	0	2			
South Carolina	0	0	5	0	2			
Utah	1	0	0	2	0			
Wyoming	5	0	0	6	0			
Iowa	2	0	0	1	0			
Kansas	1	1	0	3	1			
Colorado	1	0	0	4	2			
Oregon	1	0	0	8	1			
Washington	0	0	0	3	0			
West Virginia	0	0	2	0	0			
Mississippi	2	2	0	0	1			

*Visit CRASHLANENEWS.com

STATE CRASH TOTALS 2010 - 2012 GREATEST TO LEAST TOTAL CRASHES.	JOHN CHRISTNER TRUCKING INC DOT # 273897	TANGO TRANSPORT LLC DOT # 459762	COWAN SYSTEMS LLC DOT # 548880	MAY TRUCKING COMPANY DOT # 94081	PENSKE LOGISTICS LLC DOT # 268015	ADD A COMPETITOR HERE	ADD A COMPANY THAT WORKS WITH YOUR	ADD YOUR VEHICLE HERE
Massachusetts	1	0	0	0	0			
Maryland	0	0	8	0	0			
New Mexico	5	0	0	0	0			
Nebraska	0	0	0	3	0			
Connecticut	0	0	4	0	0			
Minnesota	0	0	0	1	0			
Montana	0	0	0	1	1			
Nevada	1	0	0	2	0			
Idaho	0	0	0	3	0			
Maine	0	0	0	0	0			
North Dakota	0	0	0	0	0			
South Dakota	0	0	0	1	0			
Delaware	0	0	0	0	1			
New Hampshire	0	0	0	0	0			
Vermont	0	0	0	0	0			
Rhode Island	0	0	0	0	0			
Alaska	0	0	0	0	0			
TOTAL CRASHES PER CARRIER	73	73	72	72	71			
TOTAL INSPECTIONS WHERE VIOLATIONS WERE GIVEN	306	188	179	181	158			

Below is the Violation Table. This includes all the violations from the commercial motor vehicles mentioned in the above Crash Table. Note that the order of this table mirrors that of the Crash Table. *Crash Lane News* found out there was no consistency in violations given according to crashes. The FMCSA and the Department of Transportation have mentioned that there is more being done to make things safer but it also seems to be in an unorganized system of management. This irregularity of crash totals compared to violation totals seems like a fabrication of data to appear that things are safer when they are possibly more aimless as to the cause of accidents than ever in the history of trade going back thousands of years. Check out the data while keeping in mind that there is no pattern of violation enforcement based on crashes. The only patterns that exist are by each state. Each state is arranged differently from the above, showing the greatest amount of violations occurring in Indiana. Below is a simple list of states giving the most unsafe driving violations. Note, when compared to the list of states with most crashes, there is really no pattern or consistency seen in traffic enforcement. The comparison between crash state totals and unsafe driving violation totals are very random in order. This list can help travelers know that traffic enforcement is taken more serious in the below states. Know that traffic enforcement is held at a higher standard. Protect yourself from getting an unsafe violation. By doing this you should also avoid more accidents, even though the order of the two lists does not match.

1. Indiana	12. Pennsylvania
2. New Mexico	13. North Carolina
3. Ohio	14. California
4. Illinois	15. Nevada
5. Louisiana	16. Iowa
6. Arizona	17. Colorado
7. Texas	18. South Carolina
8. Georgia	19. Maryland
9. Washington	20. West Virginia
10. Michigan	21. Arkansas
11. Tennessee	22. Massachusetts

23. Idaho
24. Kentucky
25. Oklahoma
26. New York
27. Missouri
28. New York
29. Missouri
30. Oregon
31. Nebraska
32. Alabama
33. Florida
34. Wyoming
35. Kansas
36. Minnesota

37. Wisconsin
38. Virginia
39. Connecticut
40. Montana
41. Utah
42. Vermont
43. Mississippi
44. New Jersey
45. Delaware
46. South Dakota
47. New Hampshire
48. Rhode Island
49. Alaska

Note, aside from the Crash list and Unsafe driving list having no consistency, the solution is simple. If you drive in one of the states towards the top of the list, drive with extra caution. Drive in a defensive way in order to avoid an unsafe driving violation.

	TOTAL	SWIFT TRANSPORTATION COMPANY LLC DOT # 54283	UNITED PARCEL SERVICE DOT # 21800	WERNER ENTERPRISES INC DOT # 53467	SCHNEIDER NATIONAL CARRIERS INC DOT # 264184	PENSKE TRUCK LEASING CO LP DOT # 327574	FEDEX FREIGHT INC DOT # 239039	J.B. HUNT TRANSPORT INC DOT # 80806
CRASH LANE NEWS INSPECTIONS WHERE THERE WAS A UNSAFE DRIVING VIOLATION ISSUED PER STATE GREATEST TO LEAST 2010 - 2012. THERE ARE 4 IMPORTANT THINGS TO KNOW IN THE FOLLOWING. (1.) NOTE THAT EACH STATE'S INSPECTION RATES VARY FROM EACH STATE'S CRASHES. THIS DIFFERENCE IS SIGNIFICANT, PROVING EXCESSIVE CITATIONS, AND AIMLESSNESS. (2.) THE COMERCIAL MOTOR CARRIERS ARE IN THE ORDER OF CRASH TOTALS FROM CRASH TABLE. (3.) FOR A HINT ON HOW TO AVOID A UNSAFE CITATION FROM AN AREA GIVING AN EXCESSIVE AMOUNT OF CITATIONS CHECK THE BELOW STATE ORDER. THIS ORDER IS OFF OF THE STATE'S UNSAFE VIOLATION TOTALS. (4.) THE DEPARTMENT OF TRANSPORTATION'S INCONSISTENCY IS VERY VISIBLE. FIRST, THE INCONCISTENT TOTALS BETWEEN CRASHES AND UNSAFE VIOLATIONS FOR EACH COMPANY IS VERY OBVIOUS. THEN EXAMINE THE INCONCISTENT TOTALS BETWEEN EACH STATE. TRAFFIC MANAGEMENT AND THE FMCSA's RATINGS IS INCONSITENT WITH THERE BEING DIFFERENT SIZE STATES, AND DIFFERENT TRAFFIC MANAGEMENT BUDGETING/CAPABILITIES FOR EACH STATE. AFTER REVIEWING IT SHOULD ALL APPEAR VERY EXCESSIVE, AND APPEAR THAT THE FMCSA'S RATINGS OF COMMERCIAL CARRIERS LISTED HERE ARE A COMPLETE FABRICATION. ONE OF THE BIGGEST INCONCISTENCIES IS THE FMCSA DOES NOT TRACK AND MAKE PUBLIC THE COMMERCIAL DRIVER FATALITIES/DEATHS OCCURING ONDUTY AND OFFDUTY. This table data is from the www.fmcsa.dot.gov.								
VIOLATION TOTALS PER COMPANY AND BELOW STATE	40094	3870	1046	2355	1934	316	754	1225
TOTAL CRASHES PER COMPANY	19422	1525	1471	975	880	826	717	675
Indiana	8219	548	236	523	467	4	156	365
New Mexico	2880	402	33	200	49	22	29	0
Ohio	2296	183	40	130	128	16	24	65
Illinois	1745	104	63	123	106	64	48	94
Louisiana	1592	178	15	58	74	1	19	47
Arizona	1506	228	23	77	44	14	26	30
Texas	1446	159	5	84	0	12	38	41
Georgia	1305	123	38	52	82	3	18	58
Washington	1268	214	16	69	0	12	17	27
Michigan	1246	96	42	80	62	6	21	50
Tennessee	1064	96	40	56	81	14	19	32
Pennsylvania	979	81	27	61	73	14	17	40
North Carolina	951	94	2	40	55	6	15	26
California	915	107	14	43	71	32	15	34
Nevada	833	144	22	43	48	3	15	17
Iowa	775	63	37	71	41	6	19	23
Colorado	737	131	43	55	22	14	25	4
South Carolina	725	70	25	33	34	2	11	20
Maryland	719	65	26	54	51	9	16	0
West Virginia	693	35	5	33	63	2	22	22
Arkansas	671	51	21	29	32	0	12	17
Massachusetts	651	39	34	27	37	10	23	29
Idaho	567	126	8	14	9	3	11	6
Kentucky	565	25	19	40	35	0	14	14

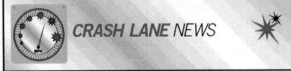

Violations per company and state. Information from public domain www.fmcsa.dot.gov. This spreadsheet is available to download for free at www.crashlanenews.com. Design is the Property of *Crash Lane News*. All Rights Reserved ©

CRASH LANE NEWS INSPECTIONS WHERE THERE WAS A VIOLATION ISSUED PER STATE GREATEST TO LEAST 2010 - 2012. THIS IS A GOOD VIEW OF EACH STATES INSPECTION RATES. NOTE THE TOTALS HERE ARE DIFFERENT FROM THE TYPE OF VIOLATION CHART WHICH HAS THE COMPLETE AMOUNT OF VIOLATIONS PER COMPANY. IN THIS TABLE THE COMERCIAL MOTOR CARRIERS ARE RANKED IN THE ORDER OF CRASH TOTALS FROM CRASH TABLE. THE CARRIERS STATE ORDER IS OFF OF SWIFTS TOTALS. THE BOTTOM COLUMN SHOWS THE INCONCISTENCY BETWEEN CRASHES AND VIOLATIONS. THIS INFORMATION IS FROM www.fmcsa.dot.gov	TOTAL	SWIFT TRANSPORTATION COMPANY LLC DOT # 54283	UNITED PARCEL SERVICE DOT # 21800	WERNER ENTERPRISES INC DOT # 53467	SCHNEIDER NATIONAL CARRIERS INC DOT # 264184	PENSKE TRUCK LEASING CO LP DOT # 327574	FEDEX FREIGHT INC DOT # 239039	J.B. HUNT TRANSPORT INC DOT # 80806
Oklahoma	493	53	17	18	28	4	8	8
New York	464	40	11	38	34	6	4	18
Missouri	442	25	12	30	14	9	12	14
Oregon	439	67	3	23	24	0	4	5
Nebraska	426	22	5	30	7	4	20	4
Alabama	421	45	10	22	30	0	2	13
Florida	415	35	15	33	13	8	5	9
Wyoming	348	48	0	13	12	1	6	2
Kansas	339	28	5	26	15	1	5	4
Minnesota	327	24	8	27	16	2	11	12
Wisconsin	325	13	24	28	22	1	15	24
Virginia	257	20	3	14	0	1	7	17
Connecticut	224	11	12	3	23	2	8	9
Montana	145	23	12	11	4	0	4	1
Utah	145	20	10	15	0	0	3	2
Vermont	129	7	22	8	0	1	3	15
Mississippi	98	15	1	7	7	0	2	3
New Jersey	69	6	0	4	3	5	1	0
Delaware	59	2	2	1	10	0	1	2
South Dakota	59	2	21	5	2	1	0	0
Maine	47	0	2	2	6	0	0	2
North Dakota	36	1	15	2	0	0	0	0
New Hampshire	26	1	1	0	0	1	3	0
Rhode Island	12	0	1	0	0	0	1	0
Alaska	1	0	0	0	0	0	0	0

Violations per company and State. Information from public domain www.fmcsa.dot.gov.
Design is the Property of *Crash Lane News.* All Rights Reserved ©

INSPECTIONS WHERE THERE WAS A VIOLATION ISSUED PER STATE GREATEST TO LEAST 2010 - 2012. THE BOTTOM COLUMN SHOWS THE INCONCISTENCY BETWEEN CRASHES AND INPECTIONS. THIS INFORMATION IS FROM www.fmcsa.dot.gov	RYDER TRUCK RENTAL INC DOT # 16130	C.R. ENGLAND INC DOT # 28406	CON-WAY FREIGHT INC DOT # 241829	US XPRESS INC DOT # 303024	FEDERAL EXPRESS CORPORATION DOT # 86876	NEW PRIME INC. DOT # 3706	YRC INC (YELLOW) DOT # 71821
Indiana	2	205	137	451	34	199	226
New Mexico	10	170	6	69	7	110	80
Arizona	4	75	12	25	7	56	34
Washington	3	160	9	21	11	56	24
Ohio	16	52	21	128	4	51	53
Louisiana	4	28	29	94	7	38	28
Texas	32	55	24	53	14	43	18
Nevada	5	85	5	20	4	31	10
Colorado	8	82	6	27	4	29	16
Idaho	4	52	3	16	1	30	11
Georgia	7	21	15	64	9	24	27
California	21	70	4	28	7	27	12
Illinois	40	79	51	71	4	33	29
Michigan	8	13	31	89	11	43	25
Tennessee	0	20	2	40	4	21	9
North Carolina	6	21	10	48	7	22	20
Pennsylvania	12	31	23	54	5	44	23
South Carolina	8	8	12	62	8	13	12
Oregon	0	35	1	13	3	14	9
Maryland	5	12	5	60	3	28	8
Iowa	0	28	24	21	4	20	17
Oklahoma	1	13	5	19	4	18	5
Arkansas	2	25	10	29	0	18	14
Wyoming	4	48	0	14	0	31	2
Alabama	0	7	9	18	1	11	9

Violations per company and State. Information from public domain www.fmcsa.dot.gov.
Design is the Property of *Crash Lane News*. All Rights Reserved ©

INSPECTIONS WHERE THERE WAS A VIOLATION ISSUED PER STATE GREATEST TO LEAST 2010 - 2012. THE BOTTOM COLUMN SHOWS THE INCONCISTENCY BETWEEN CRASHES AND INPECTIONS. THIS INFORMATION IS FROM www.fmcsa.dot.gov	RYDER TRUCK RENTAL INC DOT # 16130	C.R. ENGLAND INC DOT # 28406	CON-WAY FREIGHT INC DOT # 241829	US XPRESS INC DOT # 303024	FEDERAL EXPRESS CORPORATION DOT # 86876	NEW PRIME INC. DOT # 3706	YRC INC (YELLOW) DOT # 71821
New York	10	8	5	25	2	29	11
Massachusetts	12	4	21	19	10	36	22
Florida	14	7	4	20	8	11	7
West Virginia	9	10	13	51	3	24	13
Kansas	0	21	5	8	0	13	9
Kentucky	5	3	7	27	2	11	6
Missouri	2	11	16	16	2	12	16
Minnesota	0	15	16	12	11	11	10
Montana	0	27	1	5	0	8	0
Nebraska	9	23	5	14	0	15	7
Utah	0	23	2	1	3	4	2
Virginia	1	3	4	18	6	5	2
Mississippi	1	1	1	2	0	1	0
Wisconsin	0	13	19	5	3	1	7
Connecticut	2	0	17	3	2	10	10
Vermont	0	3	4	5	0	6	3
New Jersey	6	0	0	2	1	0	0
Delaware	1	0	2	3	0	2	0
South Dakota	1	2	2	1	1	1	1
North Dakota	0	0	2	0	0	1	0
New Hampshire	1	0	1	2	1	1	2
Alaska	0	0	0	0	0	0	0
Maine	2	0	2	1	1	7	1
Rhode Island	2	0	1	1	0	0	0
TOTAL INSPECTIONS WHERE VIOLATIONS WERE GIVEN	280	1569	604	1775	219	1219	850
TOTAL CRASHES	646	592	577	562	497	513	488

Violations per company and State. Information from public domain www.fmcsa.dot.gov.
Design is the Property of *Crash Lane News*. All Rights Reserved ©

	CRETE CARRIER CORPORATION DOT#73705	WAL-MART TRANSPORTATION LLC DOT#63585	CRST EXPEDITED INC DOT #53773	AVERITT EXPRESS INC DOT #36684	LANDSTAR RANGER INC DOT #241572	KNIGHT TRANSPORTATION INC DOT #428823	USA TRUCK INC DOT #213754	CELADON TRUCKING SERVICE INC DOT #261902	SAIA MOTOR FREIGHT LINE LLC DOT #29124	ABF FREIGHT SYSTEM INCORPORATED DOT #82866	MARTEN TRANSPORT LTD DOT #74432
TOTAL INSPECTIONS	1045	406	1045	506	1075	939	627	854	383	341	778
TOTAL CRASHES	385	342	342	316	296	289	266	263	255	263	244
Indiana	306	63	181	89	197	148	137	283	58	81	257
New Mexico	83	30	161	19	140	68	7	45	18	31	49
Ohio	94	9	77	19	51	46	74	79	8	10	45
Illinois	45	9	41	14	21	26	21	24	26	18	39
Louisiana	42	9	14	41	54	25	47	48	39	8	21
Arizona	10	28	62	3	88	82	16	16	19	10	15
Texas	19	28	28	42	62	11	34	53	23	10	18
Georgia	28	15	16	34	10	24	30	21	25	12	30
Washington	16	11	71	0	21	77	2	20	10	6	18
Michigan	16	10	9	10	46	13	12	27	26	11	22
Tennessee	24	13	16	52	26	12	24	18	9	8	16
Pennsylvania	32	2	18	2	18	18	27	9	0	15	9
North Carolina	27	9	16	40	16	15	15	22	13	11	8
California	9	3	43	2	18	78	7	10	8	2	38
Nevada	11	16	21	0	19	73	5	3	4	3	22
Iowa	21	8	22	1	0	10	8	13	10	6	10
Colorado	16	10	8	1	12	32	3	7	20	5	3
South Carolina	21	18	6	19	15	10	9	13	11	5	9
Maryland	13	10	4	7	16	15	26	5	0	4	18
West Virginia	20	3	11	20	18	6	17	22	0	12	16
Arkansas	17	11	13	17	20	8	16	16	0	4	6
Massachusetts	11	11	4	0	11	3	11	7	0	15	13
Idaho	11	1	24	0	16	35	0	5	0	2	4
Kentucky	20	8	4	19	18	5	18	14	4	1	15

Violations per company and State. Information from public domain www.fmcsa.dot.gov.

	CRETE CARRIER CORPORATION DOT#73705	WAL-MART TRANSPORTATION LLC DOT#63585	CRST EXPEDITED INC DOT # 53773	AVERITT EXPRESS INC DOT # 36684	LANDSTAR RANGER INC DOT # 241572	KNIGHT TRANSPORTATION INC DOT # 428823	USA TRUCK INC DOT #213754	CELADON TRUCKING SERVICE INC DOT # 261902	SAIA MOTOR FREIGHT LINE LLC DOT # 29124	ABF FREIGHT SYSTEM INCORPORATED DOT # 82866	MARTEN TRANSPORT LTD DOT # 74432
Oklahoma	13	8	24	10	14	5	10	6	8	6	7
New York	11	0	9	1	5	7	14	13	0	5	8
Missouri	8	4	11	4	13	7	10	5	7	7	9
Oregon	7	2	26	0	7	24	1	4	3	4	11
Nebraska	34	9	17	0	9	1	0	8	6	5	4
Alabama	10	7	7	20	17	7	2	7	0	1	1
Florida	4	10	5	11	37	9	0	2	8	2	7
Wyoming	11	4	17	0	12	7	0	4	0	1	6
Kansas	9	6	31	1	5	4	3	3	1	3	1
Minnesota	4	3	2	1	4	4	3	2	4	5	7
Wisconsin	3	7	4	4	7	7	1	2	9	2	2
Virginia	8	4	1	1	7	2	13	2	1	1	4
Connecticut	3	0	2	0	2	1	0	5	0	5	4
Montana	1	1	10	0	4	1	0	1	0	0	1
Utah	1	0	6	1	0	7	2	2	2	2	2
Vermont	3	0	0	0	2	0	1	1	0	1	0
Mississippi	0	0	1	1	0	4	0	4	2	0	2
New Jersey	1	0	0	0	1	1	0	1	0	0	0
Delaware	0	0	0	0	8	0	0	1	0	1	0
South Dakota	2	2	1	0	3	0	0	0	1	0	0
Maine	0	4	0	0	2	0	1	0	0	0	0
North Dakota	0	0	1	0	1	1	0	0	0	0	0
New Hampshire	0	0	0	0	1	0	0	1	0	0	0
Rhode Island	0	0	0	0	0	0	0	0	0	0	1
Alaska	0	0	0	0	1	0	0	0	0	0	0

Violations per company and State. Information from public domain www.fmcsa.dot.gov.

	USF HOLLAND INC DOT #75806	COVENANT TRANSPORT INC DOT #273818	CENTRAL REFRIDGERATED SERVICE DOT #21331	QUALITY CARRIER INC DOT #76600	STEVENS TRANSPORT INC DOT #79466	P.A.M. TRANSPORT DOT #179752	DART TRANSIT COMPANY DOT #75525	SUPER SERVICE LLC DOT #1972877	ROEHL TRANSPORT INC DOT #74481	TRANSAM TRUCKING INC DOT #315503	FFE TRANSPORTATION SERVICES INC DOT #109745
TOTAL INSPECTIONS	580	607	599	598	412	428	542	541	359	414	411
TOTAL CRASHES	238	234	217	184	165	164	154	144	147	134	131
Indiana	262	100	105	118	56	0	168	156	113	102	92
New Mexico	0	64	39	11	65	24	26	7	12	10	37
Ohio	67	25	42	50	26	60	28	60	43	30	12
Illinois	53	27	30	37	0	15	26	21	21	27	13
Louisiana	0	22	9	55	17	46	20	2	3	10	19
Arizona	0	31	20	9	30	13	1	13	4	2	8
Texas	0	22	13	44	40	65	33	6	1	13	30
Georgia	8	31	11	23	4	19	41	35	7	14	22
Washington	0	29	44	7	10	4	0	1	1	0	13
Michigan	53	19	3	42	9	20	6	36	28	18	10
Tennessee	15	24	14	16	6	22	16	13	7	9	5
Pennsylvania	0	16	13	13	13	14	12	22	12	12	11
North Carolina	21	20	25	8	4	18	19	22	8	9	4
California	0	12	17	6	21	2	1	3	1	0	8
Nevada	0	16	11	8	7	1	0	1	3	0	10
Iowa	22	4	21	3	10	2	23	2	7	22	5
Colorado	0	9	17	0	3	3	2	0	0	7	6
South Carolina	17	16	11	18	6	6	14	11	6	1	6
Maryland	0	11	4	9	9	11	9	7	4	4	9
West Virginia	9	7	12	20	3	17	6	31	8	0	2
Arkansas	2	16	3	16	5	24	5	3	2	8	6
Massachusetts	0	5	0	6	3	3	2	9	4	8	4
Idaho	0	9	21	4	4	1	0	1	1	0	6
Kentucky	10	12	4	17	0	0	6	38	6	3	2

Violations per company and State. Information from public domain www.fmcsa.dot.gov.

	USF HOLLAND INC DOT # 75806	COVENANT TRANSPORT INC DOT # 273818	CENTRAL REFRIDGERATED SERVICE DOT # 21331	QUALITY CARRIER INC DOT # 76600	STEVENS TRANSPORT INC DOT # 79466	P.A.M. TRANSPORT DOT #179752	DART TRANSIT COMPANY DOT # 75525	SUPER SERVICE LLC DOT # 1972877	ROEHL TRANSPORT INC DOT # 74481	TRANSAM TRUCKING INC DOT # 315503	FFE TRANSPORTATION SERVICES INC DOT #109745
Oklahoma	0	4	4	4	15	1	7	0	4	17	15
New York	1	0	1	4	7	3	3	5	8	6	3
Missouri	12	3	1	5	3	7	8	8	4	8	5
Oregon	0	10	21	4	5	0	0	0	1	0	5
Nebraska	2	6	19	0	2	0	2	0	1	20	3
Alabama	4	3	4	5	1	10	8	2	5	8	3
Florida	0	7	0	2	2	4	4	5	1	5	7
Wyoming	0	9	14	1	3	1	0	0	1	0	1
Kansas	2	5	8	2	12	0	7	1	1	31	10
Minnesota	6	4	7	2	1	0	26	2	2	4	1
Wisconsin	12	2	7	7	1	0	6	2	23	0	0
Virginia	2	1	3	2	3	7	1	7	0	1	5
Connecticut	0	3	1	7	0	0	0	5	0	0	2
Montana	0	2	6	1	0	0	0	1	3	0	0
Utah	0	0	8	0	3	0	0	0	0	0	2
Vermont	0	0	2	6	0	0	1	2	1	0	4
Mississippi	0	1	2	0	2	4	0	0	0	2	3
New Jersey	0	0	0	1	0	1	1	0	1	0	2
Delaware	0	0	0	5	1	0	0	0	0	1	0
South Dakota	0	0	1	0	0	0	0	0	1	0	0
Maine	0	0	0	0	0	0	1	0	0	1	0
North Dakota	0	0	1	0	0	0	3	0	0	0	0
New Hampshire	0	0	0	0	0	0	0	0	0	1	0
Rhode Island	0	0	0	0	0	0	0	1	0	0	0
Alaska	0	0	0	0	0	0	0	0	0	0	0

Violations per company and State. Information from public domain www.fmcsa.dot.gov.
Design is the Property of *Crash Lane News*. All Rights Reserved ©

	GREYHOUND LINES INC DOT # 44110	PASCHALL TRUCK LINES INC DOT # 105234	MERCER TRUCK LINES CO INC DOT # 154712	INTERSTATE DISTRIBUTOR CO DOT# 8273	KLLM TRANSPORT SERVICES LLC DOT # 154237	CRST MALONE INC DOT # 105790	RUAN TRANSPORT CORPORATION DOT # 55787	GORDON TRUCKING INC DOT # 190991	TRANSPORT CORPORATION OF AMERICA INC DOT # 183949	MVT SERVICES LLC (MESILLA VALLEY TRANSPORTATION) DOT # 270179	SOUTHERN REFRIDGERATED TRANSPORT INC DOT # 276010
TOTAL INSPECTIONS	196	513	509	330	423	511	232	310	380	469	320
TOTAL CRASHES	126	125	119	119	119	116	124	113	113	112	103
Indiana	0	136	110	34	106	114	46	58	123	27	45
New Mexico	9	0	57	54	34	43	7	3	19	229	29
Ohio	0	43	22	20	25	23	15	12	39	2	8
Illinois	0	13	14	3	17	20	12	8	17	11	3
Louisiana	2	49	17	1	32	23	0	0	2	37	31
Arizona	5	7	24	24	16	16	26	11	9	36	34
Texas	7	25	16	3	18	25	6	0	11	36	19
Georgia	2	17	17	1	27	15	5	0	10	12	11
Washington	5	0	15	53	4	2	7	67	0	3	8
Michigan	2	6	12	4	6	14	6	5	19	8	6
Tennessee	1	27	16	9	10	18	2	0	8	11	10
Pennsylvania	2	7	12	3	7	7	5	0	8	5	6
North Carolina	7	23	8	3	16	11	2	2	10	4	3
California	1	1	10	22	7	2	6	20	1	3	6
Nevada	0	0	10	20	3	1	5	40	4	2	6
Iowa	0	5	15	1	6	24	12	3	15	2	3
Colorado	2	1	3	12	2	9	11	15	1	7	3
South Carolina	2	6	11	1	15	13	2	0	7	1	5
Maryland	41	7	5	1	5	6	5	0	3	2	1
West Virginia	0	17	11	0	6	12	3	2	9	0	4
Arkansas	4	25	14	3	8	8	0	0	6	9	15
Massachusetts	19	0	6	0	1	2	8	0	4	0	2
Idaho	0	0	10	18	1	3	4	27	1	2	11
Kentucky	1	19	11	2	4	17	1	0	8	3	2

Violations per company and State. Information from public domain www.fmcsa.dot.gov.
Design is the Property of *Crash Lane News*. All Rights Reserved ©

	GREYHOUND LINES INC DOT # 44110	PASCHALL TRUCK LINES INC DOT # 105234	MERCER TRUCK LINES CO INC DOT # 154712	INTERSTATE DISTRIBUTOR CO DOT# 8273	KLLM TRANSPORT SERVICES LLC DOT # 154237	CRST MALONE INC DOT # 105790	RUAN TRANSPORT CORPORATION DOT # 55787	GORDON TRUCKING INC DOT # 190991	TRANSPORT CORPORATION OF AMERICA INC DOT # 183949	MVT SERVICES LLC (MESILLA VALLEY TRANSPORTATION) DOT # 270179	SOUTHERN REFRIDGERATED TRANSPORT INC DOT # 276010
Oklahoma	1	7	10	3	6	8	1	0	3	0	14
New York	11	2	6	0	5	4	1	0	3	1	0
Missouri	0	5	5	5	7	6	3	1	6	2	0
Oregon	1	0	1	16	2	3	2	14	0	5	6
Nebraska	0	41	2	6	2	14	4	2	2	3	4
Alabama	9	5	6	0	5	15	0	2	12	2	6
Florida	18	3	2	2	2	4	0	1	2	0	4
Wyoming	0	0	5	2	4	5	2	4	0	1	7
Kansas	0	1	6	0	2	8	2	0	1	1	2
Minnesota	0	5	4	2	2	2	6	2	3	0	0
Wisconsin	6	3	1	1	0	1	8	3	1	0	0
Virginia	3	3	2	0	2	3	2	0	3	0	1
Connecticut	10	0	0	0	0	2	2	0	3	0	0
Montana	0	0	2	0	0	0	0	4	1	0	3
Utah	0	1	1	0	1	3	1	4	0	0	1
Vermont	4	0	5	0	3	0	1	0	1	0	1
Mississippi	0	1	0	0	3	4	0	0	1	2	0
New Jersey	21	0	0	0	0	0	0	0	1	0	0
Delaware	0	0	4	1	1	0	0	0	0	0	0
South Dakota	0	0	0	0	0	1	1	0	3	0	0
Maine	0	0	1	0	0	0	0	0	0	0	0
North Dakota	0	2	0	0	0	0	0	0	0	0	0
New Hampshire	0	0	0	0	0	0	0	0	0	0	0
Rhode Island	0	0	0	0	0	0	0	0	0	0	0
Alaska	0	0	0	0	0	0	0	0	0	0	0

Violations per company and State. Information from public domain www.fmcsa.dot.gov.
Design is the Property of *Crash Lane News*. All Rights Reserved ©

	ARNOLD TRANSPORTATION SERVICES INC DOT # 148974	RUAN LOGISTICS CORPORATION DOT # 149350	MAVERICK TRANSPORTATION LLC DOT # 178538	ATLAS VAN LINES INC DOT # 125550	BOYD BROS TRANSPORTATION INC DOT # 92321	JOHN CHRISTNER TRUCKING INC DOT # 273897	TANGO TRANSPORT LLC DOT # 459762	COWAN SYSTEMS LLC DOT # 548880	MAY TRUCKING COMPANY DOT # 95081	PENSKE LOGISTICS LLC DOT # 268015	INSEERT YOUR VEHICLE	INSERT A COMPETITOR	INSEERT A COMPANY THAT WORKS WITH YOUR COMPANY
TOTAL INSPECTIONS	189	214	252	483	131	306	188	179	181	158			
TOTAL CRASHES	88	83	76	75	75	73	73	72	72	71			
Indiana	28	39	90	74	32	21	18	28	19	27			
New Mexico	1	8	3	42	0	92	1	3	5	3			
Ohio	20	6	17	16	8	1	6	19	10	5			
Illinois	6	8	21	22	6	9	8	9	2	4			
Louisiana	29	1	7	18	19	17	64	0	6	5			
Arizona	0	30	0	21	0	39	1	2	7	5			
Texas	0	8	8	5	4	6	21	4	0	7			
Georgia	18	7	3	21	8	1	4	11	0	10			
Washington	0	2	0	15	0	9	0	0	49	2			
Michigan	1	6	12	46	1	1	1	5	0	11			
Tennessee	0	0	12	12	10	5	3	10	2	7			
Pennsylvania	6	3	2	9	2	2	2	14	2	5			
North Carolina	15	1	9	12	3	4	3	3	1	6			
California	0	3	0	5	0	10	0	0	6	4			
Nevada	0	10	0	8	0	8	0	2	8	5			
Iowa	0	23	3	5	4	5	1	0	0	2			
Colorado	1	5	0	3	0	3	0	0	0	3			
South Carolina	11	1	5	9	5	0	1	8	1	5			
Maryland	6	0	1	16	5	0	1	17	2	2			
West Virginia	5	1	13	8	3	2	0	2	0	0			
Arkansas	6	2	10	3	1	1	31	1	8	2			
Massachusetts	4	1	0	18	0	0	0	10	1	8			
Idaho	0	2	1	13	0	12	0	0	13	0			
Kentucky	4	1	7	2	6	2	3	6	1	1			

Violations per company and State. Information from public domain www.fmcsa.dot.gov.

Design is the Property of *Crash Lane News*. All Rights Reserved ©

	ARNOLD TRANSPORTATION SERVICES INC DOT # 148974	RUAN LOGISTICS CORPORATION DOT # 149350	MAVERICK TRANSPORTATION LLC DOT # 178538	ATLAS VAN LINES INC DOT # 125550	BOYD BROS TRANSPORTATION INC DOT # 92321	JOHN CHRISTNER TRUCKING INC DOT # 273897	TANGO TRANSPORT LLC DOT # 459762	COWAN SYSTEMS LLC DOT # 548880	MAY TRUCKING COMPANY DOT # 95081	PENSKE LOGISTICS LLC DOT # 268015	INSERT YOUR VEHICLE	INSERT A COMPETITOR	INSERT A COMPANY THAT WORKS WITH YOUR COMPANY
Oklahoma	5	3	4	10	2	9	5	1	0	1			
New York	7	3	1	5	1	0	0	0	0	8			
Missouri	1	8	4	8	0	8	3	0	0	3			
Oregon	0	1	0	9	0	9	0	0	19	0			
Nebraska	0	4	1	3	0	5	0	0	3	1			
Alabama	1	2	5	1	2	3	3	2	1	6			
Florida	10	3	2	9	2	5	0	2	0	1			
Wyoming	0	0	0	9	0	10	0	0	5	0			
Kansas	2	2	2	3	1	2	1	0	0	1			
Minnesota	0	9	0	1	3	1	1	0	2	1			
Wisconsin	0	2	1	1	0	1	0	0	0	1			
Virginia	0	6	5	3	1	0	0	6	0	0			
Connecticut	1	1	1	5	0	0	0	11	0	3			
Montana	0	0	0	2	0	0	0	0	2	0			
Utah	0	1	0	1	0	1	0	0	3	0			
Vermont	0	0	0	1	0	0	0	0	2	1			
Mississippi	1	0	2	0	1	2	6	0	0	0			
New Jersey	0	0	0	1	1	0	0	2	0	0			
Delaware	0	0	0	6	0	0	0	0	0	1			
South Dakota	0	1	0	0	0	0	0	0	0	0			
Maine	0	0	0	0	0	0	0	0	0	0			
North Dakota	0	0	0	1	0	0	0	0	1	0			
New Hampshire	0	0	0	0	0	0	0	0	0	0			
Rhode Island	0	0	0	1	0	0	0	1	0	1			
Alaska	0	0	0	0	0	0	0	0	0	0			

Violations per company and State. Information from public domain www.fmcsa.dot.gov.
Design is the Property of *Crash Lane News*. All Rights Reserved ©

After viewing the Violation Table, move on to the Type of Violation Table below.

This is the Type of Violation Table, and it is important showing what the different violations are. This includes all the companies mentioned in the above two tables but lists unsafe driving violations per company. The order of commercial carriers by violations is shown from greatest to least.

The order of violation totals differs significantly from the order of companies that crash greatest to least showing an inconsistency in the ability to enforce the safety and security in the transportation industry. This table is sorted off of Swift again. It has the type of violations listed from greatest to least. Note add your own company, competitor, and car, to find your rank and comparison. The Type of Violation Table can be useful for a traveler employed or around one of the company's listed.

There is no method to the madness of citations for unsafe violations. The current system and strategy targets random commercial motor vehicle drivers and is aimless. The amount of violations are excessive and have been described to not have due process when something is automatically added to the Preemployment Screening Program without any legal defense. In summary the FMCSA, the Department of Transportation, and the Department of Justice are aimless when looking at the order of companies that crash the most and then comparing that to the inspections and type of violations. The ratings by the FMCSA of commercial motor carriers are not comprehensible because there is no pattern or visible strategy they put in place after they examine their own data years after the program started. The inconsistency of ticket distribution and what they have been considering the cause of the accidents is displayed in this type of violation table per company. The most important point is that the ratings do not mention anything about the weather being a factor. Information is in tables from public domain at www.fmcsa.dot.gov. This spreadsheet is available to download for free at www.crashlanenews.com. Type of Violation Design is Property *Crash Lane News*. All Rights Reserved ©

Number of VIOLATION for table	TYPE of VIOLATION	Type of Unsafe Violations Per Company 2010 - 2012. Each company is listed in the order of greatest to least violations. The listed companies' order is different from the other tables, showing the same that crashes and violations are not managed consistently by traffic enforcement.	Total of Unsafe Violations per Company	SWIFT TRANSPORTATION COMPANY LLC DOT # 54283	WERNER ENTERPRISES INC DOT # 53467	SCHNEIDER NATIONAL CARRIERS INC DOT # 264184	US XPRESS INC DOT # 303024
1	392.2C	Failure to obey traffic control device	7166	996	524	394	275
2	392.2-SLLS2	State/Local Laws - Speeding 6-10 miles per hour over the speed	6737	602	396	304	332
3	392.16	Failing to use seat belt while operating CMV	5298	407	215	286	185
4	392.2-SLLS1	State/Local Laws - Speeding 1-5 miles per hour over the speed limit	4946	360	307	253	232
5	392.2S	Speeding	4367	355	308	239	218
6	392.2-SLLS3	State/Local Laws - Speeding 11-14 miles per hour over the speed limit	2468	228	122	124	118
7	392.2LV	Lane Restriction violation	2236	208	137	137	122
8	392.2LC	Improper lane change	1805	168	101	98	62
9	392.2FC	Following too close	1747	123	83	96	86
10	392.2-SLLSWZ	State/Local Laws - Speeding	1248	136	62	48	37
11	392.2-SLLS4	State/Local Laws - Speeding 15	1413	121	70	68	53
12	392.2PK	Unlawfully parking and/or leaving	863	96	24	41	55
13	392.22(a)	Failing to use hazard warning	417	54	9	21	30
14	392.2P	Improper passing	351	37	20	19	9
15	392.2Y	Failure to yield right of way	335	37	20	20	13
16	392.60(a)	Unauthorized passenger on board CMV	294	42	16	16	17
17	392.2T	Improper turns	253	36	17	18	7
18	392.2R	Reckless driving	142	16	7	5	8

Number of VIOLATION for table	TYPE of VIOLATION	Proof of seasonal weather causing accidents is not seen to be a part of traffic management. Except for #23 below (Failure to use caution for a hazardous condition). Note it is toward the end of the list of unsafe violations. This is from the www.fmcsa.dot.gov	Total of Unsafe Violations per Company	SWIFT TRANSPORTATION COMPANY LLC DOT # 54283	WERNER ENTERPRISES INC DOT # 53467	SCHNEIDER NATIONAL CARRIERS INC DOT # 264184	US XPRESS INC DOT # 303024
19	392.71(a)	Using or equipping a CMV with radar detector	141	7	0	7	5
20	392.82A1	Using a hand-held mobile telephone while operating a CMV	135	12	5	9	3
21	397.3	State/local laws ordinances regulations	79	5	2	2	4
22	397.13	Smoking within 25 feet of HM vehicle	56	5	1	0	3
23	392.14	Failed to use caution for hazardous condition	36	3	2	2	2
24	392.2DH	Headlamps - Failing to dim when required	31	3	2	2	0
25	392.10(a)(3)	Failing to stop at railroad crossing — placard	24	0	0	1	0
26	392.80(a)	Driving a commercial motor vehicle while texting	21	0	1	1	0
27	392.2-SLLT	State/Local Laws - Operating a CMV while texting	12	1	1	1	0
28	392.10(a)(4)	Failing to stop at railroad crossing — HM cargo	12	0	0	0	0
29	390.17DT	Operating a CMV while texting	11	0	0	2	1
30	392.6	Scheduling run to necessitate speeding	9	1	0	0	1
31	392.10(a)(1)	Failing to stop at railroad crossing — bus	7	0	0	0	0
32	392.2RR	Railroad Grade Crossing violation	7	0	0	0	1
33	392.62	Unsafe bus operations	4	0	0	0	0
34	392.82(a)2	Allowing or requiring driver to use a hand-held mobile telephone while operating a CMV	3	0	0	0	0
35	177.804C	Fail to comply with 392.82 - Using Mobile Phone while Operating CMV - HM	1	1	0	0	0
			42675	4060	2452	2214	1879

Number of VIOLATION for table	C.R. ENGLAND INC DOT #28406	J.B. HUNT TRANSPORT INC DOT #80806	NEW PRIME INC. DOT #3706	LANDSTAR RANGER INC DOT #241572	CRETE CARRIER CORPORATION DOT#73705	CRST EXPEDITED INC DOT #53773	UNITED PARCEL SERVICE DOT #21800	WESTERN EXPRESS INC DOT#511412	KNIGHT TRANSPORTATION INC DOT #428823	CELADON TRUCKING SERVICE INC DOT #261902	YRC INC DOT #71821	MARTEN TRANSPORT LTD DOT #74432	FEDEX FREIGHT INC DOT #239039	CENTRAL REFRIDGERATED SERVICE DOT #21331	USA TRUCK INC DOT #213754
1	480	206	297	130	156	206	146	199	185	118	92	119	97	148	134
2	139	170	165	193	209	196	190	153	158	177	145	107	148	101	94
3	220	182	205	128	120	96	29	93	90	74	214	74	63	47	97
4	119	177	122	154	155	106	150	90	108	142	94	112	97	71	58
5	147	152	80	137	107	77	172	129	107	83	99	105	113	67	65
6	71	70	59	88	46	84	112	61	42	43	40	51	64	42	17
7	53	73	58	71	64	53	52	73	41	59	27	49	33	24	48
8	87	86	57	28	42	54	44	34	55	36	36	36	48	35	36
9	34	62	28	59	47	46	39	24	50	59	38	43	26	29	16
10	52	42	38	36	44	30	34	22	28	33	27	34	23	16	16
11	73	35	52	19	32	45	63	63	43	17	30	32	27	26	16
12	43	28	38	7	21	28	5	24	19	21	11	16	17	21	18
13	11	17	14	0	13	3	3	10	10	13	7	7	1	3	14
14	26	7	6	9	5	6	8	10	15	6	14	5	8	3	7
15	17	11	17	7	10	17	8	9	6	7	4	6	8	6	4
16	12	13	10	15	5	1	0	30	13	6	0	1	0	13	8
17	14	3	7	7	2	10	8	7	4	10	2	5	1	6	5
18	12	3	5	3	4	3	2	7	1	2	3	5	4	0	3

Number of VIOLATION for table	C.R. ENGLAND INC DOT # 28406	J.B. HUNT TRANSPORT INC DOT # 80806	NEW PRIME INC. DOT # 3706	LANDSTAR RANGER INC DOT # 241572	CRETE CARRIER CORPORATION DOT#73705	CRST EXPEDITED INC DOT # 53773	UNITED PARCEL SERVICE DOT # 21800	WESTERN EXPRESS INC DOT#511412	KNIGHT TRANSPORTATION INC DOT # 428823	CELADON TRUCKING SERVICE INC DOT # 261902	YRC INC DOT # 71821	MARTEN TRANSPORT LTD DOT # 74432	FEDEX FREIGHT INC DOT # 239039	CENTRAL REFRIDGERATED SERVICE DOT # 21331	USA TRUCK INC DOT #213754
19	18	2	2	6	0	1	2	4	6	1	0	5	0	3	1
20	3	11	3	2	3	1	0	2	2	3	3	1	5	1	1
21	0	1	4	10	0	7	2	2	0	1	2	4	0	1	2
22	1	0	0	6	0	5	0	0	1	1	1	1	2	0	0
23	0	0	1	1	0	4	0	2	1	2	1	0	4	1	0
24	4	1	1	2	0	2	0	2	0	0	0	0	0	1	3
25	0	0	0	0	0	0	1	0	0	0	0	1	8	0	1
26	1	1	1	0	0	1	0	0	0	0	2	0	0	0	0
27	1	0	0	0	0	0	1	0	1	0	0	0	0	0	0
28	0	0	0	1	0	0	0	0	0	0	0	0	1	0	0
29	0	1	3	0	0	0	0	0	0	0	0	0	1	0	0
30	0	0	2	0	0	0	1	1	0	1	0	0	0	0	0
31	3	0	0	0	0	1	0	0	0	0	0	0	0	0	0
32	0	0	0	0	0	1	0	0	0	0	1	0	0	0	0
33	0	0	0	0	0	1	0	0	0	0	0	0	0	0	0
34	0	0	0	0	0	0	0	0	1	0	1	0	0	0	0
35	0	0	0	0	0	0	0	0	0	0	0	0	0	0	0
	1641	1354	1275	1119	1085	1085	1072	1051	987	915	894	819	799	665	664

Number of VIOLATION for table	QUALITY CARRIER INC DOT # 76600	COVENANT TRANSPORT INC DOT # 273818	CON-WAY FREIGHT INC DOT # 241829	P.A.M. TRANSPORT DOT #179752	USF HOLLAND INC DOT # 75806	ESTES EXPRESS LINES DOT # 121018	DART TRANSIT COMPANY DOT # 75525	SUPER SERVICE LLC DOT # 1972877	OLD DOMINION FREIGHT LINE INC DOT # 90849	PASCHALL TRUCK LINES INC DOT # 105234	CRST MALONE INC DOT # 105790	MERCER TRUCK LINES CO INC DOT # 154712	AVERITT EXPRESS INC DOT # 36684	ATLAS VAN LINES INC DOT # 125550	MVT SERVICES LLC (MESILLA VALLEY TRANSPORTATION) DOT # 270179
1	57	113	72	114	21	48	73	60	73	67	58	58	55	52	66
2	116	106	60	106	107	87	71	134	84	103	107	109	102	87	100
3	100	62	193	62	126	112	104	50	132	51	59	65	81	82	43
4	101	58	60	52	129	77	74	98	60	76	80	87	64	64	50
5	52	86	71	49	72	74	73	29	41	50	38	45	36	39	57
6	39	43	29	31	23	42	24	44	38	39	44	33	32	51	27
7	29	37	19	62	26	29	44	45	32	39	25	21	44	16	13
8	25	29	41	16	28	33	15	11	22	17	14	17	16	12	26
9	30	24	23	39	33	25	23	30	20	18	27	36	36	26	26
10	21	13	9	29	13	20	21	11	11	17	14	16	19	21	25
11	28	16	15	13	18	18	21	19	17	11	23	18	8	25	16
12	6	16	7	20	6	4	6	8	14	26	11	8	12	9	15
13	2	8	2	17	2	0	5	4	2	17	9	4	7	1	10
14	4	1	1	2	2	4	4	5	3	9	7	5	3	2	5
15	3	3	3	5	2	4	3	2	1	2	4	3	4	3	2
16	4	2	0	1	0	0	1	5	1	5	11	5	1	13	2
17	2	6	4	3	1	1	1	4	2	4	2	2	2	2	2
18	1	3	6	0	0	0	2	2	3	1	0	0	0	1	3

*Visit CRASHLANENEWS.com

Number of VIOLATION for table	QUALITY CARRIER INC DOT # 76600	COVENANT TRANSPORT INC DOT # 273818	CON-WAY FREIGHT INC DOT # 241829	P.A.M. TRANSPORT DOT #179752	USF HOLLAND INC DOT # 75806	ESTES EXPRESS LINES DOT # 121018	DART TRANSIT COMPANY DOT # 75525	SUPER SERVICE LLC DOT # 1972877	OLD DOMINION FREIGHT LINE INC DOT # 90849	PASCHALL TRUCK LINES INC DOT # 105234	CRST MALONE INC DOT # 105790	MERCER TRUCK LINES CO INC DOT # 154712	AVERITT EXPRESS INC DOT # 36684	ATLAS VAN LINES INC DOT # 125550	MVT SERVICES LLC (MESILLA VALLEY TRANSPORTATION) DOT # 270179
19	1	5	1	3	5	0	2	3	2	1	3	3	0	8	6
20	5	1	3	0	3	1	2	4	2	0	1	1	5	3	0
21	2	0	2	0	1	0	1	0	1	0	1	0	1	0	0
22	7	3	2	1	2	3	0	1	2	0	0	1	1	0	0
23	0	2	0	0	0	0	0	0	1	0	0	0	0	0	0
24	0	1	0	0	0	0	2	0	0	0	0	0	0	0	0
25	0	0	5	0	1	1	0	1	1	0	0	0	1	0	0
26	3	0	0	0	0	1	0	0	0	0	0	1	0	0	0
27	0	0	0	1	0	0	0	0	0	0	0	0	0	0	0
28	6	0	0	0	0	0	0	0	1	0	0	0	1	0	0
29	0	0	0	0	0	0	0	0	0	0	0	0	0	0	0
30	0	0	0	0	0	0	0	0	0	1	0	0	0	0	1
31	0	2	0	0	0	0	0	0	0	0	0	0	0	0	1
32	0	1	0	0	0	0	0	0	1	0	1	0	0	0	0
33	0	0	0	0	0	0	0	0	0	0	0	0	0	0	0
34	0	0	0	0	0	0	0	0	0	0	0	0	0	0	0
35	0	0	0	0	0	0	0	0	0	0	0	0	0	0	0
	644	641	628	626	621	584	572	570	567	554	539	538	531	517	496

Number of VIOLATION for table	STEVENS TRANSPORT INC DOT # 79466	FFE TRANSPORTATION SERVICES INC DOT #109745	TRANSAM TRUCKING INC DOT # 315503	KLLM TRANSPORT SERVICES LLC DOT # 154237	WAL-MART TRANSPORTATION LLC DOT#63585	SAIA MOTOR FREIGHT LINE LLC DOT # 29124	TRANSPORT CORPORATION OF AMERICA INC DOT # 183949	ROEHL TRANSPORT INC DOT # 74481	ABF FREIGHT SYSTEM INCORPORATED DOT # 82866	INTERSTATE DISTRIBUTOR CO DOT# 8273	PENSKE TRUCK LEASING CO LP DOT # 327574	SOUTHERN REFRIDGERATED TRANSPORT INC DOT # 276010	JOHN CHRISTNER TRUCKING INC DOT # 273897	GORDON TRUCKING INC DOT # 190991	RYDER TRUCK RENTAL INC DOT # 16130	MAVERICK TRANSPORTATION LLC DOT # 178538
1	118	72	80	67	60	28	44	68	39	63	61	47	31	86	58	32
2	46	60	72	63	82	60	66	63	53	70	46	55	67	51	49	53
3	80	79	34	48	27	117	56	44	72	33	38	49	39	35	55	29
4	27	57	55	59	70	54	77	60	42	25	20	30	36	29	22	45
5	54	40	50	41	55	39	29	35	41	40	80	21	36	21	31	22
6	19	14	24	29	27	20	17	16	20	11	14	14	20	14	21	16
7	20	21	33	39	18	20	22	27	18	10	3	10	5	10	5	17
8	19	15	12	16	16	28	17	19	13	15	24	17	11	12	23	8
9	8	23	13	16	28	17	29	15	15	15	11	25	13	12	6	16
10	17	14	16	0	13	5	12	14	9	12	5	18	15	4	5	12
11	5	11	9	11	10	5	11	5	13	14	15	14	12	15	8	3
12	7	11	12	18	4	3	6	5	0	9	2	13	11	2	3	3
13	3	6	5	11	1	3	1	2	0	3	0	7	6	0	1	2
14	1	5	4	3	2	3	2	4	5	8	4	6	1	6	6	2
15	6	4	3	1	2	4	2	1	3	4	0	2	5	4	0	1
16	3	1	1	1	0	0	1	0	0	3	3	3	0	3	2	0
17	4	1	5	3	1	1	1	2	0	7	0	2	1	7	0	2
18	4	1	3	2	2	2	2	0	1	0	1	1	1	1	0	0

Number of VIOLATION for table	STEVENS TRANSPORT INC DOT # 79466	FFE TRANSPORTATION SERVICES INC DOT #109745	TRANSAM TRUCKING INC DOT # 315503	KLLM TRANSPORT SERVICES LLC DOT # 154237	WAL-MART TRANSPORTATION LLC DOT#63585	SAIA MOTOR FREIGHT LINE LLC DOT # 29124	TRANSPORT CORPORATION OF AMERICA INC DOT # 183949	ROEHL TRANSPORT INC DOT # 74481	ABF FREIGHT SYSTEM INCORPORATED DOT # 82866	INTERSTATE DISTRIBUTOR CO DOT# 8273	PENSKE TRUCK LEASING CO LP DOT # 327574	SOUTHERN REFRIDGERATED TRANSPORT INC DOT # 276010	JOHN CHRISTNER TRUCKING INC DOT # 273897	GORDON TRUCKING INC DOT # 190991	RYDER TRUCK RENTAL INC DOT # 16130	MAVERICK TRANSPORTATION LLC DOT # 178538
19	2	1	1	3	0	2	0	0	1	3	4	0	7	0	1	0
20	1	0	0	1	2	2	1	1	1	1	1	1	0	0	1	1
21	0	0	1	1	0	2	2	1	3	0	0	1	1	1	1	0
22	0	0	0	2	0	1	1	0	2	0	0	0	0	0	0	0
23	0	0	0	1	1	1	0	0	0	1	0	0	1	1	0	0
24	0	0	1	0	0	0	0	0	0	1	1	0	0	0	1	0
25	0	0	0	0	0	1	1	0	0	0	0	0	0	0	0	0
26	0	1	2	0	0	0	0	0	1	1	2	0	0	0	0	1
27	0	1	0	0	0	0	1	0	0	0	1	0	0	1	0	0
28	0	0	0	0	0	1	0	0	1	0	0	0	0	0	0	0
29	0	0	0	0	0	0	0	0	0	0	1	0	0	0	0	1
30	0	0	0	0	0	0	0	0	0	0	0	0	0	0	0	0
31	0	0	0	0	0	0	0	0	0	0	0	0	0	0	0	0
32	0	0	0	0	0	0	0	0	0	0	0	0	0	0	0	0
33	1	0	0	0	0	0	0	0	0	0	0	0	0	2	0	0
34	0	0	0	0	0	0	0	0	0	0	0	0	0	0	0	0
35	0	0	0	0	0	0	0	0	0	0	0	0	0	0	0	0
	445	438	436	436	421	419	401	382	353	349	337	336	319	317	299	266

Number of VIOLATION for table	RUAN TRANSPORT CORPORATION DOT # 55787	ARNOLD TRANSPORTATION SERVICES INC DOT # 148974	FEDERAL EXPRESS CORPORATION DOT # 86876	GREYHOUND LINES INC DOT # 44110	RUAN LOGISTICS CORPORATION DOT # 149350	TANGO TRANSPORT LLC DOT # 459762	MAY TRUCKING COMPANY DOT # 94081	COWAN SYSTEMS LLC DOT # 548880	PENSKE LOGISTICS LLC DOT # 268015	BOYD BROS TRANSPORTATION INC DOT # 92321	ADD YOUR COMPANY HERE	ADD A COMPETITOR HERE	ADD A COMPANY THAT WORKS WITH YOUR COMPANY HERE	ADDYOUR VEHICLE HERE
1	25	50	41	25	24	22	52	33	27	24				
2	49	41	27	43	52	32	22	32	18	7				
3	37	29	39	6	38	40	22	31	51	23				
4	33	17	22	18	24	13	13	15	20	26				
5	29	19	26	7	23	9	16	10	12	9				
6	12	17	15	52	7	10	10	16	5	7				
7	7	16	7	17	10	11	8	8	4	7				
8	10	5	13	7	9	5	7	6	7	6				
9	21	6	13	4	15	5	2	7	5	3				
10	2	7	3	10	6	9	8	5	3	6				
11	9	8	13	35	2	4	9	13	5	3				
12	2	9	2	0	1	17	9	5	1	7				
13	0	12	0	0	1	15	5	0	0	3				
14	3	0	1	3	1	2	1	0	1	0				
15	2	2	2	0	5	6	3	0	1	1				
16	1	2	0	0	0	0	0	0	1	0				
17	1	1	2	1	0	2	1	0	0	1				
18	0	1	1	0	2	0	1	0	0	1				

Number of VIOLATION for table	RUAN TRANSPORT CORPORATION DOT # 55787	ARNOLD TRANSPORTATION SERVICES INC DOT # 148974	FEDERAL EXPRESS CORPORATION DOT # 86876	GREYHOUND LINES INC DOT # 44110	RUAN LOGISTICS CORPORATION DOT # 149350	TANGO TRANSPORT LLC DOT # 459762	MAY TRUCKING COMPANY DOT # 94081	COWAN SYSTEMS LLC DOT # 548880	PENSKE LOGISTICS LLC DOT # 268015	BOYD BROS TRANSPORTATION INC DOT # 92321	ADD YOUR COMPANY HERE	ADD A COMPETITOR HERE	ADD A COMPANY THAT WORKS WITH YOUR COMPANY HERE	ADD YOUR VEHICLE HERE
19	0	1	0	0	0	0	0	0	0	2				
20	1	1	3	0	2	3	0	4	3	3				
21	2	0	0	0	1	0	0	4	0	0				
22	0	0	0	0	0	0	0	0	0	0				
23	0	0	0	0	0	0	1	0	0	0				
24	0	0	0	1	0	0	0	0	0	0				
25	0	0	0	0	0	0	0	0	0	0				
26	0	0	0	0	0	0	0	0	0	0				
27	1	0	0	0	0	0	0	0	0	0				
28	0	0	0	0	0	0	0	0	0	0				
29	0	0	0	0	1	0	0	0	0	0				
30	0	0	0	0	0	0	0	0	0	0				
31	0	0	0	0	0	0	0	0	0	0				
32	0	1	0	0	0	0	0	0	0	0				
33	0	0	0	0	0	0	0	0	0	0				
34	0	0	1	0	0	0	0	0	0	0				
35	0	0	0	0	0	0	0	0	0	0				
	247	245	231	229	224	205	190	189	164	139				

*CRASHLANENEWS.com plans to update information about the FMCSA and the weather continuously.

The top violations are failure to follow a traffic control device and speeding. This is where the traffic enforcement strategy is mainly put in place. Speed traps are nothing new. Most travelers know, see, and sometimes speed too fast through them getting a violation. After reviewing all these tables one of the main points to be clear on is that speeding is being enforced the greatest. Below is a simple list of the unsafe driving violations in the table summarized in the order of greatest to least. A traveler using a commercial motor vehicle should know these in order to prevent themselves from doing them. This unsafe violation list is also preventable by travelers using other forms of transportation like regular Class C passenger vehicles, motorcycles, or bicycles on the road. An interesting thing is some of the distracted driving unsafe driving violations are also something travelers should be aware, avoiding the use of their smartphones while driving. Speeding is enforced the greatest. The greatest 20 unsafe driving violations are bolded below.

Note, item number 23 is underlined, **392.14 Failed to use caution for hazardous condition.** This particular violation is an interesting one. It has been given to travelers that did not adjust their speed due to the weather, or adjust their speed to avoid an accident. This unsafe driving violation is placed towards the end of the list. It is definitely not the number one violation. But, it is important in that it relates to the issues of the weather. When this ticket is given to drivers in severe weather or other hazardous conditions the roads were considered open and passable by the Department of Transportation, and traffic enforcement, but also considered hazardous by traffic enforcement. This can be a confusing subject because this violation is traffic enforcement's management of unsafe driving, specifically through the severe and hazardous conditions that they allowed the public to drive in. This violation when enforced is as close as traffic enforcement gets to the issue of managing traffic in a safe way during a severe weather event or a disaster. The interstate and roads are left open many times in severe weather and in hazardous conditions. One solution that can prevent the accidents that result from drivers failing to use caution for hazardous conditions, would be for the Department of Transportation and traffic/law enforcement to close the interstate and roads at the right time. When there is a known hazardous condition ahead of time the road can be temporarily shut down. These interstate closures happen in severe winter storms. With the few closures that do take place, this situation has not been perfected and managed the same that speeding has. The lack of management during these times adds to another point of what is being left out by the FMCSA on its safety rating program. This violation is proof that the weather is sometimes the cause of the unsafe violation and crashes, but then the weather is not mentioned to cause the eventual accidents that occur. Many multiple vehicle pileups are occurring annually and in winter because the interstates and roads do not get closed. Closures can be fit into the existing system at the right time to avoid the low visibility of severe weather, and closures or warnings should be made once the first accident occurs, preventing a pileup. These issues can be managed better. Until they get attention there will be accidents, pileups, and a lack of accountability as to how it all happened.

1. **392.2C Failure to obey traffic control device**
2. **392.2-SLLS2 State/Local Laws – Speeding 6-10 miles per hour over the speed limit**
3. **392.16 Failing to use seat belt while operating CMV**
4. **392.2 – SLLS1 State/Local Laws – Speeding 1-5 miles per hour over the speed limit**
5. **392.2S Speeding**
6. **392.2 – SLLS3 State/Local Laws – Speeding 11-14 miles per hour over the speed limit**
7. **392.2LV Lane Restriction Violation**
8. **392.2LC Improper Lane Change**
9. **392.2FC Following too close**
10. **392.2 – SLLSWZ State/Local Laws – Speeding in a work/ construction zone**
11. **392.2 – SLLS4 Speeding 15 or more miles per hour over the speed limit**
12. **392.2PK Unlawfully parking and/or leaving vehicle in the roadway**
13. **392.22(a) Failing to use hazard warning flashers**
14. **392.2P Improper passing**
15. **392.2Y Failure to yield right of way**
16. **392.60(a) Unauthorized passenger on board Commercial Motor Vehicle**

17. **392.2T Improper Turns**
18. **392.2R Reckless Driving**
19. **392.71(a) Using or equipping a Commercial Motor Vehicle with radar detector**
20. **392.82A1 Using a hand-held mobile telephone while operating a Commercial Motor Vehicle**
21. 397.3 State/Local Laws ordinances and regulations
22. 397.13 Smoking within 25 feet of Hazardous Material Vehicle
23. <u>392.14 Failed to use caution for hazardous condition</u>
24. 392.2DH Headlamps – Failing to dim when required
25. 392.10(a)(3) Failing to stop at railroad crossing – placard
26. 392.80(a) Driving a commercial motor vehicle while texting
27. 392.2-SLLT State/Local Laws – Operating a Commercial Motor Vehicle while texting
28. 392.10(a)(4) Failing to stop at railroad crossing – Hazardous Material Cargo
29. 390.17TD Operating a Commercial Motor Vehicle while texting
30. 392.6 Scheduling run to necessitate speeding
31. 392.10(a)(1) Failing to stop at railroad crossing – bus
32. 392.2RR Railroad Grade Crossing violation
33. 392.62 Unsafe Bus Operations
34. 392.82(a)2 Allowing or requiring driver to use a hand-held mobile telephone while operating a Commercial Motor Vehicle
35. 177.804C Fail to comply with 392.82 – Using Mobile Phone while operating Commercial Motor Vehicle – Hazardous Material

Note, the above list is as accurate as FMCSA's rating system. The real list of what is occurring to cause accidents the most is an unknown. The real list of what happens is not identified by Law Enforcement and the Department of Transportation for a few reasons. The main reason is the inconsistencies between the crashes where violations are given, and the rest of the unsafe violations. Another leading reason why this above list is not accurate, is, it does not mention the weather. All Commercial Carriers have winter driving training for their drivers so they know it is an issue. Carriers will then still send their drivers out on a route during a winter blizzard, and after a winter blizzard, mainly because the Department of Transportation have the roads open. Commercial Carriers has to follow the road closures and when the roads are open according to the Department of Transportation across each state. Each State's management of closures has varied greatly. There is no public rating available about the accuracy of road condition reporting by each State's Department of Transportation. The end result has been the placement of many inexperienced travelers in situations they had not been able to travel safely. Inexperienced travelers continually end up in accidents. A majority of accidents that occurred were because these travelers trusted the State's Department of Transportation. They trusted that the roads had been safe to travel on, but the roads really had patches of debris. A rating based on the fact there is a considerable amount of debris allowed on the road for certain States would be an answer to some accidents. Some States leave debris on the road for days and weeks, while also leaving the roads wide open. This failure is being caused by the Department of Transportation across the United States. Rating these State traffic enforcement strategies is a suggestion. This rating should use the management of the weather as a starting point across each State. The benefits of a Management rating, debris rating, and weather rating would decrease season accident trend totals immediately. The solution here is to develop a rating system for each state's Department of Transportation ability to more accurately enforce traffic. That would be a great rating for the public, giving them the knowledge of what state is being regulated the safest. The data from these lists provide some of the more obvious suggestions and areas of concern. But the suggestions and information provided in this book is not an official government rating system. This report is a reflection of what went on from 2010-2012. A similar example also took place before those years and currently in 2014. These lists order are predicted to be similar in the future for few reasons. One main reason is the existing lack of government accountability. The lack of transparency about the United States government is a real problem and can affect the public for years, which is what has already happened with these ratings, and the aimless data put out by the FMCSA.

When compared to the Blooming into Disaster Meter, speeding and many of the above mentioned types of violations are not on there. Many items on the Blooming into Disaster Meter are considered a disaster by

FEMA, including severe winter storms, severe thunderstorms, tornadoes, hurricanes, floods, and more. Many departments in the U.S. government are tracking these problems but more consistent management can be done. Speeding is not considered by FEMA to be a disaster, and this is a contrast to traffic enforcement's strategy focusing on speeding while also allowing traffic to pass through severe weather every year. This may be one of the more interesting areas of difference about what is the most important for public safety between the federal government and state government. Traffic accidents versus disaster management has also been a big topic that could be used by more of the commercial carriers as to why the FMCSA rating is not comprehensive. When it comes to damage, injury, and fatalities, all both get thought out in detail between these two agencies but not in an interagency system of management. What is aimless is the inability of the Department of Transportation and the FMCSA to recognize the pattern of the severe weather causing the higher levels of accidents in the winter months.

The weather causes disasters, accidents, injuries, fatalities, and damage. Be aware of winter storms and prevent an unsafe trip that is speeding too fast through the storm. This can sound repetitive but the same message is important for many different reasons. Winter trips may be one of the most dangerous things a traveler can do. The real issue is that with all the types of violations shown here, none are from the point of view of someone being forced into a weather disaster, or forced into a circumstance that causes an accident. That would be a great rating to include, as to the forcing of a driver into a current disaster, and forcing a driver into a disaster's aftermath. It occurs annually during all four seasons but is never rated. The big picture of what causes an accident has been hidden. It is not public for the convenience to local, state, regional, and federal government. By not closing down interstates, roads, and other parts of the infrastructure when a disaster such as severe weather occurs, there are no additional budget and government resources needed. It eliminates the need of the non-profitable traffic enforcement, as opposed to generating income from speeding fines and traffic court fees. Also that kind of enforcement, meaning the closing of roads during severe weather would not generate revenue. It would also lead to public complaints, and that is possible why closing the roads is not regularly done. The public and businesses have the power to persuade the Department of Transportation and the legislators that road closures should occur more often in order to eliminate preventable accidents occurring in severe weather. The reason the public and legislators need to get involved is that the current methods have not eliminated all the accidents, because the current method is not comprehensive. The closing of roads at the right time has not been used enough. Traffic enforcement has not been perfected even after the biggest public rating system ever with the FMCSA, and both failed with the continued accident patterns in severe weather. An additional rating on road closures on a city, county, and state category, would be a great public rating to have. The public would know what area they are traveling in, and how that area's government is able to manage the roads. A rating on the closing of the roads at the right time, and which cities, counties, and states can do it from greatest to least would be perfect. This would prevent a weather disaster or other natural disaster combining in with regular traffic and unsafe violators.

There are many other solutions available out there like having a better communication system put in place. The Wireless Emergency Alerts are warning travelers of major disasters with smartphones. That is just the beginning of a regional warning through mobile phone companies and there were some warnings that existed prior to that. Unfortunately, these were confusing some travelers. The problem of confusion when traveling when getting warnings and alerts may still exist even with the Wireless Emergency Alerts because the aftermath of the disaster may not end up as part of the warning. This is a public concern because even when the disaster, blizzard, severe thunderstorm, and hurricane is over, the damages and chaos occurring in the area may not be considered by those that send out the Wireless Emergency Alerts when they should be. Wireless Emergency Alerts are discussed in detail in chapters 4, 5, 6, and 7. The importance of a good warning system when the roads remain open is obvious. News about the weather has been available through the National Weather Service/NOAA and through local and nationwide news about the weather. With these sources, there have still been accidents by the drivers sent out into severe weather. Prior to the ratings and prior to the Wireless Emergency Alert the public was stating there was not enough transparency.

Even now with these two systems there may still be an issue of sending commercial drivers into severe weather. That poor system of management affects the other traffic on the road and the public's perception of how accurate the FMCSA really is.

In a perfect traffic enforcement system each local, state, and regional area would be able to communicate what type of unsafe driving violation is being enforced and where publicly. Each area has its own strategy of traffic enforcement and the level of transparency varies. Unsafe violation enforcement is discontinuous as a result. This is done many times with traffic signs, regarding the speed limit, but with the list above there is a complex traffic enforcement system. As of 2014 traffic enforcement appears to be more of a game. It is filled with public deception, involving an unknown competition for promotions sought out by traffic enforcement officers. The need to get promoted over the reality of what is really unsafe is a false strategy from the beginning before the speed trap is even set up. Because of that, many in the public believe that traffic enforcement is not an attempt to make things safer, but for a few local agencies' monetary gain spread out like a maze across the 50 states. If traffic enforcement was all about public safety, commercial drivers and other drivers of Class C vehicles would not be able to say they had witnessed tornadoes, hurricanes, blizzards, and the other disasters. This truth about traffic enforcement is usually not transparent in the news, but should be.

Texas

A traveler who is driving a car or truck could use the crash rates and facts to help him or her travel with more awareness. This can help in planning a trip. Crash rates can also help while en route of the trip. When looking at the crash data look at the state of Texas. Some states do have more crashes than others; Texas, for example, is usually the highest out of the larger companies, middle size companies, and even some of the smaller companies. The crash table is sorted with Swift being the greatest, which has Texas crash totals being the highest of any state. For Swift, Texas is placed on the unsafe driving violation table after Indiana, New Mexico,

Arizona, Washington, Ohio, and Louisiana. The amount of violations is still high but it does look like some other states hand out a great deal more tickets for unsafe driving violations. This can lead to the discussion if Texas should hand out more unsafe driving violations to reduce the overall crash rate. This is usually determined by the state and the local communities' support of programs. Each state has a different policy and way of enforcing violations which is another issue aside from the numbers.

A contributing factor for Texas having the most accidents includes the population density, the size of the state, the location to the border of Mexico, and the speed limits. Some more than others can be argued to cause the crash rate in Texas, but the fact remains that there is something going on there. Any traveler of any vehicle should know that for commercial motor vehicles Texas has the highest amount of crashes. If all motorist know this, some extra distance and possible caution can be applied while driving near and around a truck.

Indiana

Indiana is the leading state to get an unsafe driving violation in a commercial motor vehicle. The volume of traffic is one reason. Another reason is that most law enforcement personnel in charge of controlling traffic try to hand out tickets when their command tells them to. These enforcers are doing what they were told to do. The local, county, state, and federal government give law enforcement these orders allowing them to legally control traffic, and in Indiana traffic is a big focus area.

The traffic density is higher east of the Mississippi River resulting in a greater presence of law enforcement. Indiana may also have a higher standard for truck drivers compared to other states, explaining the high rate of unsafe driving violations. In fact, compared to many other states their violations are extremely higher than any other state in the country, which can raise the question of whether their ability to hand out unsafe violations is actually making things safer.

This is an interesting state to discuss the difference of the violation rate and the crash rate. For Swift Indiana falls after Texas, California, Arizona, and Missouri. Indiana does have many crashes, being fifth out of all the states listed, which can also be why the violation rate is as high as it is. Drivers going through Indiana should be aware of the high violation rate and high crash rate, while remembering that unsafe driving violations are enforced there very strictly and at a high standard.

Another issue that surprises some is that the overall size and population of the state is not as big as others in the area. Compared to Texas's population and size, Indiana is only a fraction but still gives out as many unsafe driving violations. With the high level of standards for drivers Indiana must be a safer state to drive in. This safety relies heavily on the fact that the violation distribution can make a difference and reduce accidents.

Companies Shut Down by FMCSA in the Crash and Violation Graphs

Some of the shut down companies from 2010–2012 are on the FMCSA.dot. gov website. All these are very small companies and the real safety issues get forgotten about when making an example of the following. There is no mention that usually the smaller companies suffer shutdowns compared to larger companies on the FMCSA, but this can also be an inconsistency.

- C & D Transportation Inc DOT # 2096634.
- Demco Trans Inc DOT # 1719805.
- Heartland Charter & Tours DOT # 1460491.
- HP Distribution LLC DOT # 869516.
- J & A Transportation Inc DOT # 1869103.
- Judson Mobley Logging Inc DOT # 590038.
- LEX EXPRESS. DOT # 824116.
- MTI Transportation LLC. DOT # 2296470.
- Peace of Mind Relocation. DOT # 1727253.
- Three Angels Farms.

There were no violations listed or crashes listed on the following companies and were not include in the chart. But the rating would have been only one or two crashes and violations. Knowing these companies were shut down by FMCSA for a reason can give another traveler the information on what is considered unsafe. Each company receives a letter and the FMCSA actually publishes the letter on its website.

- Ben Gordon DOT # 926441.
- BM&L TRUCKING LLC, affiliated company IDM Transportation Inc.
- Reliable Transportation Services, Inc.
- Terri's Farm.

Crash Lane News Critical Review of FMCSA

A critical review can start with FMCSA mention of shut down companies, and how the FMCSA website improves safety and security through visible company data. Despite these programs in past years, there are still accidents as well as a very high rate of violations. There are still going to be accidents no matter what FMCSA does to manage commercial motor vehicles' information from this point on. The question remains if shutting down companies actually make things safer. The displaying of shutdown companies by the FMCSA is just a fancy presentation and is really based on an old system of how to regulate traffic. The old system was not developed to benefit the average traveler's safety.

Information presented by the FMCSA covers up that sometimes accidents happen no matter what the circumstances. There is also no mention that some accidents involving commercial motor vehicles were caused intentionally by lighter forms of traffic.

Some accidents also have unpredictable circumstances. The FMCSA has attempted to place the reason of all the accidents and violations into five basics, which is misleading. The point is that FMCSA should mention there are many other factors that cause accidents if they plan on a public display of carriers' and drivers' information. Without these additional examples the presentation as is should not and could not be taken as the full report of what threatens travel. A traveler should develop and describe some additional factors that cause accidents. This list can vary for each traveler and benefit him or her, knowing there are more overall causes of accidents. This also takes away some of the fear and blame that has been built about traveling near commercial motor vehicles. These critical points are good for truck drivers and their companies. This discussion creates more of an explanation of the issues that exist about the FMCSA and law enforcements strategy, which will also allow the government to improve and make the current rating system more accurate. This rating system does use the input from advisors who are employees of trucking companies currently, which should be noted as a good thing but did not prevent the current inconsistencies.

The Proof of the FMCSA Data Inconsistency Is in the Weather

One inconsistency begins with the weather as an uncontrollable force. The weather has threatened travel since the beginning of trade thousands of years ago. How the FMCSA, DOT, and law enforcement do not blame the weather more is an issue. The fact remains that of the five basics mentioned to cause accidents, none include the variable issue of the weather.

An accident and violation is observed, and annotated, based on finding the human error, placing fault on one of the vehicles. The weather may be considered a factor by law enforcement into why an accident occurred but it is not usually referred to as the primary cause for the accident. It is also definitely used against the driver with the argument as why he or she was driving in bad weather.

Many truck drivers have driven through bad weather and natural disasters. The weather and natural disasters have contributed to accidents, but most of the blame for violations and accidents focuses on a list of legal violations that only the driver can cause. The fact these drivers have more experience traveling through severe weather safely is usually disregarded when there is an accident and/or violation.

Another point about the weather being a factor is that the FMCSA does not mention any violation regarding the company sending a commercial motor vehicle straight into severe weather. This may be the way it is because of the argument that the company could not have predicted the storm in advance. This can be a good point although with all the satellite and storm predicting available in the news and on government websites like the www. weather.gov and www.noaa.gov, there could be some accountability. Some major storm systems can be seen in advance and one can predict some of the conditions that may cause a disaster for the area.

Many storms cause accidents and violations. In many situations it is the company that is sending the driver into the location of where a storm is going to occur. A driver should request to be rerouted or to change loads since he or she is the operator of the vehicle. It is the driver's driving record that would get a violation or accident added, but communicating this to the company is not always an option. Many companies have a forced dispatch. This is a management system of drivers in companies forcing their drivers to travel through and to anywhere. These same storms and locations have been later considered a state and federal disaster area. Drivers that want to keep their job do what the company says, by traveling through these storms and disasters. This can result in an accident and violation later blamed only on the driver.

Many companies and law enforcement consider extreme weather as a safety issue. These same companies then require drivers to travel and navigate through these storms. Sending an employee into a storm is not illegal because of the unpredictability of the weather even with advance weather reports. Companies are managed in a way to send a driver into the situations that cause violations and accidents. They do not get held accountable publicly by the FMCSA. This does not mean that every accident and violation is caused by management issues. This also does not mean that these problems should be placed up on the Internet like the current placing of violations and accidents. The traveling public should know that management is allowed to focus on blaming the driver when it was their company policy and planning causing the violation and accident. The point is there are many third parties involved in causing violations and accidents and the display of safety data according to the FMCSA fails to mention any of that. These are real issues that should be brought up to really explain safety.

Because of the way things are managed by the carrier (trucking company), DOT, FMCSA, and law enforcement, there are no regulations and laws preventing a company from sending a driver through extreme storm systems. There is no law or regulation about sending a driver into a disaster area mentioned by the FMCSA. This is an inconsistency. When an entire transportation industry of the United States looks at the FMCSA website they are not getting the real story. The solution to this issue of the misleading safety situation requires revision from the way violations are approached and who they are distributed to.

A traveler should look at the Blooming into Disaster Meter on the homepage and know that not one of these disasters are mentioned to cause accidents according to the FMCSA, when in reality they all cause accidents. Some of the disasters include severe winter storms/blizzards, hurricanes, tornadoes, lightning storms, fires, earthquakes, floods, severe summer heat, economic collapse, manmade disasters, hacker attacks, diseases, and more. The categorizing and classifying each disaster with some additional causes taking some or all the blame off the driver should be reworked to make the system more reliable. The chance of this change is low because it would require widespread support and possible additional laws being amended and passed at the state and federal levels of government.

The FMCSA News & Alerts section on the front page of its website mentions federal and state emergency declarations for states affected by disasters, although these disasters have not been considered to be the cause of some violations and accidents. This is very confusing to someone trying to be safe and learn about safety data. This news and alert section on the front page is an additional example of an inconsistency with the present data and ratings of a company's drivers. Some examples of weather and disasters that contribute to accidents and violations mentioned in the above tables include severe winter weather, severe rain, severe lightning, severe thunder storms, tornadoes, hurricanes, floods, earthquakes, tsunamis, manmade disasters, and many more. The story to what commercial drivers navigate through safely is not mentioned by the FMCSA and drivers are not awarded for being safe in these conditions that law enforcement, carriers, shippers, receivers, and the rest of the transportation place them in. This is a forgotten side of the current rating system as well as a forgotten side of a Department of Motor Vehicles ability to have a consistent driving record.

In summary, this discussion is ongoing about the FMCSA data at the professional, governmental, and public levels. The objective of mentioning these inconsistencies leads into the reason to present the three tables of the data. The information for each table is taken from the www.fmcsa.dot.gov

website. This information in the Crash Table, Violation Table, and Type of Violation Table are accurate according to the FMCSA. Keep in mind some of the questionable issues of their ability to present the collected data in a real way that describes safety issues.

The FMCSA strategy has also been up for public debate because of the order of crashes per company being compared to the order of violations. Remember to view this book and information from the point of view that there are ways to improve everything instead of blaming one area alone continually.

Check out the interviews on the next page. Note there are many situations the driver is put in because of management's policies and gross domestic product. Many situations have nothing to do with safety and are difficult to alter at the driver's end due to a lack of reasoning at the manager's end. The way the current FMCSA only places violations to have been caused by the driver is easy to show to be the result of a rating. The company does get a lower rating as a result of unsafe drivers that crash or get pulled over for inspections that result in citations and safety violations. The FMCSA management of drivers is not improving the overall system, some would say. The office is not stated as being unsafe and causing some of the problems that may factor into accidents and violations. There is no safety rating of dispatchers, or of the safety department, truck stops, each state's DOT, the local law enforcement, and warehouses, as a contributing factor to accidents and violations. The FMCSA is lacking the entire reality of how the industry operates still to this day. This causes the continuation of many accidents in severe weather because management can force drivers into it, and a high volume of violations year round because citations are handed out based on a company's ratings in many examples.

The cycle of a poor rating results in more inspections and a lower rating. This cycle is the current way the FMCSA plans to keep things safe, instead of altering its point of view. The current system of ratings has been in place and there are still accidents. Only the driver loses his or her job because of things that occur on the road. Management and the company get the rating according to the FMCSA but there is no need for them to improve the way they send the drivers out because they get to place most of the problems at the drivers' end as the result of the FMCSA five basic areas. This issue of management being the possible cause is also why the FMCSA has been trying to make things more transparent with a rating, but all the while failing to really use the drivers' point of view about safety. The rating is really not going to changed the way management sends out drivers into severe weather that causes accidents and increases poor ratings, and increases inspections and violations. The driver was the one living on the road, driving on the road, and surviving the accidents that occur as a result of the inexperienced drivers out there as a result of a high turnover rate, the weather, and poor management policies connecting everything. **Good luck, and travel safely!**

The Future of Travel

Misrepresented data causes many victims and surviving family members of fatal accidents, to immediately blame Commercial Drivers, and Carriers. This blame occurs even when these vehicles and drivers did not cause the accident. This blame originates based on the size of the Commercial vehicle. Blame has also been falsely occurring because of how the scene of the accident appeared. The size of the truck sometimes leaves a larger skid mark on the road, or also was crashed into by a few vehicles being its size is larger, making the truck look like the cause falsely. The biggest source of the blame though has been the public rating system by the FMCSA that misrepresents accident data, and unsafe driving data.

This is not being written with the arrogance that none of the arguments against the Commercial industry are real. The forcing of Commercial drivers into severe storms where an accident is more than likely to occur has been the reality still unchecked. But, if there is misrepresented information from the beginning, like if the Department of Transportation allowed these Commercial trucks onto the road in these severe storms the truth is not coming out later in their own description of what happened. Because of that the future is going to have to require the government to be more transparent instead of just hearing that the government is more transparent. When the public was told that the FMCSA is going to improve transparency about the Commercial industry those that drove, and even some companies had an open mind, thinking it would benefit their company since they have a safety office. This has not been what happened though in that the transparency created has not included more of the Commercial Carriers side of what happened, and it definitely does not include the driver's point of view of what happened.

There is no doubt that the Department of Transportation its FMCSA agency, and law enforcement, knowingly allowed Commercial vehicles to travel through unsafe situations like disastrous storms (severe thunderstorms, blizzards, hurricanes). These same Commercial vehicles were also allowed to travel through these same areas where a disaster's aftermath was ongoing. The problem is that then the same government agency being the Department of Transportation, which allowed this to happen, then places every single violation infraction up on the internet. There is a great deal of data being manipulated in a false way. It is like some how the U.S. government is forgetting they had the final authority of the roads being open. It is unfortunate to also conclude with the reality that the company overview page has been knowingly posting a misrepresentation of data of what occurred, and who is really to blame. There is only so much blame a Commercial Carrier and a Commercial Driver can get before the government that controls the road explains the issues of there been traffic allowed to flow through disaster areas where an accident has a higher probability to occur. The FMCSA is making the Commercial Carriers appear to be the cause of more than its share of injuries, fatalities, and have fabricated data, posting it online. The FMCSA company snapshot is posting a report that does not directly list the vehicle that caused the accident being the Commercial truck or passenger cars. Then the FMCSA mentions that there was an injury or fatality, without revealing even a sentence of which vehicle was the cause, and all of the data they describe is very misleading without mentioning which vehicle started a pile up, and clarifying which vehicle was not the cause. The U.S. government has fabricated data in the past and this is one of the biggest examples of this again here. It is ruining a drivers and companies record when there is an accident pile up and the Commercial vehicle has avoided the worst part of an accident. To later be associated permanently with what occurred with each vehicle, being a fatality, or being an injury, even if some other passenger vehicle motorist caused the accident. Also the motorist that died may have been the cause of the accident to begin with, but the FMCSA has been using the mass punishment system. This is also very aimless because many Commercial vehicles have been followed by passenger vehicles, and if there is low visibility, with disastrous weather when these vehicles collide it can appear that the Commercial vehicle is falsely the cause just because of that grouping of data. The FMCSA is about as aimless as it can get when describing what is happening in every company, city, and state.

The later arguments, no mater how believable, and how many witnesses there are, can be seen by those in the Commercial industry that have lived the known examples of misrepresented data skeptically. No Commercial driver wants to cause an accident. Commercial drivers do not want accidents because they lose their jobs, and when they see the existing blame, and existing distortions of data describing their company's injuries and fatalities, these drivers view these more serious accident reports as having much more wrong with them. It is common to state these reports, and the FMCSA rating system, has more problems with being accurate and being comprehensive to include the weather as the cause, for the entire public to believe them.

All this can confuse someone new to the FMCSA, and new to the Commercial industry. In an even simpler explanation, when there is an obvious effort to mislead which is what is happening, the information about the cause either from the weather, or from the Commercial drivers side, it actually causes there to be false beliefs once an accident is being investigated by insurance companies, law enforcement, and the survivors. This may seem like a very small argument and only in favor of the Commercial Carriers and the Commercial Drivers, but the focus as them always being the cause is a huge misdirection as to what occurred, especially if the roads were open. But if every company is being viewed to be more dangerous than they are on their carrier overview page, at FMCSA.dot.gov, it is an important argument. This argument is important as long as there is that misrepresentation, and it is likely to stay in place. The end result of false information will take away from putting the right amount of attention towards the more real problems of managing traffic in a more prepared way that prevents open roads in severe weather. Some problems like the government's failed ability to close the road for a few hours or a day are real. That problem and more like it really occur, and still have not been acknowledged or made public. Many problems that can make things safer can be made from the point of view of the Commercial Carriers, and the Commercial drivers. That side of safety not always been taken seriously. As the result the suggestions by the Commercial industry is predicted to not get added into the FMCSA's data. This will prevent many known problems from getting the government's attention in a way to be managed. One area of concern is the focus of the FMCSA on issues like a seat belt violation, or an inspection finding something tiny on the maintenance that was already in the shop attempted to be fixed by the driver. There is not much mentioned about the studying of road closures at the right time and place. It is seen that road closures are not the Department of Transportation's strategy enough and that can be the leading solution out of this discussion and book. Road closures are simply not something being studied enough, or put in use enough, and road closures can be a very easy way to prevent accidents when used along side the science of the weather.

In the future, because of fabrications, failures, and false data presented by the FMCSA and law enforcement, there will be a continuous amount of accidents. When there is dishonesty in describing something as serious as the cause of a vehicle accident, there is a definite distraction that is misleading the public as to what is the most important problem affecting traffic. The FMCSA is also misleading the local and state governments, including their law enforcement, and their state department of transportation. These local offices that handle traffic are prevented from having real clarity, on what the real transportation problems are. These will all be preventable accidents, with preventable injuries, and with preventable fatalities, while only appearing to be the fault of the Commercial driver and carrier. The reasons is the current system is not comprehensive, by not including more of the issues mentioned by the National Weather Service/NOAA, and the issued of forced dispatch into and through a storm. There will also be accidents in the future if the roads are open during these severe weather events because of the Department of Transportation. Some accidents will occur in the future because of all these mentioned points. It is unfortunate knowing that the current Department of Transportation system is actually causing some of the injuries and fatalities, while also not being accountable even with all the transparency being advertised to exist.

Some of these hazards and the aftermath issues, foreseen to occur, can be prevented. This can begin with a more accurate system of unsafe violation and accident data being presented. A presentation of a more accurate point of view is still needed. Not all injuries, and fatalities mentioned by the FMCSA and the Department of Transportation were caused by Commercial Drivers and Commercial Carriers. Even if these big trucks were in the same storm, and accident, many times their vehicle is going slower and not the cause. The current FMCSA system in its entirety is misleading the public. It is also not protecting the public as well as it could be, by not including more information about the weather and the Commercial point of view. In the future, if a Commercial vehicle did not cause the accident that should be noted in the report. In the future the amount of information mentioned by the FMCSA about Commercial Carriers listed publicly should be more proportionate to reality as to what occurred and caused each individual accident. The mention of there being an injury or fatality should be eliminated if the cause is not also included; being the accident is caused by the Commercial Driver, caused by the weather, or caused by the other vehicles.

This eliminates the scenario where a truck had been crashed into by other vehicles after an accident, then is made out to appear like they are the cause of the accident by the FMCSA falsely by not including what had happened. Many trucks are going slower than other traffic, as the result of different vehicle specifications, and Commercial trucks also stop sooner many times, to only later be included in an accident report that does not include that very fact. But with that, these trucks also get crashed into after the accident started. This has made trucks appear to have made contact with other vehicles and be the cause, when really they were the vehicles hit. In the future, and for the best interest for travelers the FMCSA needs to publicly state in their reports that many accidents are not caused by Commercial trucks If this truth is not mentioned and the changes to the presentation does not happen there will be a continued view as to what is happening, and this can have a negative long term affect on public safety.

When going beyond the carrier overview and examining the crash indicator page the crashes with injuries and fatalities are combined in one total. On the carrier overview page they are separated from fatality and injuries without the cause stated which is confusing, and now it is even more confusing as to why they would combine the totals. The FMCSA also states beneath the overview page totals why they do not include the causation. Most reading this would think there was an explanation and answer but there is nothing other than the outcome that there is deception as to the cause. The withholding of the cause of the accident on the FMCSA website is not really explained in that they do not want the public to know the cause. The FMCSA admits to withholding the cause. That somehow is acceptable by their logic. But then use all accidents caused or not caused by the Commercial driver for the Carriers' ratings leads into false information.

The FMCSA website http://ai.fmcsa.dot.gov/SMS/InfoCenter/default. aspx#question1204 has the below as of June 2014.

Why are all crashes used without any determination as to responsibility?

The Carrier Safety Measurement System (CSMS) Crash Indicator considers a carrier's accident involvement, without any determination as to responsibility. State-reported crash data are used to calculate the Crash Indicator measure of relative crash involvement. State-reported crash data does not have information regarding fault. The CSMS algorithm, by design, ranks Carriers in comparison to other Carriers. All Carriers are treated the same way. In the case of the Crash Indicator measure the carrier's crash rates are being compared to other Carriers' crash rates without any determination as to responsibility of individual crashes. Therefore, there is no relative disadvantage to any particular carrier. To eliminate misinterpretation, a caveat is placed wherever CSMS Crash Indicator-related values are shown. The caveat states, "A motor carrier's crash assessment (Crash Indicator BASIC measure and percentile) and the list of crashes below represent a motor carrier's involvement in 24 months of reportable crashes without any determination as to responsibility" When a Crash Indicator percentile is relatively high, it suggests that a further examination of causes is needed, and if correctable, action should be taken by the motor carrier. CSMS calculations are applied uniformly to all Carriers and are adjusted for exposure. For a more detailed explanation of the calculation of the Crash Indicator and its components, please refer to the SMS Methodology document.

Crash Lane News discovered that all the current micromanaging of certain areas like the 5 basics of a Commercial company does not matter, when later seeing there are still many accidents and false presentations of data. The main reason these 5 basics appears to not be working is that there are still many fatal accidents. It is good to try to prevent accidents using data, but the way this has been managed by the Department of Transportation is false. The FMCSA has led the public into thinking they are in more danger than they are, when traveling around Commercial vehicles. These government offices use the hype that there was a recorded accident or unsafe violation, while being disconnected from the reality of what occurred, what was the cause, and what was the weather.

The future should have ways to prevent accidents with the use of data. The solution will not be found with the current FMCSA rating system. Planners in the Commercial industry that want to make things safer will have to be smarter. The FMCSA will need the more commonly known issues drivers face on the road. The future will have to be more successful. The descriptions of things getting safer and more transparent are only a written message, without any meaning. Without real meaning, or proof, and real results, improving public safety, there is the issue of false reporting. With the issues known by the public about the government, the government has fooled many using fear tactics with the accidents Commercial vehicles are in to also be a part of the reason there is a fatality. Internal government accountability has been complicated. The FMCSA is self defeating. If change cannot be made that would actually clarify what happened, it is a failure. The future of this truth occurring may be impeded. But, with all the delays, change in the United States has occurred many times before through investigations, legislation of laws, amending laws, and voting. An internal look as to how Commercial Carriers and Commercial Drivers are becoming falsely presented by the Department of Transportation should occur. The highest levels in the government include the Supreme Court, Congress, the Senate, and the President, and they should look into these issues as soon as possible. The problem should get attention in 2014, not ten, twenty, thirty, or forty years from now.

The future can be predicted to be bleak for some Commercial companies. Investors tend to move their money somewhere else when a business is losing customers. This has been happening in the Commercial industry based on this FMCSA U.S. government rating system. This change has been catastrophic when a rating is unfavorable for a trucking company. The result is that the FMCSA's rating system has completely changed the economy since about 2006. These companies have been trapped with a bad FMCSA rating. Their support of the change mentioned in this report to their Congressman is a start. Their support of change at the Executive level of the Department of Transportation would also fix the misrepresentations.

False data is continuous concern. Many businesses rely on the U.S. Government for its data for business. More importantly, the public uses the government's point of view about safety and security when making decisions about travel on every trip. U.S. Citizens can travel within the United States and the world free. But, if the information given to the public is misleading and fabricated, then they will not be safe. The public should finish reading this section about the FMCSA knowing some things stated by the U.S. government about Commercial companies is not accurate. With this critical view, the U.S. government also has offices and departments put in place specifically for the public. Many offices work with the media and press to appear transparent, and some help the public more than others. The rest of the book includes some helpful and hopefully more accurate departments in the government.

For questions and comments email crashlanenews777@gmail.com
This page is available online at the link http://www.crashlanenews.com/Dashboard.html

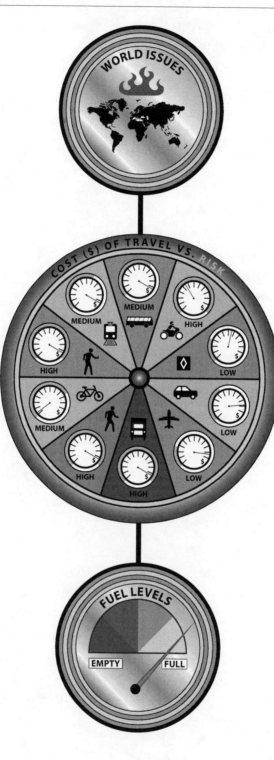

Travel Budget Page

A travel budget can be a complicated issue when taking into account the cost of oil. The cost of oil at the global level affects the price of gas and fuel in the United States. The cost of gas and fuel in the United States is affected by each state's pricing system based on the available priced supplies from refining companies. There are also other factors that contribute to a state's prices. Local areas of a state have different prices, resulting from the business providing the gas and fuel to the customers. A business's ability to run a business in the best interest of a customer is reflected in the price of gas being high or low. Some of the bigger sized businesses of gas and fuel stations also affect the local prices when they have a low cost of gas available. As a result of this summary, the travel budget meter was developed to try to portray these issues into one graphic. These issues are complicated and require an explanation along with the graphic.

The Travel Budget Meter consists of three meter parts. The overall point of having this meter is to include the factor of security along with the different prices related to the forms of travel. Travelers should make their own travel budget meter while observing which form of travel is safer. This should be done individually because each area's location is going to affect the different cost of travel along with the different risks. These risks should include a local area's accident and disaster rate as a starting point. There are many other risks a traveler can also add to the personal cost versus risk plan to travel. The goal of having this list and information is so a traveler can find out what is the safest and most cost efficient way to travel. There are some cheap ways to travel, but traveling cheap does not always mean you will be safe. Travelers need to remember an important lesson about the quality of safety compared to the different available prices, and the available forms of transportation. It is not recommended to travel using an unsafe form of transportation. This is especially true if a traveler is able to have that safety information ahead of time, prevent from even using an unsafe form of transportation, or method from the beginning. It is important that each traveler knows their area's safety recommendations, and avoid unsafe situations.

The first part is the top meter. There is a picture of the world inside with a flame above it. This represents that the global issues in the world contribute to the price of travel in the United States. The global issues are included in the Blooming into Disaster Meter on the homepage. These are disasters that are also factors into the world economy and security, both affecting travel. The title inside this meter is "Global Issues." This map of the world, flame, and title "Global Issues" in a meter then connects to the middle meter mentioned as a "Travel Cost versus Risk." The connection between the two symbolizes the global issues connected to the price of safety and security on a trip in the United States.

The second part is the middle meter. This meter is titled the "Travel Cost versus Risk," and shows the different types of transportation in a circle. Each type of transportation also has a meter inside that has a dollar sign to represent the cost as well as an out meter to represent the risk. The amount of risk is typed as being low, medium, or high. Risk can also be related to the location's disasters as well as the global disasters that may threaten travel in a certain area in the United States. Global threats to travel in the United States has been a concern as a result of the September 11, 2001 terrorist hijacking of airliners. The global threat of terrorism creates some risk of intentional accidents being caused in the form of an attack. Many issues related to unsafe driving make up most of the risk, and rarely is a terrorist attack considered but rather an accident. Travelers should make a distinction between the government's ability to identify accidents and their own common sense of what they experience. Many major news outlets tend to cover what the government wants to report related to traffic accidents and other global issues, which may not be the entire story.

These are estimates based on data provided from the National Highway Traffic Safety Administration. The NHTSA lists the different types of travel as well as the rate of accidents and fatalities. This can explain a summarized risk for pedestrians, pedacyclists, trucks, cars, buses, and motorcycles. Depending on the state the traveler is in, their cost of travel will differentiate to this meter's cost per vehicle type.

A good source of finding prices for gas stations across the United States can include looking up some of the nationwide and local gas stations online, where they list and update the price of gas and fuel. Once the price of gas and fuel is determined for a state, other costs should be looked at to determine the total cost of travel. A traveler should know that the cost should rise for travel that has a higher risk of accident and injury due to medical expenses that may occur as a result of the type of travel.

Rail and airliner accident deaths and injuries per the cost of travel are low per amount of the population that uses that transportation. On the meter their risk is low but at the same time their cost is mentioned as being high. The train and light rail has some of the lowest travel fares, beating the bus system across country. Note that the cost on the meter should be lower.

Airline prices continue to rise and the meter showing the cost on that is about where it should be. Considering the distance that can be traveled along with the faster rate of travel, the cost is listed as low. This risk is also mentioned to be low because the DHS and the TSA have been increasing security for airlines, reducing the risk of a future incident.

Hitchhiking is another issue though, and hard to really view on a government rating on the death and injury totals. Some of these deaths are a part of the pedestrian totals and totals of deaths in other vehicles. There is a risk to hitchhiking that also has nothing to do with the possibility of an accident causing an injury or death, which is why this risk is high.

The third part of the Travel Budget Meter is the actual fuel levels. A traveler should know that the global issues affecting the safety and security of travel can also affect the fuel levels. This means that the supply and demand for gas and fuel can rise and fall based on global disasters, particularly war and the global economy. A traveler should also know that this affects the United States more than other countries because more of the population travels. There is a reliance on the world in the United States more than is usually mentioned in the local news and government. When it comes to the cost of travel and the risk, these issues are a factor.

Fuel and gas levels are also affected by the type of transportation. This is important when considering how to travel. Certain types of transportation can travel greater distances with less fuel, keeping tanks filled longer. A vehicle's ability to get good gas mileage really keeps the trip moving at a longer amount of time. The less amount of time spent stopping to get gas and fuel reduces some risks of accidents and injuries. There is a risk when having to pull off the road in an unknown area to find a gas and fuel station. A traveler should plan fuel and gas stops ahead of time. A plan ahead of time can prevent one from getting lost looking for fuel and gas, having an accident while looking for fuel and gas, wasting gas and fuel while looking for gas and fuel, and make a trip to a gas station known to have good prices and other services. Someone who is constantly traveling can forget or miss a planned stop. A traveler can make a checklist of places to get gas and fuel. Make a plan to get fuel and gas in a safe and secure way while adding your own *preferences* into your plan.

This page is available online at the link http://www.crashlanenews.com/ Travel_Budget.html

4

FCC's 10 Steps to Smartphone Security and the CTIA-The Wireless Association Interview

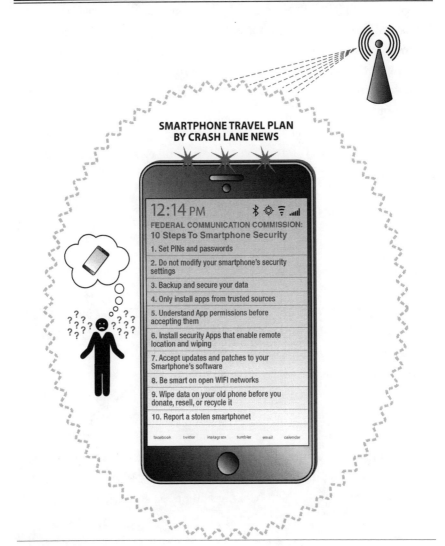

SMARTPHONE TRAVEL PLAN
BY CRASH LANE NEWS

12:14 PM

FEDERAL COMMUNICATION COMMISSION:
10 Steps To Smartphone Security

1. Set PINs and passwords

2. Do not modify your smartphone's security settings

3. Backup and secure your data

4. Only install apps from trusted sources

5. Understand App permissions before accepting them

6. Install security Apps that enable remote location and wiping

7. Accept updates and patches to your Smartphone's software

8. Be smart on open WIFI networks

9. Wipe data on your old phone before you donate, resell, or recycle it

10. Report a stolen smartphonet

facebook   twitter   instagram   tumbler   email   calendar

Smartphone Page

The Future of Travel and the Smartphone

The current use of the smartphone is shaping travel. The Federal Communications Commission's (FCC) government website http:// www.fcc.gov/smartphone-security includes helpful information a traveler can use to be more safe and secure. This is a good public announcement, communicating the need for users to check their own security while using a smartphone. The FCC mentions these steps to be important for the mobile operating systems of the Android, Apple iOS, Blackberry, and Windows Phone. This is important for the future of safe travel in the United States. Smartphone users need to develop a plan for their own communication security. The first step is to stay aware that there is an issue with securing personal data. A traveler should have a smartphone communication security plan.

Crash Lane News includes the FCC 10 Steps to Smartphone Security Plan in italics below. Information on how a traveler can secure personal data while traveling is included in the plan.

1. Set PINs and Passwords

To prevent unauthorized access to your phone, set a password or Personal Identification Number (PIN) on your phone's home screen as a first line of defense in case your phone is lost or stolen. When possible, use a different password for each of your important log-ins (email, banking, personal sites, etc.). You should configure your phone to automatically lock after five minutes or less when your phone is idle, as well as use the SIM password capability available on most smartphones.

A traveler should know the first step on the FCC list is to set pins and passwords. This means to have a password required on entering and using the phone. This can be the most important step according to the FCC.

A smartphone secured with a password gives the user a relatively safe period of time to report the missing or stolen phone. With a password, the threat of a tech savvy person hacking a phone is still a reality. Travelers should ask their service provider what their options are after they report the missing phone. One procedure is to have the service provider block the phone from being used and wipe the data. More information about this is mentioned in step 10.

2. Do Not Modify Your Smartphone Security Settings

Do not alter security settings for convenience. Tampering with your phone's factory settings, jail breaking, or rooting your phone undermines the built-in security features offered by your wireless service and smartphone, while making it more susceptible to an attack. A traveler should keep the Smartphone Security Settings as is when they receive the phone. This allows for some features to be used like the above mentioned setting of a password. The reason is that when some security settings are altered the phone's regular functions of security can be bypassed and lower the amount of cyber security.

Travelers should keep the Smartphone Security Settings as is when they receive the phone. This allows for some features to be used like the above mentioned setting of a password. The reason is that when some security settings are altered the phone's regular functions of security can be bypassed and lower the amount of cyber security.

Jail breaking may be tempting to someone who is traveling but it can make the security of the phone unstable while on a trip. It can corrupt or disable the password settings that would block someone from using a missing and stolen phone. Jail breaking also corrupts and disables many of the other nine steps mentioned by the FCC.

Additional issues can arise related to jail breaking a phone. Jail breaking is known to disable software on a smartphone. Security applications on the phone can be defeated. This can also affect all the security of other the applications. Password information may be available as well as access to accounts.

The main thing to remember is jail breaking changes the phone's original security settings. The original settings are put in place for the user's benefit.

3. Back Up and Secure Your Data

You should back up all of the data stored on your phone—such as your contacts, documents, and photos. These files can be stored on your computer, on a removal storage card, or in the cloud. This will allow you to conveniently restore the information to your phone should it be lost, stolen, or otherwise erased.

A traveler should know the importance in backing up data on the smartphone. The increased use of a smartphone can shift what needs to be secured and saved. The replacement of the personal computer with a smartphone means that the user needs to have a plan to backup information. Backing up data can provide some recovery of information when a phone is damaged, missing, or stolen. On a trip the ability to replace a smartphone in a day is an option but replacing the information on it may not be as easy, which is why it should be backed up.

A suggestion is to back up some information online. This can give a user more accessibility to their information. Where ever they are on a trip in need of backed up files it would be available by logging into an online account. The only issue here is to make sure a provider does not close an account if not active. Backing up information online can safeguard some information from being lost or missing when backup to another computer, thumb drive, or disc.

Research the most convenient available way to back up data through contacting the smartphone service provider. Research customer's reviews of backup services provided by different companies such as Google and Dropbox. Research and record personal experiences backing up information and what works best.

In addition to online back up, keep a short emergency list of contact information on a printed paper. A hard copy of information can be a great offline source should the use of a technology device become unavailable due to weather, natural disaster, lack of power, no Internet access, or other event. Printing all files may not be possible when taking on a trip but choosing some to print and take should also be an option to have on a trip.

4. Only Install Applications from Trusted Sources

Before downloading an app, conduct research to ensure the app is legitimate. Checking the legitimacy of an app may include such thing as: checking reviews, confirming the legitimacy of the app store, and comparing the app sponsor's official website with the app store link to confirm consistency. Many apps from untrusted sources contain malware that once installed can steal information, install viruses, and cause harm to your phone's contents. There are also apps that warn you if any security risks exist on your phone.

A traveler should know that there are some things to watch while installing smartphone applications. A phone's existing security settings will give a warning on untrusted applications. One issue would be the prevention of an application being downloaded that has a virus or malware, or changes the security settings. Each smartphone setting is different and may block different applications, so knowing some basic information on what to block allows a user to make informed choices.

5. Understand Application Permissions before Accepting Them

You should be cautious about granting applications access to personal information on your phone or otherwise letting the application have access to perform functions on your phone. Make sure to also check the privacy settings for each app before installing.

A traveler should know about application permissions before accepting them. When certain applications are downloaded know that information is being gathered from the phone. Having location of events public is sometimes good for advertising a business but when it comes to the reality of having a safe and secure trip, the GPS of a trip may not be to your advantage. Being an informed smartphone user is vital to the success of your trip.

6. Install Security Applications That Allow Remote Location and Wiping

An important security feature widely available on smartphones, either by default or as an app, is the ability to remotely locate and erase all of the data stored on your phone, even if the phone's GPS is off. In the case that you misplace your phone, some applications can activate a loud alarm, even if your phone is on silent. These apps can also help you locate and recover your phone when lost. Visit CTIA for a full list of anti-theft protection apps.

A traveler should know the importance of installing a security application for a smartphone and how to do it. Mobile protection applications are provided on many smartphones without much effort from a user. Some security applications from smartphone service providers have a cost like $3 per month. Plan to have your smartphone secured before the trip.

7. Accepting Updates and Patches to Your Smartphone's Software

You should keep your phone's operating system software up-to-date by enabling automatic updates or accepting updates when prompted from your service provider, operating system provider, device manufacturer, or application provider. By keeping your operating system current, you reduce the risk or exposure to cyber threats.

There are two different types of updates. One is for software and another is for some of the applications on the phone. Manufacturers send updates for software on smartphones to correct errors while updating the security. These updates can also be set to be automatic or to be done manually by the user. The updates may be set only when a phone is connected to a Wi-Fi network. Set application updates to auto or manual based on whether there is access to Wi-Fi. Updating over Wi-Fi saves the use of monthly data in the service provider package. Keep your updates current to ensure safer personal data.

8. Be Smart on Open Wi-Fi Networks

When you access a Wi-Fi network that is open to the public, your phone can be an easy target of cybercriminals. You should limit your use of public hotspots and instead use protected Wi-Fi from a network operator you trust or mobile wireless connection to reduce your risk of exposure, especially when accessing personal or sensitive information. Always be aware when clicking web links and be particularly cautious if you are asked to enter account or log-in information.

A traveler should know that open Wi-Fi networks may not be secure. Anything going over the Internet has the possibility there are more than you and the recipient watching it. People can hack Wi-Fi networks and watch what some people are using This can also allow a hacker to get inside a smartphone to see passwords, contact information, messages and other information. Some smartphone service providers have recommended Google's suggestions to find the best security and antivirus options.

9. Wiping Data on Your Own Phone before You Donate, Resell, or Recycle It

Your smartphone contains personal data you want to keep private when you dispose of your old phone. To protect your privacy, completely erase data off your phone and reset the phone to its initial factory settings. Now having wiped your old device, you are free to donate, resell, recycle, or otherwise properly dispose of your phone.

A traveler should know the advantage of wiping personal data off the smartphone. The wipe prevents a refurbished phone from retaining some of the previous user's information. Many computer users backup their data before a wipe as should a smartphone user. A data wipe can be done by going to the smartphones settings. Once there a user can set a phone to return to default settings and to reset everything on the device. When a wipe is done the right way the device goes to original state at purchase and default settings when the phone was brand new.

10. Report a Missing or Lost Smartphone

The major wireless service providers, in coordination with the FCC, have established a stolen phone database. If your phone is stolen, you should report the theft to your local law enforcement authorities and then register the stolen phone with your wireless service provider. This will provide notice to all the major wireless networks without your permission.

A traveler should report a missing or lost cell phone to his or her service provider first. This can allow for the service provider to block the future use of the phone. Some service providers also will have an alarm go off on a phone that alerts someone that a phone has been stolen or missing in the area. Report the lost phone to the hotel or other establishment. Follow procedure to retrieve the phone or obtain a new phone through the service agreement. Check insurance coverage before traveling. Be vigilant in planning for the trip to ensure personal data.

Conclusion to Smartphone Plan

In summary, the plan mentioned by the FCC and in the above can keep a trip safer and more secure. A traveler should apply this information to their own comprehensive travel plan. Visit the FCC http://www.fcc.gov/smartphone-security website's 10 steps to smartphone security. Once there the FCC asks which mobile operating system is used and when entered there are additional links and suggestions available for each system. A traveler should buy *Crash Lane News* to find a fuller and more in-depth explanation of security issues and how to plan to defend against them. Travel safely.

This page in available online at the link http://www.crashlanenews.com/Smart_Phone_Plan.html.

Interview with CTIA.org, CTIA-The Wireless Association

Information security is a big travel issue for local and regional trips in the United States and abroad. The use of electronic devices like a smartphone has the risk of information leakage. A regular phone call or accessing mobile data can become threatening. The safety of a secure office or at home is usually taken for granted. The following interview with the CTIA-The Wireless Association can help improve information security awareness of the public. The following includes an expert's point of view about how to travel in a more secure way. That point of view can be added into a traveler's personal security plan.

The following is an interview with the CTIA-The Wireless Association, www.ctia.org, an international organization representing the wireless communications industry. Membership in the association includes wireless carriers and their suppliers, as well as providers and manufacturers of wireless data services and products. CTIA advocates on behalf of its members at all levels of government. They coordinate the industry's voluntary best practices initiatives, sponsoring the industry's leading wireless tradeshows. CTIA was founded in 1984 and has seen the changes from the hilarious bulky 1980s cell phones, morphing through time to the current smartphones.

The interview focuses on information security in relation to the security issues of smartphone security.

Stolen Cell Phone Database

One of the more significant projects managed by the CTIA, as of November 2013, is the creation of the stolen smartphone database. The stolen smartphone program is currently active in many parts of the country. There are also some updates being added while the database is currently processing data. This program is going to bring some needed continuity for information security after a smartphone is lost or stolen.

The database works by tracking the phones alert number, which sounds like a type of serial number. This number identifies each phone. In the event that the phone is stolen, there is a certain alert attached to every device. That alert has a number that is entered into the database. Therefore if someone is in possession of that lost or stolen device, they would not be able to use it. They would also not be able to reinstitute service on it. That stolen smartphone database is one way to deter theft. The fact that smartphones are the most popular device in a theft resulted in this program being launched.

CTIA, CEO Steve Largent, stated 27 November 2013, "Today, I am pleased to confirm that the global, multi-carrier, common database for LTE smartphones has been finalized and implemented in advance of the November 30, 2013 deadline. The matter of stolen devices is extremely important to the wireless providers, which is why they worked so hard over the last year to meet each deadline on time. As more countries and more carriers around the world participate in the 3G and 4G/LTE databases, criminals will have fewer outlets since these stolen phones would be blacklisted and could not be reactivated. Another important element to stopping stolen phones is consumers. To assist users, we offer a list of apps to download that will remotely erase, track and/or lock the stolen devices. We also remind consumers to pay attention to their surroundings. Similar to your purse or wallet, it's best to not call attention to your smartphone and create an opportunity for a thief to steal it. We continue to believe that combating stolen cell phones will require a comprehensive effort. We encourage consumers to use currently available apps and features that would remotely wipe, track and lock their devices in case they are lost or stolen, and our members are continuing to explore and offer new technologies. We also strongly support and need Senator Schumer's legislation to pass that would impose tough penalties on those who steal devices or modify them illegally since it would help dry up the market for those who traffic in stolen devices. We also need more foreign countries and carriers to participate in the global stolen phone database to prevent criminals from selling stolen devices internationally. By working together with everyone, from the wireless companies, law enforcement, policymakers and consumers, we will make a difference."

In summary, this means that there is more being done by the CTIA and the government in regard to preventing thefts.

Wireless Emergency Alert Advice from CTIA

The Wireless Emergency Alert is a National Initiative. They work at three levels. One is the Presidential Alert level, which has never been used thankfully and hopefully never will be. That is a significant thing. Another use is to communicate a public safety threat. This alert can be initiated at various levels by public safety officials. It could be a hurricane, tornado, earthquake, snowstorm, heavy rain, environmental issues; those are more common. There are also Amber Alerts. The mentioned are now distributed through the wireless emergency alert program. The WEAs are an effective program and growing the safety measure. They are geographically based. If a traveler is from the western states but traveling in a different region like in the eastern states, and if there was an event happening back West, he or she would not get the alert information on the device. The reason is his or her phone is not in a state in the West; it is in a state in the East. If a user was from somewhere else and he or she traveled and something was to happen in proximity of where the smartphone is, then he or she would be notified. It is important to only send relevant information at that moment. This can reduce possible unwanted messages that could also be a distraction and create other issues.

Wireless Emergency Alerts are a very good way to communicate a threat to the public. Overall it can increase the government's communication of information, while accurately managing public safety. Users should be impressed with the government for the Wireless Emergency Alerts if they actually save lives. One reason is it is opening up an additional way to communicate issues that may help protect the public from disasters that only the government would know about. There is difficulty on the way the government manages public safety in their ability to increase the communication of information between the public and government's departments. Aside from the existing use of the U.S. Post Office, aside from the weather radio warnings, or aside from the regular telephone, this Wireless Emergency Alert is the first of its kind for the public.

Passwords

One of the first suggestions the CTIA mentions is to make sure to utilize the password function on the phone. Passwords are described as a big step a person can take to protecting themselves. This can also be the easiest step to take for information security. Users should visit the device's settings page and set up a password.

The good thing about passwords is that is available on your device from purchase. There is no need to download anything. In addition to making sure to have a password, keep the device's original operating system intact. Do not reset the default security settings to the device. There is a habit that people are getting to change some of the regular software settings on a device. The problem with these changes is they can lead to later security issues, corrupting the function of having a password.

Having a password set and keeping the integrity of the smartphone protect the smartphone user the most. Many users are excited about shiny new technologies like the smartphone but sometimes forget they need to have some access controls put in place to safeguard their information, being these default security settings. The example of jail breaking a phone to receive free applications, downloads, or service can cause someone who is desperate to get something for free temporarily. This is illegal and a mistake to do. This may occur in the time before the next paycheck, making the wrong short-term decision. The easy out for the short term also affects their information security from being unknowingly compromised.

Know how to choose a more secure password. Take advantage of customizing passwords or pin numbers. These can be to a series of different numbers. Numbers for a password and pin should be more difficult to break or for someone other than you to figure out. An estimated 70% of the passcodes used are ten different combinations. That is pretty remarkable when you think about it. The 320 million and growing total subscribers in the country have the ability to set the passwords and protections on the devices, yet the vast majority of them are a combination of ten numbers. These 320 million subscribers are not doing the best they can. Having a good password is the most basic step to protect the device from being broken into when out of an owner's possession. That is a very big issue and a good reason to add some additional thought into lengthening a password. For a password have ten or more digits if possible, and use different numbers or letters for a password. In the example that the smartphone only lets you use four numbers, rather than using 1234, or 1111, or 0000, use a more random sequence. Create a password that is not as predictable as repeating the same number, and use a number that is not popular. Many smartphone users are choosing the easier way using predictable numbers and this puts them at risk of having their information security violated, compromised, and stolen. In summary, it is recommended to use the pins and passwords that come with the device. Then make sure passwords are not obvious to a stranger.

Wiping Data

Another very popular function today with smartphones is enabling the ability to use remote locking or remote wiping. This is possible in the event that you lose the device. It is encouraged that people have remote wiping as an available option. This wiping works in a situation when a user becomes disconnected from his or her device. Even though the device is out of their control they can remotely wipe their personal information. The owner can also lock the phone so it cannot be easily used by somebody, once lost or missing. The reason to wipe data is because these phones can store a large amount of data and have more sensitive information. When a user does lose a phone the last thing a user should want is for someone to look and navigate through the device's information. This could cause information security problems later on a larger scale, for example, with some of the information being misused in an identity theft crime. A user's information may not be the only thing at risk as well, in that their business contacts and friends' information may also fall prey to information crime. If someone can have unauthorized access to another user's device the risk and threat level of misused information is high. Information on the smartphone is considered personal information, and a user would not usually share information with someone they do not know, so why have it available when an unknown person may find, or steal a phone? Eliminate the risk of saving information on the phone by wiping the data if it ends up lost and stolen. Remote wiping and locking is a real solution available for smartphone owners.

Public Wi-Fi Security

Smartphone security is at risk from public Wi-Fi threats. Areas where there is Wi-Fi include coffee shops, Internet cafes, travel centers, libraries, universities, and other stores that offer Wi-Fi network connections. In addition to these areas there are literally tens of thousands of places to access Wi-Fi around the United States. Most of these access points are legitimate, but there are criminals that turn a legitimate access point into something that threatens an unsuspecting user's device. There are some Wi-Fi spots that are setup by hackers. These also look like they are legitimate Wi-Fi spots.

Wi-Fi security threats exist in the form of hiding in plain sight. When seeking them out it may not be easy because there are so many legitimate ones and only a few problem ones, and the problem ones may not want to be found, so can be difficult to identify. These Wi-Fi traps setup by hackers are called honey pots. The honey pots trick people unknowingly, thinking they are in a safe Wi-Fi area. The honey pot then allows a hacker to get the user's information when a user signs into the honey pot. The hacker then has direct access to an unsuspecting user and their network, which is a clear avenue into a device. Once a hacker and a honey pot have this access it extracts certain information from a computer, with the added possibility of infecting it with some kind of malware that will later block a user from finding how their computer was hacked. Many hackers try to just shut down a user's computer and are incapable of getting the information. In the event there is a sophisticated hacking operation getting information, the evidence of this can be disguised when a computer stops functioning. It is too late for a user's device at this point and this has been an issue for laptop users at these Wi-Fi honey pots for awhile. It is the same basic risk but now on a smartphone.

Alert! Smartphone users, avoid using fake WI-FI hotspots, these are known as honeypots

Designed and Property of *Crash Lane News*

CTIA urges people to be aware of the Wi-Fi network they are accessing. Verify that it is the legitimate Wi-Fi name by asking customer service or someone who is an employee and knowledgeable about that. One example of this is if a user is at a business offering public Wi-Fi, make sure the right Wi-Fi network is located and verified before connecting the device. If at a travel center make sure it is a travel center's correct link to the Wi-Fi or other access. There are ways to verify it on the Wi-Fi access website where there is a name. Be aware of using legitimate Wi-Fi access points. Do not leave yourself open to potential intrusions caused by the honey pot scam and hackers. That problem is becoming more important as more and more Wi-Fi hotspots pop up around the country. Remember the vast majority of Wi-Fi hotspots are accessible and available. But some are not what they appear to be, and the traveling public should be aware of this.

Be Aware of the Surroundings

Literally, be aware of your physical surroundings. This can include the present location where the traveler is or is passing through. If a user is traveling on a train or a bus, try to be aware of the risks. A small smartphone device is easy prey. Once left alone for a few minutes it can get pocketed in a theft, or become lost. For those basic reasons, maintain possession of a smartphone device at all times when out in public and do not lend it to a stranger. Do not flash it around. It is a potential target for a theft, and be mindful that these devices end up missing and stolen. Be aware of the potential problem of a theft. A user should know there are times when he or she may not be able to pay attention to the environment and people around, and take steps prevent certain episodes from happening. Something can go missing when you least expect it to happen, so try to take extra precautions to secure the device. People can be a little cavalier, clueless, and naive sometimes when traveling on short trips. The ability to remember this advice is important and can prevent the device from ending up missing, and compromised from an act of carelessness. Smartphone users have to be aware of where they are, while also paying attention to what is happening around them while using their phone. Remember it is a very valuable device, which is currently very popular and attractive. A user should treat it like he or she would a wallet or a purse, as another valuable. Get used to the automatic locks that require passwords that were previously mentioned and are available. Set the unlock password, and take the precautions that you would for any other valuable. Those are the main points for travelers.

Proper Use of the Phone

Use a smartphone to help you on a trip. Before leaving plan and find a safe time to use the device. When using it make sure to remember the above mentioned best practices on how to keep the device secure while in use.

Make sure that when on a trip that useful information is included on the device. This means to have all the important contacts on the smartphone. Some examples of some useful contacts that are good to have saved in advance include that of an emergency contact, doctor, dentist, the car insurance office point of contact, information for AAA, and other travel services. Some personal contacts that should also be saved are those of relatives, friends, and people who can help in relaying a message in case of emergencies. The mentioned should be accessible ahead of time, so that when a user does need them, it is available. When things are not saved and then needed it can create another headache in the event of an accident. The security of the device is important, but it is also important to be able to use the device so it can be beneficial to the user on a trip.

Distracted Driving

There are many current issues going on with vehicle safety and the smartphone that may also affect the future of traveling safe and secure. Many applications are restricting use when the device is moving at a certain speed. There are also applications available to download that will apply that safety feature to the smartphone, preventing its use in motion. That is a popular application with a lot of parents, hoping to prevent young drivers from being tempted by these distractions if possible. It is not just for young people. All kinds of offerings are available for adults that tempt them to use their smartphone while driving. The smartphone is one of the latest distractions for all types of drivers: young, adult, and for senior citizens. Every user wants to load applications onto a device and sometimes cannot help to resist the temptation from not picking it up in traffic. Many drivers cannot resist picking up the phone when driving as well, making these preventative distracted applications a real tool of safety to insure attention is to the road. Many application developers and carriers are sometimes working in concert and sometimes separately come up with new techniques to make the vehicle experience even safer. An app that helps to prevent distracted driving is a good thing for traveling as well helping the drivers around you be safer and focus on the road.

CTIA mentions drivers should only be using a smartphone when they absolutely have to. For the most part, a call can wait until the next stop, break, rest area, and service station. A driver should never text message when he or she is driving. There are very few circumstances where a phone call is essential. There are safe ways you can still be connected and use the phone. Just pull over to a well lit, safe, and secure area. It is recommended to limit the use for during the most extreme driving conditions that may cause the more hazardous situations. Common sense can usually persuade someone to have all their focus on the road while driving in extreme weather, but distractions also occur with the use of devices. Stay off the phone in bad weather.

Avoid stressful conversations when driving and make driver safety a priority. Stay off the phone in heavy traffic. Use common sense while also following those suggestions. Most of the traveling public out there would hope that people would adhere to the regulations against distracted driving, making everyone safer.

There are many applications out there now that talk to the user, giving him or her verbal instructions about driving, which may mainly include directions for the trip. These are GPS enabled applications, and using them is increasingly popular. CTIA-The Wireless Association believe GPS is extremely helpful. The voice component is useful and worth considering. The last thing you want is to have a location application that you have to watch. Having a voice component is an important part if deciding to use a smartphone while driving at all.

Applications

When it comes to getting new and exciting applications, it is tempting for everyone to download as many apps as they can because then a smartphone will have everything on it. Whether he or she is in service or out of service they do not have to download anything and just use the app. With all the different applications, there is also a wide variety of permissions. The way to know or learn about this application permission is at the app store. All the app stores run independently.

In the United States, we have highly secured app stores compared to many around the world. Because of that the smartphone infection rates are the lowest around the world. Smartphones in the United States have a malware or virus infection rate of about .02 percent. That low .02 results from the work the application community is doing, securing the apps available there. Applications in the USA are made to be reliable and legitimate. This quality control, when it comes to security, is also the result of what the carriers have done. Carriers such as AT&T, T-Mobile, Sprint, and Verizon have financial investments of billions of dollars to make sure the proper technological precautions and safety steps are put in. When it comes to applications in the U.S., carriers, developers, and other parties involved do a pretty good job of providing safe applications.

One recommendation, when it comes to downloading applications or accepting content, is that it is from a legitimate source. Applications using text messaging is a popular way for these bad actors to get access to your device. A smartphone user might receive a text message from a strange source or it appears too good to be true, then if he or she clicks to open it or see it, he or she has just now invited in the bad actor. Only accept applications and messages from trusted sources. Only download material from legitimate or recognized websites or brands. Those are steps the smartphone users can take to secure their device and information.

These are good examples from the CTIA of additional steps that can be taken in addition to the FCC's 10 Steps to Smartphone Security.

5

Travelers Should Know
Typhoons Are Hurricanes

The below is a story put together from NASA about the Typhoon Nabi made available to the public through www.NASA.gov. This is an important weather event due to its describable damage, as well as how it affected the United States interests in Philippines, Japan, and South Korea. A survivor's account of Typhoon Nabi is included after the NASA article. This point of view is included to show the need for real disaster preparedness, when there was no known plan or special instructions at the time. Many in the United States do not follow the weather overseas in that area of the Pacific, South Korea and Japan, regularly. Because of that fact, some incidents that were historical, and significant, were not turned into front page news back in the United States. Crash Lane News wants readers to consider this before reading. It is important to know that United States military is stationed throughout the region where Typhoon Nabi passed, and it affected many for the worst in the area. Typhoon Nabi was powerful enough to cause damage, injuries, and fatalities. With its devastating impact, it was also known to possibly be a disaster ahead of time, while some of the less informed did not get the right amount of warning until the day of the storm, knowing that their lives had become a part of the military's well known strategy of sacrificing lower ranking soldiers, forcing them into the weather's disaster, and other dangers like cities in hostile areas within South Korea. This happened many times over the years and resulted in some preventable incidents considered accidents caused by the weather, and other preventable events in combat. Those that were in the military under such circumstances that were forced into these preventable and avoidable events did not have the right leadership beyond the platoon, company, and battalion level. As a result they also did not have the right preparedness, equipment, and relief, causing panic, injuries, and fatalities. The region was warned ahead of time about this event, but for some in the military, and especially those on duty forced to work out in the weather, Typhoon Nabi is still unforgettable. This typhoon/hurricane is very memorable to the survivors, being it was a very hazardous experience. Its description follows in precise detail by NASA, giving the scientific background of the storm being tracked. A report by a government agency is good for future reference, while also supporting a storm survivor's point of view. US Army soldiers travel across the world learning about these types of natural weather hazards. Sometimes these servicemen are seen as unpopular, unneeded, excess, expendable, and purposely forgotten about, being then coincidentally, forced into these near news headline making situations, that never really make the news headlines enough. Unreported events like these, do not lead into military awards and military promotions. The survivors on duty at that time receive no real credit. Some in the military, mostly those in the lower ranks, learn the more unfortunate things like a lack of disaster preparedness. This is all a contradiction while the US military claims to stress about it back on the training bases in United States because it is a part of their schedule. When a Typhoon is able to be forecasted days if not a week in advance in the Pacific, and there is little awareness brought to those in it, its disastrous events become a brief history to those that saw its force and power while on duty during the storm. A disaster like a Typhoon threat overseas are occasionally forgotten about by a few, but many times known about by all. The higher ranking commanders in the United States military have a good sense about the weather in the United States and abroad, but with that there are some events that still occur. These reasons will be explained after the NASA article. While reading the NASA article, note that it is important to know there is a certain predetermined plan the military puts in place. Conditions considered unsafe back in the United States according to other government agencies and department are not always considered unsafe if in the military. No matter what significant weather event is forecasted to occur, or what manmade disaster has already taken place in the region, there is the chance of that predetermined planning forcing the unfortunate few into an avoidable hazard.

Hurricane Season 2005: Typhoon Nabi 09.08.05.
Latest Update - September 8, 2005 11:28 a.m. EDT

Typhoon Nabi was a Category 2 typhoon in the western Pacific when the Moderate Resolution Imaging Spectroradiometer (MODIS) on NASA's Terra satellite captured this image on September 6, 2005 at 11:05 a.m. Tokyo time. It had sustained winds of around 160 kilometers an hour (100 miles per hour), and it was heading north across the southern end of Japan. The eye of the storm is roughly centered in the image, and the thick storm clouds completely hide the island of Kyushu. To the northeast of the eye, the smaller island of Shikoku and the largest Japanese island, Honshu, are also under the clouds.

These clouds brought a deluge to the southern islands and caused dangerous landslides in the region's mountainous terrain. The landslides killed several people on Kyushu. As high waves pounded the coast, as much as 51 inches of rain may have fallen in 24 hours as the storm moved slowly northward into the Sea of Japan. The Japanese government had ordered evacuations for more than 100,000 people in the southern islands, according to reports from BBC News. Flights, road traffic, and ferry services were disrupted, and hundreds of thousands of people and businesses lost power. + High resolution image. Credit: NASA image created by Jesse Allen, Earth Observatory, using data obtained from the MODIS Rapid Response team.

Typhoon Nabi Hits Southern Japan

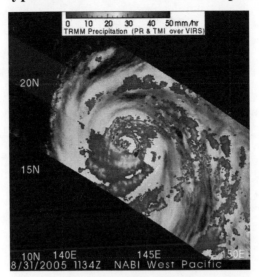

Typhoon Nabi, once a powerful super typhoon, made landfall on Japan's main southern island of Kyushu with sustained winds reported at 126 kph (78 mph). Nabi, which means "butterfly" in Korean, continued on over the southwestern tip of Honshu, triggering mudslides and flooding along the way, before heading out into the Sea of Japan. The storm left 17 dead and 9 missing in Japan, many as a result of mudslides. Four people were also reported missing in Korea.

The Tropical Rainfall Measuring Mission (TRMM) satellite has followed Nabi's progress across the West Pacific. TRMM was Launched back in November of 1997 to estimate rainfall over the global Tropics and has proven itself to be a valuable platform for monitoring tropical cyclones, especially over remote parts of the open ocean. With its array of active and passive sensors, TRMM can look into the very heart of these storms. These two images of Nabi were taken by TRMM and capture the storm during both its intensifying and weakening stages.

The first image was taken at 11:34 UTC on 31 August 2005 just after Nabi had entered the easternmost part of the Philippine Sea and was in the process of intensifying. The image shows the horizontal distribution of rain intensity within Nabi. Rain rates in the center of the swath are from the TRMM Precipitation Radar (PR), while those in the outer portion are from the TRMM Microwave Imager (TMI). The rain rates are overlaid on infrared (IR) data from the TRMM Visible Infrared Scanner (VIRS). TRMM reveals that Nabi has a small, closed eye with intense rain (dark red areas) in the southwestern half of the eyewall. The eye is surrounded by tightly spiraling rain bands (green and blue arcs), all features of a maturing cyclone. The intense rain near the center indicates were heat is being released into the storm and driving its circulation. At the time of this image, Nabi as a Category 2 typhoon with maximum sustained winds estimated at 95 knots (109 mph) by the Joint Typhoon Warning Center. Nabi, which was in the process of intensifying, reached Category 5 intensity by 18 UTC on the 1st of September with sustained winds estimated at 140 knots (161 mph).

The next image shows Nabi at 08:29 UTC on 5 September as the large eye of the storm is bearing down on southern Japan. This dramatic image from TRMM reveals some important clues about the storm. The eye is now very large but still closed with no rain visible in the broad center. The storm is still relatively strong but in the process of slowly spinning down. The large eye indicates that the wind field has spread out, something that can occur in the later stages of strong tropical cyclones, making it unlikely that the storm can reintensify. At the time of the image, Nabi was a Category 3 typhoon with sustained winds estimated at 110 knots (127 mph). Nabi would continue to weaken as it approached the coastline. TRMM is a joint mission between NASA and the Japanese space agency JAXA. Credit: NASA, Hal Pierce (SSAI/NASA GSFC) and caption by Steve Lang (SSAI/ NASA GSFC).

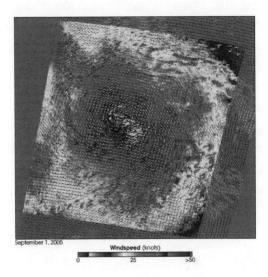

The calm eye of Typhoon Nabi stands out like a bulls-eye in the center of the concentric circles of color that make up the storm. The colors represent wind speed, with purple and pink showing the highest winds, while tiny barbs show the wind's direction spinning around the eye of the storm. The white barbs indicate regions of heavy rainfall. The image was created using data collected by the QuikSCAT satellite on September 1, 2005, when Nabi was growing into a powerful super typhoon with winds of 260 kilometers per hour (160 miles per hour, 140 knots) and gusts to 315 km/hr (196 mph, 170 knots). At the time this image was taken, however, Nabi had winds of about 213 km/hr (132 mph, 115 knots) with gusts to 260 km/hr (160 mph, 140 knots), making it the equivalent of a Category 3 hurricane on the Saffir-Simpson Hurricane Scale.

The wind speeds shown in this image don't match the winds reported by the Joint Typhoon Warning Center. This is because QuikSCAT measures near surface wind speeds over the ocean based on how the winds affect the ocean. The satellite sends out high frequency radio waves, some of which bounce off the ocean and return to the satellite. Rough, storm-tossed seas return more of the waves, creating a strong signal, while a mirror-smooth surface returns a weaker signal. To learn to match wind speeds with the type of signal that returns to the satellite, scientists compare wind measurements taken by ocean buoys to the strength of the signal received by the satellite. The more measurements scientists have, the more accurately they can correlate wind speed to the returning radar signal.

Typhoons and hurricanes are relatively rare. This means that scientists have few buoy measurements to compare to the data they get from the satellite and can't match the satellite measurements to exact wind speeds. Instead, the image provides a clear picture of relative wind speeds, showing how large the strong center of the storm is and which direction winds are blowing. To learn more about measuring winds from space, check out NASA's Winds web site. + High resolution image. Credit: NASA image courtesy the QuikSCAT Science Team at the Jet Propulsion Laboratory

Reference

NASA.gov. Retrieved from public domain online from NASA in 2013. Typhoon Nabi NASA story and images

http://www.nasa.gov/mission_pages/hurricanes/archives/2005/h2005_nabi.html

NASA image courtesy the QuikSCAT Science Team at the Jet Propulsion Laboratory

Crash Lane News' Point of View About Typhoon Nabi

Many News agencies report only what the Department of Defense releases. News agencies only cover these press releases because there is a partially open and transparent government in the United States. News agencies believe the citizens in the United States want to know about the military, and that it is best to tell the public what the Defense Department wants the public to know. There are limitations as to what gets included in each story.

It is also important to include what happens within the Department of Defense when it comes to management of the weather and disasters. But, as a result of there being some restrictions on the news, this information does not always make it into what is being reported. Most released news stories exist where the Department of Defense is planning on deploying military personnel. This could be to South Korea, Afghanistan, Iraq, Africa, basically anywhere. While this news of a deployment is announced, the Department of Defense may leave out what happens while the unit is there. The point is that the follow up story is not always as transparent as the original news release.

One example of something left out includes the weather. A military unit may experience everything from the unpredictable weather disasters of a thunderstorm with lighting to a predictable event like a Hurricane. The mentioned NASA Typhoon Nabi weather report mentions the weather. It includes a list of events including the area of South Korea. But, it did not mention that the United States military was out in the path of the Typhoon. An official weather report by NASA can help describe some more remote areas of the world, but at that same time it will not always include the entire story. Some reasons it was left out could be that the degree of damage that the military faced was not catastrophic enough, being there was no fatality. That kind of reasoning is temporary, and is not a good enough reason in the long term. This is a good example of what Crash Lane News is about. Note, the United States government released some information about the Typhoon. With that report the listed information seemed to leave out how the weather affected the safety of the United States military stationed throughout Japan and South Korea. This issue is very similar to the before mentioned discussion about the winter weather not being discussed by the Federal Motor Carrier Safety Administration, FMCSA. There is definitely something missing about the weather from both examples, and what is missing is causing crashes or fatalities. Cover ups exist in every government. This cover up about the weather seems at first to not matter here in this book, but now that it is being discussed, hopefully it will start the discussion of what needs to be managed more accurately.

The point of view in the following paragraphs mentions some of the distractions management has to work with. Many of these distractions are simple problems, and most of them can be avoided. But these also somehow cause a lot of failure when they are not avoided from the beginning. This discussion is important because it will show there is a strategy of sacrifice in the Department of Defense. This sacrifice strategy was well known by many that served in the military in the post 9/11 era. The strategy of sacrifice when compared to other departments in the United States government is also usually replaced with one of preparedness when it comes to government employee's safety. This also includes there being more preparedness for the military stationed within the United States. The strategy of sacrifice has been identified to occur within the United States in the private businesses, and the general public. One leading example of there being sacrifices within the United States is within the Commercial transportation industry.

The Department of Transportation has been sacrificing Commercial businesses reputations and their Commercial drivers. This example is in reference to the previous points when the Department of Transportation is leaving the roads open in severe winter weather, and leaving the roads open during disasters. It is important to know that no plan has to be predetermined indefinitely, and the strategy of sacrificing a few to the weather is something that is preventable. Changes can be made to military missions, and they are made many times. The military alters travel plans, and considers all the risks in order to avoid severe weather, but things like preparedness for a Typhoon sometimes will get left out.

The following is a background of events, leading up to Typhoon Nabi. Distractions affecting management's ability to have preparedness occurred. Prior to Typhoon Nabi there were some other weather and natural disasters which might have stole the spotlight for that year. A surprised turn of events before Typhoon season can create a diversion to the need for that specific season's preparedness. When looking back, some of the distractions the U.S. Army in South Korea struggled with appeared to be a part of the continuous year of disasters. One of the biggest of these was the reason for being in South Korea in the first place. It was the issues of North Korea's threatening proliferation of weapons of mass destruction and missiles. Another distraction was being stationed in an area of South Korea that was hostile against the United States. The reasons were stated that the United States did not help South Korea enough in the 1980s to support democracy. Many anti-American hostilities were known to be only opinions because there were also many South Koreans that wanted the United States there. Another distraction was the issues caused by the Indian Ocean Tsunami. The entire region was affected permanently due to that Tsunami. All these distractions filled the year with many questions. Some are still left open ended.

A United States Army unit located in South Korea, on the most southern region of the peninsula endured the Typhoon Nabi storm system. This unit was on a mission, also considered a deployment, and was named the 2-1 Air Defense Artillery Unit. Many in the military have mentioned that no one deploys to South Korea, but that is not true for this story and mission. It was a deployment according to command based on the area going into and the mission itself. The ADA unit was located in the city of Kwangju, at a Korean Airbase. This Korean Airbase is adjacent to the Kwangju Airport. At that time the city never had much U.S. military there other than an Airforce unit. This new Air Defense Artillery unit was working to support the 35th Brigade located at Camp Osan. There were a few different companies within the 2-1 ADA Battalion to include HHC (Headquarters), Alpha Company, Bravo Company, and large Maintenance Company. The planners within the Battalion's command had scheduled Bravo Company to be on duty the month of the Typhoon which was September.

A line of events during this unit's mission started with a published article in the Stars and Stripes and other news agencies in 2004. From August 2004 to November 2004 military equipment and personnel were transported to South Korea, from Fort Bliss, Texas. Many members in the military also did not know that when an Air Defense Unit moves it is considered a deployment. The Department of Defense released information to the public about the threat from North Korea. This was sent to news agencies during the years and months before 2004. Some of news stated the Defense Department's strategy to be one of deterrence. This strategy of deterrence has been the strategy since the end of the Korean War. With the United States and South Korea's management strategy public many agreed it sounds like it would make the region safer. For example, deterrence is mentioned to be preventing an invasion by the North Korean military into South Korea. The deterrence currently in place, according to the South Korea's government, and according the United State's government is working, even though it is considered one of the longest military conflicts in World History.

Deterrence is not everything, meaning that deterrence is usually only what is seen on the surface of the conflict. This brings about the idea of there being a contradicting strategy occurring. Contradictions can be found anywhere, but, when they occurred in 2005, and when they occur at the global level there are concerns. One example of a contradiction was why go into a hostile area of South Korea. This particular area had a Massacre back in the 1980s, and blamed the United States for not helping protect the protestors that were trying to have a more democratic government. Even though some of the leaders in Gwangju wanted the United States there, it did not mean that the hostilities from the 1980s would be forgotten. Avoiding a hostile area is something recommended when abroad by the Department of Defense and by the Department of the State. Why was avoiding a hostile area not done from the beginning in this situation? The only answer as of 2014 could be that there was a certain amount of greed and corruption. Corruption in any government can force something to work temporarily in a failing and unmanageable way, mostly for show. The problem in this example was that the infamous massacre from the 1980s was not anticipated to cause as much anti-American protesting as it did. Many U.S. Army Soldiers could not have expected the hostilities of what became a reality, but also had a new respect for the local population's regional history.

The point of all this is that there were man made problems that year that caused many distractions. These manmade distractions affected the safety of the unit prior to the later Typhoon weather and other natural disasters. The failures of a military mission's command at the highest and at the lowest level rarely get reported in the news. This is done by the Department of Defense to avoid the reality that a contradiction occurred. The problem here was that the United States government was supposedly maintaining deterrence against North Korea, but the way it was done brought local hostilities, and bad memories back to life. Most of these ended up being visibly seen in protests against the United States at the Kwangju Airbase. A military partnership between countries can be complicated. A protest is not going to end the mission of deterrence but it obviously causes a disruption, and later became a security issue. In this year there were solutions available. Some decisions and planning can be done ahead of time, preventing a mission from becoming threatened and exposed to a disaster. But for some reason in this unit, that kind of planning was not happening accurately enough. The level of unpredictable things was very high during 2004-2005 by command.

Towards the end of December 2004, the Indian Ocean Tsunami wiped out the lives of hundreds of thousands. South Korea was unaffected with a direct Tsunami wave, but the region's transportation and resources were impacted. The main cause of the high death rate in the areas that were hit directly was a lack of emergency alerting. The Tsunami's size was described to be unlike any event in the region ever witnessed or heard about before then. Even though the United States was not directly hit, this Tsunami disaster added to the stresses of the U.S. Military. It was one more concern on the list, and ended up being one of the biggest examples of the need for a better Tsunami warning system in that region of the world. The needed relief for the Tsunami relief drew attention away from the regular military planning for the United States, South Korea, and Japan. Everything is interconnected. That all occurred within the first 2 months this Air Defense Artillery unit was there. The Tsunami disaster should have been more of a warning to this unit. Many in the unit had a relentless amount of optimism about the year ahead, and high level of morale, not being able to see what already happened and what little was done to prevent it. Many maintained a false positive outlook through the entire year, and still believe that everything was successful.

After the Indian Ocean Tsunami's devastation was spread by News agencies, and finally reaching the unit in South Korea, the season of winter had already arrived on the peninsula. The notoriously cold South Korean blizzards really test those out in it for days doing work. Cold weather is not so bad to work in while in a heated office, or sitting in a heated vehicle. For those out in the snow and ice a winter is really a momentum changer. The cold can cause a significant amount of stress, causing to further distractions. Many that had some high morale began to turn during the winter season. Many in the military are forced into winter storms every year in South Korea. That type of forcing is preventable.

After the South Korean winter melted, spring arrived. Spring in 2005 was considered protest season by command. The management of problems between the hostile protestors and the South Koreans that wanted the Air Defense Artillery created additional distractions. By this time it literally was one bad natural disaster event and severe weather disaster after another. Instead of the weather becoming mild and things going smooth, protestors began protesting. Distractions allowed the later incoming weather threats to have an additional unnecessary negative impact. The unit's readiness and morale was a casualty by spring. Many things like South Korea's protest season was a surprise. This is true even though there are protestors every year in South Korea, and there is even military training in advance, and warnings about it by the military and Department of the State. The U.S. Soldiers forced to be on duty during the severe winter weather, and forced to be on duty while hearing protesting near the base became intimidated. Many Soldiers became frightened. Some did not trust the local businesses anymore, staying on post 24/7. Some just lived life as usual, not letting the protesting change their activities, and way of life. All of the exposure to it was preventable. But, instead of eliminating the placement of United States military members in harms way, it was a strategy of sacrifice.

The United States military throughout South Korea are weekly protested. Many protests have been in the news in South Korea. Some protests get press coverage in the United States and other countries. The story about the 3000 person sized riot May 2005 outside the Kwangju Airbase's main gate was one of these news stories reported globally.

The reason why there was coverage was the size of the protest being so big. A build up of hostilities originated from the U.S. Army having an increased presence. That was preventable. This area historically resents the United States more than many other areas within South Korea. The massacre of students in the 1980s is the main reason. The massacre is remembered so much now because there was a large amount of injuries, and casualties. The massacre in the 1980s lead to eventual support throughout the entire country of South Korea to change within government. The United States arrival to Kwangju may have appeared insensitive to these massacre survivors. This was not what the United States intended, and many U.S. service members really learned for the first time about the

United States handling of global politics the hard way with a lot of regret. Many U.S. military learned of these hostilities with embarrassment while some seemed more watchful. Many were actually sympathetic to South Koreans, thinking they were there to make the defenses newer with an Air Defense Artillery unit. It may not have been the best strategy long term, and was only temporary, but even that short time seemed to be a huge public relations failure for the United States and the prodemocracy protestors.

May 2005 Protest/Riot

The main failure of public relations between the United States and the local Kwangju area was the eruption of violence before the anniversary of the May 18 Massacre 2005. Despite the deterrence the Air Defense Artillery unit had been described to be providing, the South Korean protestors planned to use violence. Some rioters were tearing down fencing using tools they brought. Some of these tools were rope, breathing masks, and wire cutters. Some rioters were throwing debris and dangerous objects they brought with them, like a fire extinguisher. The activities were numerous, and were all causing destruction to the perimeter fence at the Kwangju Airbase.

There were also many anti-American messages shouted over an amplified speaker phone leading up to the riot. One message was, "Yankee go home!" The U.S. military and American civilians were referred to as Yankees in Kwangju, South Korea. This happens even if most Americans are not from New York, and do not identify themselves to be a part of the history where the word/name Yankee originates from. Some considered calling themselves Yankees but realized it was under a negative context. Anti-American messages were also painted on the street during all this. The paint and messages were visible for days after the May 18, 2005 riot. The rioters brought an American Flag and burned it, destroying it. Pictures of it being burned during the protest/riot with South Koreans in the background were in the news and on social media. Along with the rioter's violence, and threats, other messages of indifference from the area became clear. The previous smaller weekly protesting seemed harmless to a certain point but things became more serious when the Airbase was damaged.

This specific protest caused significant delays to traffic in the local area surrounding the Airbase. The protest/riot disrupted the nearby Kwangju Airport, and the local street traffic was disrupted near the Airport. The Airbase traffic was also disrupted. The rioting also disrupted the local businesses traffic in the area, causing a financial loss during the rioting, and afterwards when the public was scared to travel near the area. The protest/riot had an overall negative impact on many sides but mostly a message was in fact made against the United States being there.

The summary of the events received widespread media coverage across South Korea, and was also back in the United States. It was later mentioned that North Korea sympathizes with the May 18, massacre from the 1980s. This sympathy from North Korea is likely not 100% genuine. It is an effective and strategic use of a real event that was a massacre, and tragedy, turned into its own propaganda tool against South Korea and the United States. It is an example of the twisting of something serious about the struggle for democracy in South Korea, by a country like North Korea, which really limits democracy more than any country in that region. The manipulation of something for personal political gain is done in politics constantly. But when it comes to affecting security across a few different countries, manipulation is really just another example of why a peace treaty has not been agreed to by all.

In May 2005, there was a large amount of preparedness by South Korea's government. That was the largest amount of prevention managed that year, second to the Air Defense Artillery mission. If it was not for the Republic of Korea Soldiers (ROKS), and the South Korean Police, another massacre may have occurred in Kwangju. They prevented all the rioters from entering the base. By the time the rioters got far enough to do more damage, many had tired, and proven a point they were in "charge," which is really all the riot ended up being. With the success of the riot police, the rioters also did make it in too far, resulting in the use of tear gas. Tear gas subdued further violence, and damage, to a certain point.

Kwangju, South Korea, attained the democracy they sought out since the 1980s, but in 2005 they still wanted to make a point they remember.

The United States was forced to respect both sides of that riot. Many U.S. Airmen, and U.S. Soldiers witnessed the protest and riot from within the base. Some vividly described the seen intensity between the two sides. A riot, and protest 25 years later at the Kwangju Airbase, of all places shows there is that memory. Memory is powerful, and unfortunately can be manipulated. What had originally happened may have passed and turned into personal politics but it is still respected.

This is not the first time the United States knew of the May 18 massacre. There were previous apologies by the United States and there were dramatic changes in that area of South Korea. The proof was that 2004-2005 Air Defense Artillery mission, helping provide a missile defense system to the entire southern region. With all that proof there was a failure by the United States to gain Kwangju's respect. With the fact there were so many things going wrong, a new respect was found between the U.S. military stationed there and the South Korean riot police and military. Being in riot gear for hours can test anyone's patience, and endurance. South Koreans have a high amount of readiness, preparedness, and are able to mitigate protests/riots to prevent injuries, and fatalities. Their system of management seems more accurate but the fact remains that they also approved and welcomed the United States military to be there knowing the history might be unsettled. The more unreported and less well known massacres can also flare up years later if not remembered by all sides. It is amazing how some people in South Korea want the U.S. military to be there, even when there are these large sized anti-American protests/riots.

Before the huge protest and riot, the U.S. Army believed they were going to be there providing support and protection from the missile system being tested in North Korea. The fears the U.S. and South Korea had at that time was that the North Korea was proliferating/building up nuclear weapons. There were also reports of North Korea testing weapons, and testing the missiles. The fear of those advancement's being combined, while carrying weapons of mass destruction long distances frightens the entire region. North Korea causes many concerns about the region's stability in the long term. Residents near the demilitarized zone are at a constant alert that something may happen. The local businesses in South Korea and in the surrounding region constantly fear the fact there may be an interruption of sales, and an interruption of steady profits from war. A return on an investment may also seem unpredictable if another full scale war can fire up at any given time between the South and North Korea. Money and unpredictability tend to not last long together. Foreign countries nearby and investing allies around the globe like the United States fear the threat of North Korea's activities and additional war. Peace is always the better solution. But, in this example, obtaining that peace is not always able to be agreed upon and then managed. This is true even if peace benefits all sides of a conflict, because in this specific region there is an additional complex history.

The solution of deterrence was used, because peace was unmanageable due to the circumstances. Peace is not an easy thing for leadership to find, because it usually the countries profits and investment returns may be a financial loss. Because of greed, and pressures on the local leadership from that same countries capital, there are many examples of massacres of civilians throughout world history. The main reason this keeps happening is that war is profitable, but there have been other causes of massacres other than money to include religious and political extremists. A conflict with some civilian casualties can be seen as a victory by leadership, even when it is that same countries citizens. That issue about profit and massacres is used by governments in a type of business model, and it has been used by every country in the world. Some countries handle massacring their own civilians with a better control of the press, and with the help of hiring public relations officers, presenting the governments side of the story in a more favorable way. False reporting by a government can lead to a news cover up. This kind of activity prevents many citizens of that same country from ever knowing when the government caused a massacre. This is also true when a government let an ongoing massacre continue to escalate into more violence, causing more preventable casualties. If it will make the existing government look bad in a way to loose political power things like a massacre will be edited out of government press releases, and the news agencies of that country may not ever publish what occurred.

Despite uncomfortable facts that there is anti-American protesting against the United States, many U.S. military personnel stationed in Kwangju liked the area. Even with the known weekly protesting hostilities, there were many excited about living and working in South Korea. One reason is the farther south cities like Kwangju, offer a more mild winter. It is still freezing in Kwangju, but with less severe blizzards. Another reason was being in foreign area of South Korea considered at the time, and even now an unknown. A deployment to a new area in South Korea was an exciting thing for some. Many in the U.S. military enjoyed spending money off post, buying things in an area less frequented, just because it seemed new to Americans. Some also liked South Korea because they were able to learn something new like about the food, and about the rest of the culture. Many also appreciated living in a developed foreign country in East Asia literally on the other side of the world away from the United States. East Asia's culture is so different from Europe, and the western world, but still has some similarities when it comes to transportation, leading many to believe they could survive happily while stationed there in the first few months.

The result of some military enjoying the area was a positive on the local economy. The money spent by some Soldiers helped build up some support in favor of the United States. Most of this was local businesses that were near the Airbase and partly owned by South Korean military, but still there were some friends made. It is kind of easy to open a bar and make a profit where a few hundred military are stationed. The United States military money is accepted once converted or as it is in some off post businesses in South Korea. Support to build these South Korean businesses that would accept U.S. Soldiers and airmen existed because the U.S. provided the mentioned deterrence to North Korea.

The U.S. was welcomed to a certain point because they brought the area money. Many other South Korean locals in Kwangju provided their services to the United States getting jobs on and off base. This helped smooth over the anti-American protesting, and the later rioting that occurred, in the area near the base.

Support of the United States is still strong in many areas of South Korea, and even in Kwangju, but some of the events of 2005 proved the May 18 Massacre is still a very sensitive issue. It would have been better to place this Air Defense Artillery unit in a less hostile area even though it was mentioned as convenient to be at a South Korean airbase. There were some U.S. military bases that far south and having the unit there from the beginning would have been smoother with the South Korean public.

A history of a place where the U.S. military is stationed affects that U.S. unit's success. History, if negative, can contribute to the mentioned diversions to the United States mission. The mission of providing deterrence was clearly forgotten about by some of the protesters rioters, but at the same time being in that hostile of a place was avoidable. Deterrence is similar to preventing an accident. Deterrence could prevent a later war with fatalities, injuries, and property damage. There has not been total destruction in the area of South Korea since the Korean war but that does not mean that it will not happen. But if making deterrence causes a riot, causing injury, causing fatalities, and causing property damage, the deterrence is not being managed the right way. Deterrence is useful if proportionate to the threat. Deterrence is supposed to protect the South Korea public, but only works if it has the South Korean public's support. Through all these issues of providing deterrence the right way, the weather can sometimes get unintendedly left out.

Typhoons and the US Military

Protesting season is spring, and protests last beyond spring through summer but not at the same amount. The summer changes the amount protesting with the heat, and with vacations. As summer arrived in 2005, Typhoon season's activity started. Typhoon Nabi was a category 2-3 storm system, when reaching South Korea, and Japan. The Typhoon caused catastrophic damage as mentioned in the NASA report. The storm was also identified and reported as being a category 4-5 before reaching Japan and South Korea. This storm's catastrophic damage affected travel in a few different countries along its path. It was being considered a category 5 in some places before nearing Japan and South Korea.

It is important to learn the language to describe the weather and know how to describe a plan to prevent from traveling in it. To start, Typhoons and Hurricanes are considered the same type of storm. The categories used to describe the size are also the same.

The Typhoon Nabi storm affected the coastal areas the most. These types of storms increase the regular sea levels, causing storm surge. Storm surge causes flooding. Flooding from a Typhoon/Hurricane affects the populated areas along the coast the most. There are also other dangers that occur to include the winds and the lowered visibility. This typhoon's winds were powerful enough to affect the areas more inland. Cities off the coast usually do not get affected as much, but it does not mean that high winds will not cause damage inland.

A Typhoon with this size on course to hit Japan and South Korea always needs to be in the weather forecast before it is expected to arrive. Awareness within the military is needed to be able to receive important weather information. If alerted/warned ahead of time there can be some preparedness. For servicemen at a place of work in a remote area, like where this unit was located, a Typhoon warning can add to an already existing level of stress. But knowing there is a large storm system coming ahead of time, can provide those forced to work in its condition's to make a plan to stay indoors, or stay in a severe weather shelter.

A lack of disaster management exists in the military overseas if there is no communicated warnings and prevented action taken. A lesson for command was that a lack of disaster management scared the members that were on duty during Typhoon Nabi. The reason this occurs is that at that time, there were many issues of security all having nothing to do with the weather. Management had to provide security into its plan, knowing the possible hazards from the weather, but at the same time was not able to communicate the details of the forecast to those on duty at the time. The U.S. Command in Kwangju had a strategy of keeping of some personnel out in the path of an incoming hurricane/typhoon providing security. It was a contradiction similar to sending a unit of deterrence into an area that is hostile to the U.S. Having only a couple people on guard was also another act of sacrifice, and a perfect example of what command should not do to their Soldiers in a disaster. To go further, it is widely known that the uneducated, and those not very knowledgeable about these situations end up forced in them the most while in the military, and also while working in the private sector for businesses back in the United States. Being forced into a weather disaster is possibly the most dangerous thing to experience.

There are also other hazards, and other traps, forced upon U.S. citizens abroad, and in the United States.

The fears experienced by those on duty in South Korea led to many discoveries. The most basic finding was that those not informed about disaster preparation were being placed on duty. It was a clear contradiction, while also not being informed of the procedures to take in a Typhoon. The lack of that instruction was later considered by those experiencing the storm as an intentional placement of them in harm's way, by the command. Later these Soldiers discovered many in the unit had known about the storm's forecast. The unit had known about the need for Typhoon preparedness. The Soldiers ordered out on duty in the storm were told they would die. Some Soldiers in command verbalized to lower ranking Soldiers that they will die in other situations leading up to this as a threat. This happened in the months and happened again the day of this storm. Command was wrong a few times that year. Both Soldiers survived threats, and both survived management placing them in Typhoon Nabi's path. Both left South Korea alive. There was later a U.S. soldier casualty at that same Airbase. The casualty was from a lightning storm striking the area, and according to the news it killed the soldier. The news reported that the lightning incident was under investigation in 2006. Since then, nothing more was reported regarding the incident, and after that unfortunate story, and the Air Defense Artillery unit had left that Airbase.

One of the Soldiers that survived the 2004-2005 Tsunami, and survived the Typhoon, was not surprised to hear someone became a casualty. It is unfortunate to say it like that, but the reality was there were too many near death experiences in the time they were in South Korea, while also being told that they would die. When later learning someone did die was a later kind of scary reality, but it was something the some within the U.S. Army force to occur. Forcing an unsafe situation involving the weather is something that unit had also expected after its first year. There is no benefit to the U.S. Armed Forces to force their own soldier to become a casualty, but it happened frequently since 2001. The reason why could come from a hundred of different reasons. Lower ranking Soldiers and even some higher ranking ones could present many in a list, with most or all reasons leading back to the failure of leadership to keep Soldiers protected from harm. The way the soldier was being placed on duty during the Tsunami and talked to, led him to believe a different story or how this later lightning incident really happened. Knowing he was not a witness to it there was nothing really that could be done.

This same soldier later realized his troubles in the Army were in part linked to the home state he was from in Southern California. The soldier ended his term of service with the Army in 2005. After the threats and being forced in the Typhoon it seemed right. He received a honorable discharge for completing his first term of service, but wanted to try to finish college, and get a civilian job. The soldier was still obligated to serve, being placed in the inactive ready reserve. He later received a misdemeanor of Public Intoxication on the 4 th of July, by the Los Angeles County Courts in Pasadena, California. A year after surviving the Tsunami he was in Court being told he was being charged with a crime. The soldier was repeatedly being laughed at, following each sentence read by the Judge. When being read the court paperwork of what the police claim occurred this laughter at the end of each sentence was intimidating. It also seemed strange at first, but the former soldier recognized the Judge's name, being Dorothy Shubin. Another soldier in the Air Defense Artillery from 2004-2005 back in South Korea had the same name. This soldier named Shubin while in South Korea went to talk the soldier being charged a few times. Shubin even mentioned his mother was a Judge. Remembering all this in September 2006, after surviving a Typhoon the Judge's son had not been on duty in, was suspiciously bizarre. Strangely, the District Attorney Palavi Dhawan, also had a mocking laughter while reading her paperwork about the incident and that the State of California wants to charge the former soldier. It is weird to remember the failures of the U.S. Armed Forces, while also being told the procedures of the court by Judge Shubin, and being told the options to get a lawyer, or to plead guilty then.

The soldier figured the mocking laughter was a very bad sign. Both the Judge, and the District Attorney wanted to laugh and they did. Both the Judge and the District Attorney wanted to charge the inactive duty soldier to get something on his record, and they did. Since he knew the Judge's name from the following year filled with forced disasters, and since the soldier did not know the Court system, he pleaded guilty.

The plea was hoping to eliminate court costs, and time spent fighting a misdemeanor charge. He believed his charge would most likely end up with a guilty decision from a Judge based on the mocking laughter from the very beginning, so why not plead guilty. Looking back, giving a Judge and District Attorney the satisfaction of saying guilty was not the right thing to do. It only temporarily ends the harassment of those that follow, committing conspiracy. An important lesson learned is that the misdemeanor was proof that the Hometown where he was from was in fact following him to get something on record. That misdemeanor was only the beginning of something on record. What the people of California had already tried to cause him in the U.S. Army, forcing him in the Typhoon, and with the death threats, continued and still occur in 2014.

Note, forgiving those that seem to cause intentional hardships, and forgiving those that force hazardous situations is a difficult suggestion. Some would state forgiveness is not the solution when disaster recovery should be. Disaster survivors should try to use forgiveness for themselves anyways. The reason is that forgiveness helps to manage the memory of a traumatic event with more stability and continuity. This means that an overreaction to an event can be prevented, keeping the goal of the final destination in sight. It can reduce mass panic. Forgiveness also helps survivors to find closure to an event. Closure can help a survivor to have the confidence to start traveling again. A traveler able to forgive all, and move on to the next trip, is really going places, and will have more opportunities for their future. This is especially true compared to someone that gets trapped in a conflict at every stop on a route. Conflict will always exist and if not managed in a way to bypass it, it can become the end of a trip, job, and even life. There also are times where it may appear that every stop along the way may have been tainted and filled with unavoidable trouble. When this problem is so consistent keep things prioritized to accomplish the common goal of completing the trip. Remember that forgiveness should not be confused with ignorance of a threatening situation, and many hazards can be prevented if recorded and known about. Forgiveness is also needed to acknowledge the need to prepare and avoid a repeat. Many situations can be avoided even ones that seem staged and planned. Prevent yourself from being at the wrong side of a disastrous event over and over again in life. Forgiveness can provide more relief to the stresses of feeling used and manipulated. It can also lift the burden of fear that exists at many places of work across the United States and the rest of the world. With the need for forgiveness, do not forget the issues of being forced into a disaster. Keep that experience recorded, and remember it for future reference. The use of a negative experience can later be a good example for future managers of what not to do. The solution is to try to list ways to prevent unsafe situations for your self first. Then describe the list to management in a simple way, appearing helpful. A list should help communicate a message of prevention, and if professional in appearance and sound it will be taken more serious with respect. Try to remember through an attempt to communicate this, some things get forgotten about by management anyways. Reminders also help keep and hold management's attention. Through the recording of disasters, and through communicating suggestions to management, a better way to avoid a disaster in the future is an option.

Remember that reporting such issues as mentioned may not always be accepted favorably. Later after the Hurricane and the say in court, the inactive soldier decided to find a real job away from the Army. Due to the circumstances the inactive soldier did not want to reenlist, knowing now that he had a criminal record. This inactive soldier also felt his time in the service was not really honored even if he was only in there a for one term of service, and he felt like his taking a risk to serve was just used wastefully by the Army. Furthermore it seemed like there was so much more going on in the background, and those seeking revenge/reprisal from California definitely caught up to make their point of view known and as one of authority. At this point, the soldier was slowly learning that using of people that volunteer to serve with honor is very similar to what occurs in South Korea. All the time spent to get soldier's money back from them is planned out, sometimes in part by their own command. The government is a system. It can be manipulated to benefit those in charge the most, and to easily take advantage of the lower level personnel, conveniently making them out to be the problem once their usefulness is determined to be over. The inactive soldier pieced together that using of someone to start a violent riot against the United States was also a more dangerous reality occurring at that time. People can be manipulated by unseen conspirators to do something irrational, and sometimes even a crime. The using of people in the Commercial transportation industry to do the work is another huge example of this problem. U.S. Citizens that attempted to work a legal job, and contribute legally have been targeted as being an unsafe problem increasingly. This is true even though there are more "regulations" and "government transparency about safety" than ever about the Commercial transportation industry. Instead of praise and awards for accomplishing something productive, workers in the U.S. are falsely made out to be unsafe in a fabricated hoax. When there are fabrications of unsafe situations, and exaggerations of unsafe activity against workers that had in fact at one point help build the country and economy it is really a poor example of the U.S. government's strategy. But with that fact known by the public and by some in the government, there are still many U.S. Citizens in the Commercial industry mass punished. This is described to occur when the entire Commercial Carrier is given a poor safety rating about the 5 BASICS, and their drivers later receive more inspections. This mass punishment has been resulting in more violations from the increased amount of inspections, and not from what the company actually does. There are many things left out about the FMCSA's data being the entire and full story. Many have witnessed or have been a victim of a color of law violation when traveling for work. There are many lower level workers working in transportation in the public's view that has been falsely made out to be the problem. The FMCSA data had also become well known around this same time in 2006. The United States federal government's point of view about the industry became more transparent than ever so there were more critics than ever about the Commercial companies, their employees, their supporters, and their investors. Manipulation that only targets the working class exists within the United States government. Manipulation that can lead to a massacre is in the U.S. just like anywhere else in the world. But manipulation that leads into a massacre is not always viewed and talked about openly, and as transparent. The government has attempted to communicate some issues they believe can lead into a disaster and massacre through ready.gov, and the Department of Homeland Security, but remember these communications do not ever admit to the U.S. government's involvement as being the cause. Manipulation that has lead to some color of law violations against U.S. Citizens comes from Government agencies, transportation planners, and the management in the Commercial company. Coincidentally these offices and workers stay employed longer, but many times the same lower level workers get blamed for the same unsafe things over and over. Many massacres no matter how big overseas or small within the United States tend to originate from those leading a Government agency or large business organization. These are the real problems being managed by the middle, and lower working classes. The right to live free, is seemingly more impossible, without government transparency that actually managers disasters better. Many citizens being used are not really causing any serious trouble, but are falsely made out to be a threat. It really comes down to who is in charge. Those in charge profit the most, making certain individuals out to be a danger to others, it is an easy to view pattern seen on many government websites, and in public places. The ability the government has to distinguish between a real threat, and a self created hoax in the United States has not been perfected since 2001. The U.S. government has had some serious difficulty in finding an accurate system to provide Homeland Security to the public. Many programs are seemingly to benefit profits, resulting in a slow moving process to secure the United States' borders. At that time in 2006, the real issues of bringing those that caused 9/11 to justice had not become very transparent and public. If U.S. citizens are continually made out to be a threat because it is more profitable and easy for law enforcement the actually issues that cause 9/11 will have some continuity courtesy of the United States government.

This can seem overly critical, and there are many good government programs that have made things safer since 9/11. But, the fatalities in the United States military since 9/11 could have been handled with better strategy and ethics. A better plan could have been used to better guard and protect U.S. Armed Forces service members, and to better protect the citizens of the United States. There are some very complicated situations that occur, distracting management from being accurate. These failures to protect the U.S. citizens from harm, on the United States governments end are even more obvious when looking at the failures within the FMCSA. Many do not want to admit it, but the United States government has turned some of its own Soldiers, and has turned some of its own citizens into the threat, all with the profiting off its citizens and profiting off 9/11 in the background. That failure is one of the biggest distractions affecting the Department of Defense's missions at the global level. The government has gotten lost a few times when it comes to providing an accurate plan to mitigate threats, and instead tends to blame its own personnel to save themselves.

This next question may sound off topic to all the distractions occurring in this story about a Typhoon. The inactive duty soldier that got arrested, and plead guilty to the public intoxication misdemeanor in 2006 questioned to himself, "When will the U.S. Army and South Korea sign a peace treaty with North Korea? They profited off him being on guard duty during a Typhoon in September 2005, and then profited off him having him pay a fine for a misdemeanor in September 2006, and they profited off the court costs, but when will peace be found? Is keeping the armistice agreement, and war with North Korea ongoing for the government to take advantage off its uneducated citizens?" Unfortunately, the answer is YES. This system of profits happens throughout the United States government and military and happens throughout other countries governments that work with the United States. It seem unethical and a crime to massacre citizens on a low level incident such as a public intoxication incident on the 4 th of July, to massacre a citizen at a higher lever incident like forcing them into a Hurricane, or violence filled riot.

A Failure to Provide Readiness from Weather Disasters

The failures that occurred within the United States Army in South Korea in 2004-2005 seemed to keep continuing even after many had left the active duty military. If a U.S. military unit does not have the ability to prevent injuries and fatalities from a weather disaster then it will never be ready for any other type of manmade threat. The Soldiers that survived the Typhoon in South Korea also received delayed announcements that contained warnings about the area being hostile. These alerts were mainly based on the area's security, and some contained information about threats against the U.S. citizens, and military personnel in Kwangju. Many of these alerts were made public through the Department of the State, but unless a

U.S. Army soldier had internet access and knew how to look it up online, they would have to rely on their superiors. One warning announcement happened months after the Air Defense Artillery arrived, and after the May riot. It stated that the city of Kwangju had Al Qaeda, and North Korean insurgents. After the news coverage of the protest and riot, it was not surprise to hear something like a threat was there. If Al Qaeda or North Korean insurgents were there it was not a stunning revelation after the riot. At that point to lower ranking Soldiers had wandered South Korea off duty in the months leading to the memorial riot, and also noticed some examples of not being welcome in the area. The delay of the warning did confirm the failure of the unit's command to protect their own mission and Soldiers.

The reason being the 3000 anti-U.S. rioters having the force and presence they did, may have been exploited by an extremist to help support their cause against the South Korean government and United States Armed Forces. The point about forcing someone into a weather disaster can also be made about forcing someone into a manmade disaster like riot. Those exploiting something genuine like the memorial of the May 18 massacre in the 1980s energized those around them. They were able to turn a protest into a riot, while taking a step away from what they created when the rioting began in May 2005. Forcing others into a situation that gets someone else killed is something the public in South Korea and the United States should be aware of. Civilians get forced into these types of traps the most, and unfortunately the news tends to show the view from above of what happened, instead of the details of how the public was manipulated into becoming involved in protesting which may also become a riot. These situations are usually considered free speech but they also have ended in violence and massacres. Use extra caution if someone in leadership is forcing others into something unsafe, even if it is worded as being official duty. The real question is why would the U.S. military even go there to begin with? And, why did they not inform their Soldiers and airmen stationed there what the threat was from the first day, instead of after a riot? The delay of important information was a sign that there was poor management from above the battalion leadership, and poor communication within the lower ranks within each company. Failure was proven to exist between all the members of the unit by the time the first year had passed. With that, this first arriving unit had no fatalities. Considering the circumstances, that was a miracle. When later looking back at all that occurred in 2004-2005, it is a surprise there were only a few injuries.

The Soldiers who get forced into these situations the most and survive them the most are always lower in rank. These Soldiers were also lower in rank. The result of the leadership placing them on duty knowing there was a Typhoon rolling in for a two-day storm without preparedness is a continuing safety issue. This unsafe system of management the Armed Forces allows has led to other problems, causing preventable injuries and fatalities. Many lower ranking members that volunteered in the military after 9/11 became injured and a casualty as a result of failures of the management to protect them. The public display of what lower ranking Soldiers do wrong is common within the culture of the military, hoping it deters misconduct. But, the public display of what the high command does is not transparent. The few news reports about misconduct at higher levels is still far from the truth of what has happened. The reality is the public will possibly never know what their taxes really paid for. Those who volunteered to serve in the United States Armed Forces overseas took some of the biggest risks to serve under that type of management.

News

The truth about what the leadership in the military does is rarely reported in the news. One reason why is that if it would get reported, the access the news agencies had would get blocked. It is easier for the news agencies to report something in favor of the command. The main news headlines this unit made that year was that the U.S. Army was providing an Air Defense Artillery Unit to protect South Korea. There are many that served in the military, looking at the news reports of what happened as being only a fraction of what took place. The more real stories may be considered negative. When there are critical stories written and released, there is also the following issue of later censorship. Sometimes this is done in a way to be purposely unnoticed. Many news stories that become the target of censorship end up getting eliminated altogether, protecting the news agency, protecting sponsors, or protecting the "public's interest". The end result is that many stories that are written for the public, that become the subject of censorship, never get an audience. In some examples these stories squeeze through the obstacles of censorship, ricocheting between the blockers of news, getting some attention. But this happens in a way where there is a loss to reaching the big audiences. For that reason, the build up of support to change management's handling of some of these unmentioned problems is important. It is important that the public knows there are cover ups about problems considered unmanageable by the current system of government in the United States. All of these problems to include the problem of the threat of massacres can be managed the right way with some transparency.

The known concealment of the failures of management within the U.S. Government, U.S. Army, and the News Agencies, covers up some preventable examples of endangerment. This cover up is continuous. The public should know it is likely to exist. The public can use extra caution when deciding to travel. Some Soldiers and airmen in the military state that being in dangerous situation like a Typhoon is what U.S. Service Members in the Armed Forces signed up for. This is the real attitude even knowing the reality of there being possible fatalities. Knowing that some Soldiers and airmen consider those next to them to have their lives wasted to a storm, or sacrificed to some other hazard lowers morale. The buddy system in the military is not always present when it is actually needed. The hoaxes about a local population, or a hoax about a threat, and a hoax about a member of the Armed Forces create a distraction. When someone really needs help, in many examples, no one is there at the right time. This same problem is well known in the transportation industry. That bad timing is why there are real casualties. The reality is no one signs up to be in a Typhoon storm, or another hazard/disaster where there will be certain death. This Typhoon had predicted and seen winds at 130+ per hour, and what should have happened was to have all military personnel's place of duty at a designated storm shelter. Or to have instructions about where to be to withstand the storm as it passes. There is always the challenge to management in the military to be able to be an efficient leader at the right time, and timing is unpredictable making the prevention of these situations not always an option.

The experience of survival is thrilling, energizing, and it is an amazing thing to be able to describe. After the fact there were some forced into a hazardous situation with the intention that they would be injured and die, it was widely known that the storm and many things occurring in South Korea are preventable. The members in the United States Armed Forces became witnesses to poor system command, and more importantly they discovered they were lucky to be alive when learning how many casualties there were.

They were saved because the Typhoon's winds were reduced when they reached the South Korean coast. They were reduced again when they traveled inland towards Kwangju. The U.S. Army unit was also lucky that the winds and storm did not cause fatalities, and injuries in their location. Unfortunately, many in the unit did not understand what happened to those forced out in the storm in that situation and prior to that event. What is being forced on the few is never cared about if it does not happen in the first person point of view. The example of forcing the few into a disaster, causing a casualty, is also not always a part of the public's awareness of what took place, if it is not reported later in the news. This was exactly what took place in 2005. Things just do not become public, even though there were some news stories about the unit in South Korea and some weather reports made by NASA. What really happens to the average citizens and lower level workers forced into these disaster is never on the front page described in a way that the United States government was manipulated by a few, forcing the unprepared situation to occur. There are many different points of view of what happened when it comes to a disaster, and the public's point of view if critical of the government is rarely reported out to the public. Those that volunteer to serve in the United States military overseas, have since learned about being forced into dangerous situations, all forced situation also coincidentally unnoticed by the rest of the public back in the United States. What it takes to wear the U.S. Armed Forces uniform costs the volunteer the most, while many volunteers have had their beliefs in if their service, and what they are ordered and forced into is really what is right. Many employees and military that served overseas have had their beliefs and trust of the government altered permanently for the negative, knowing what tends to go wrong, usually at their safety's expense.

Many that experience trauma while in the Armed Forces automatically have a change in their belief towards negative, while also trying to piece together what was the real problem. Many in the Armed Forces since 9/11, have spent time figuring out how these avoidable events that take place while overseas were managed in a way where they were at times singled out, being forced in a disaster or another situation where the threat level is high. This trauma leads into fear and regret. It is true even if they survive, and are able to have a somewhat normal life after a deployment, or after ending their service with the U.S. military. With that, some of the same Soldiers that survived the chaos enjoyed spending time off post in between disasters like nothing was happening. Some U.S. military members were able to make friends with the locals, and some made friends with the R.O.K. Soldiers and airmen. Some U.S. military even reenlisted to stay in South Korea for another year, or reenlisted to change their job or to change their unit assignment.

Typhoon Nabi and Hurricane Katrina

The later news of the seriousness of the aftermath of the hurricane disaster in New Orleans, Louisiana, with Hurricane Katrina, put some of the hazards of the category 2-3-4-5 Typhoon Nabi into perspective. There was a considerable risk that R.O.K. and U.S. Soldiers and airmen on duty in South Korea faced. The main difference between the two events was their location's approximate location to the path of the storm. The Airbase was located more inland, while also away from the storm surge on South Korea's coast. The atmosphere over South Korea created a buffer pushing the incoming winds, weakening the path of the storm. The storm was also losing strength before arriving to South Korea. Hurricane Katrina was merciless on the Louisiana coast to include the population living in and around New Orleans. The storm surge was more of an issue for that event. Both occurred the same year and both affected the United States while only one of them became an unforgettable and very infamous storm. The location a traveler is in regarding the larger storms of a Hurricane is the main determining factor of if they will survive.

The second most important difference was the communication. The residents of Japan, South Korea, and the United States have access to radios and Weather News, but there were still injuries and fatalities. There were more injuries reported for Hurricane Katrina than for Typhoon Nabi. For the U.S. military there are many ways to avoid the placement of personnel in the path of a Hurricane, but sometimes the issues of manipulation will override the need for preparedness. Communication of a weather forecast does not mean anything if not listened to. In the United States many government offices, military, and the public go to a storm shelter when a Hurricane is in the area. Overseas this is not always the policy with the mentioned example in South Korea. Another part of this communication issue is that the Hurricane Katrina storm was more powerful, affecting more people in densely populated area. U.S. Citizens are able to get a warning from News agencies and U.S. Government ahead of time, but were not all able to evacuate. The heavily populated areas within the United States have some individuals that need help. Otherwise, citizens that are stranded or forced into a powerful weather disaster will suffer if not assisted, and the later news of the hazards of a few citizens in an aftermath will occur.

Another issue showing some difference between the two storms is that the management of disasters within the United States has been somewhat public information. As for what happens to U.S Armed forces members when it comes to the weather on a deployment or stationed overseas there may not be that same amount of available public information about the weather. There is also less accountability. For that reason more can go wrong for the U.S. military overseas when it comes to a Hurricane/Typhoon, even if the storm is rated smaller. As for the U.S. governments ability the system has not been perfected. FEMA does provide relief to states declared disaster areas which are an example of good management. But with that good management, the public should remember any kind of relief will be provided on FEMA's terms and conditions. This can include small print on their paperwork, and include some last minute changes to their policies about what they will, and what they will not provide relief for. Their relief can change as well because each event is given a certain budget. Also, FEMA does not usually provide assistance for an evacuation ahead of time. This is important to know they do not do this because an evacuation is really one of the biggest parts of being "prepared." The public should know the best strategy and meaning of preparedness should include how to avoid being in the disaster ahead of time. When U.S. citizens are left behind in these storms, they later tend to mistrust the U.S. government and its agencies like FEMA. FEMA and the government use words like "preparedness", "emergency management", and "public safety" many times but how many examples of failures do these agencies admit to while also promising that they will not be repeated to perfect disaster preparedness. Trust in a system that cannot be updated can dissipate. Some citizens' end up lost in a predicted Hurricane, and stuck in its aftermath for days, and some blame can end up on all sides as to what went wrong to include the U.S. government. Unfortunately, many federal government agencies like FEMA, only show up after the storm. Luckily, many areas threatened have local groups that help provide storm preparedness resources and seeking this out is a real solution. Local areas really need to have their own local emergency management plan. U.S. Citizens should not rely on the U.S. government when it comes to weather disasters, and other natural disasters. Have a personal preparedness plan. In 2014 there is not a public rating about how U.S. citizens view FEMA's handling of disaster relief. Some believe that with all the things that are being communicated by the government something like that would be a priority, but it tends to get lost in the issues of the government's priority of being transparent in a way that could actually boost preparedness. An emergency preparedness rating that compares events and compares locations could save many lives. Why that type of rating is not created is a real mystery. If the public knows they are in an area that has a poor FEMA relief rating, they would have extra motivation to evacuate ahead of a predicted event like a Hurricane, or even move. Not having that communication goes back to the U.S. government's failure to protect U.S. citizens from the harm of disasters. With that critical statement of the U.S. government, the citizens of these areas with a lack of disaster preparedness can correct their own lack of preparedness, and correct the lack of disaster management at the government level. U.S. Citizens can vote for government officials that provide disaster preparedness, while voting for those officials prioritizing the need to evacuate an area for the more major events like Hurricanes.

Some man made problems for Hurricane Katrina and made problems for the Armed Forces service members overseas are worse than they have to be. The ability to have a plan that reduces injury, reduces damage, and prevents fatalities is one of the most important things. Some serious management problems that occur lead into a worse aftermath. This can cause low morale throughout the public and a military unit. Low morale can lead into illegal substance abuse and drug use. Low morale can cause members of the Armed Forces to be absent without leave. In South Korea at the Kwangju Airbase AWOL Soldiers were the unit's daily news stories. Some were missing altogether, and the story of what happened is still unknown due to a lack of accountability. Low morale is preventable, and it is not an excuse to commit abuse, but has been observed as partly the cause. Low morale and poor leadership accountability has led to physical abuse. Low morale also leads into the serious problem of sexual abuse. There are many programs trying to keep accountability of low morale problems and misconduct. A real challenge for these programs is when the military has stationed a unit in an area the United States is not normally in. Low morale and its effect can occur in an area off the map regardless of a program back in the rear where the main force is stationed. There have been many U.S. military that were victims to low morale and its cause of problems. Then these same personnel are left without a real management system to account for what happened afterwards. Low morale tends to make things more difficult than they have to be. Low morale has been described like the feeling that what experienced took place never ever happened. It is difficult to believe in a mission or any job when knowing that some nearby their place in the military did not acknowledge and did not try to prevent internal abuse between military personnel. Low morale occurs intentionally. Low morale's effects are manipulated strategically. This is more complicated to describe, but it is basically one conspirator trying to achieve personal gain over someone else. If a competitor is humiliated with examples of abuse then it is likely they will suffer eventually some form of low morale. At times they will also no longer believe in the mission 100%. Temporarily, the harassing conspirator will have accomplished eliminating their so called competitor, but the after effect of the abuse can be considered to not yet be fully determined. Timing is a big issue in correcting low morale. When low morale is left to freely exist in a work place there are consequences affecting productivity, and the health, and the welfare of all military and civilian personnel. There were even reports of racism, abuse of rank, and unsafe driving. Management that causes low morale is preventable. Aside from low morale these problems are also able to be recognized and preventable even with low morale. There are many programs making them manageable but sometimes even these are corrupted and lacking in the ability to make a difference. It really could not be worse than facing a disaster like a category 3 Typhoon at the last minute. With the management problems that existed, threats were not able to be managed by those forced in them. This unit also seemed to force Soldiers to work together knowing there were some complaints, and reported incidents, similar to human resources type of issues in a private business. When unit level problems are occurring at a high rate, and at crossing points of time throughout a year in a foreign hostile area, leading up to being forced into a place of duty unprepared for a hurricane/typhoon shows there is some intentional hardship being created. This type of management was common in the U.S. military, instead of planning that would have prevented such incidents, with many in command at high levels well beyond the platoon level. It is surprising how high up in command a preventable disaster was allowed to be experienced by only a few. When command has endorsed such decisions there have been injuries, damage, and fatalities. Similar failures resulted in the high rate of casualties in other units deployed to Iraq and Afghanistan. Since 2001, many lower ranking Soldiers in South Korea, Iraq, and Afghanistan were forced into these avoidable disasters. Many were unprepared, and put in these situations without a line of communication to their command. This type of management resulted in preventable fatalities, and preventable injuries. The solution to these rarer events can be found, and the solution can be applied for future U.S. Military personnel, and future missions.

Currently, there is very limited oversight into these injuries, and fatalities. Icasualties.org is a website listing combat casualties, and those missing in war. Many of the descriptions of incidents in the news are limited to all the causes as to what took place. The weather can affect a unit's overall morale affecting their readiness, and affect those individual service members placed on guard duty in a Hurricane. Incidents of injury and fatalities reported in the news and other outlets do not always mention that the weather played a role in the casualties in war. The weather should be mentioned more if it partly affected an incident, if not entirely be mentioned as a cause of what later happened. It should also be mentioned that the weather has not been managed the same overseas, as has it been managed at the training bases back in the United States. The mention of equipment failure, to include a casualty's access to a storm shelter, as to the cause in every casualty is not mentioned in the U.S. government's news releases to the public. There are many questions that anyone that was ever stationed overseas in the U.S. military could come up when it comes to the weather, and disaster management.

One Solution is for the Department of Defense to Provide all in the US Military with Wireless Emergency Alerting Smartphones

After learning disaster management has failures, there is usually the discussion brought up about equipment failure as what to correct instead of management's planning. Blaming lower ranking personnel and their management of equipment is the easy way out and occurs in many business and in the United States military. The failed military vehicles that did not provide the United States Armed Forces the right mobility, while lacking armor contributed to management's failures. It is easy to say there is not the right equipment but the plan itself is doomed from the very beginning, because equipment specifications are known about before any decision is made. The lack of the right amount of armor and strategy to avoid known hostile areas was a failure to protect volunteers in the U.S. military from harm. These failures affected travel throughout the entire world later, because the enemy, and same security problems, seemed to always have an advantage. More importantly, these kinds of failures faced by the military directly affect the safety of travel back in the United States. The issues of the military not avoiding the weather overseas and the issues of failed equipment cost the United States tax payers every year. These same problems add to the risk of another incident when unchecked overseas, and even back in the United States.

The long-term solution is to increase the communication of information that can eliminate these forced situations without the right preparedness. Some of these situations are mainly management based in the military. Equipment can help change some of these problems, but if management is literally trying to sacrifice someone for unknown reasons like revenge or reprisal adding something new like a smartphone is just one more thing that would have to get bypassed. With the more complicated issues of how some soldiers get chosen as the one to sacrifice, a smartphone that communicates to each individual service member needed alerts about the weather and disasters is a suggestion. This could help the entirety of command to see the threat of the weather and disasters clearer. If there are more eyes watching these types of alerts during the more difficult situations while of being in a foreign area, being in hostile area, and in combat, command can do more to provide its own personnel with better level of force protection.

The example of the new Wireless Emergency Alerts on a smartphone would have been a great addition to those who served in the military in the past 14 years since 9/11. Many disasters could have been managed better with that kind of communication. The past reality is command uses a tradition of management referred to as, "a chain of command." A chain of command starts with the high ranking members going down to low rank. This system of management is for the higher ranking member's ease of decision making, and to make it easier to give orders. This system of management usually halts the needed transparency, and needed available access to information preventing some of the injuries, and fatalities that occur to all service members, high ranking, and low ranking when forced into a weather disaster, or a massacre. Damage to property also occurs in these situations where there is a lack of communication. A chain of command type of management allows more risk and more threats planned to be managed by only the lower ranking service members in a military unit. There is a lot of avoidable incidents publicly occurring with this allowable system of sacrifice. This has occurred in the U.S. Armed Forces and has also occurred in the transportation industry because management in both situations is not seen by the public as the cause of what was avoidable to happen. The situations of sending some personnel into a something like a typhoon, hostile area, or combat, while considering these same personnel may become injured and killed are common as a result. There are solutions that can help prevent losses.

A smartphone distributed to every service member can make the current system of management for the military more updated to 2014. The benefits can start with the phone's receiving weather alerts, Wireless Emergency Alerts, and smartphones available to those on duty. The prediction of this solution occurring for the lower ranking Soldiers is that it will most likely not happen unless they buy a smartphone. The continuation of the younger and lower ranking members in the military being forced into some preventable situations will exist, while not being reported in the news. In the years after 9/11 there was a big issue and discussion about how there is a lack of transparency in the United States about information relating to Homeland Security and disasters like Hurricane Katrina. The lack of transparency in the military, and what later happened to many of those that volunteered to serve the United State is horrific. But with all the casualties, injuries, and failures, change to correct these errors can be made. Trust in a system that is filled with cover ups is a hard thing for anyone to believe in, especially a volunteer military force, but trust can be made again.

6

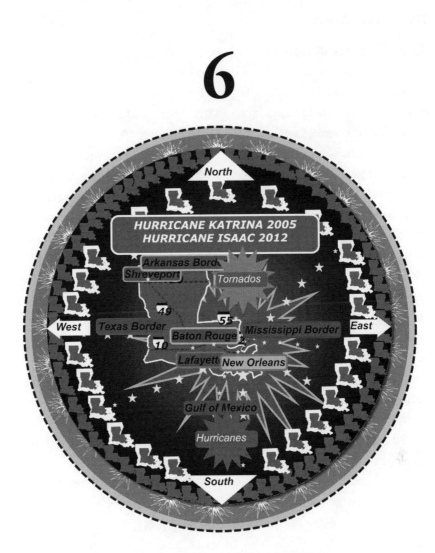

Designed and Property of *Crash Lane News*

About Hurricanes in the United States

Includes Louisiana NOAA Office Interview, and Travel Advice through Gulf Coast States

The Louisiana NOAA/National Weather Service Office has experienced weather forecasters and meteorologists, providing helpful information to the public. Some of their meteorologists witnessed many severe weather events. This is including Hurricane Katrina back in 2005 and Hurricane Isaac in 2012. The Louisiana NOAA office has a good point of view for a traveler to know about when it comes to severe weather and travel.

Louisiana is located on the Gulf Coast, along the Gulf of Mexico. The states that border Louisiana include Texas, Arkansas, Alabama, and Mississippi. When it comes to severe weather, this region has had its share of disasters. Most disasters occur in the form of hurricanes and severe thunderstorms.

The following report includes some of the problems that the local residents and travelers face in that region. Some specific examples used are mentioned by the National Weather Service office to have occurred during Hurricane Katrina and Hurricane Isaac. Some helpful suggestions are included of how to avoid problems and travel safely when in a region threatened by hurricanes and other severe weather. Knowing the information in this report can add to one's existing knowledge of Hurricane Katrina and also explain some of the larger issues that develop after a disaster. One main problem mentioned in detail is the transportation infrastructure becoming unusable. This problem caused delays in Louisiana and the region. It is important to note that when a storm is finished many travelers assume it is safe to travel when there could still be significant damage to roads. This can be a complicated situation in the middle of a trip and some solutions are explained.

Hurricane Katrina had a huge effect on travel and it has been used as reference many times to discuss disaster preparedness. Hurricane Katrina is still a bad memory for survivors, but it is also still a mystery in how the issue of a storm that was warned about in advance had later caused so much confusion, damages, and the loss of life. The sad thing is there was a warning about Hurricane Katrina in advance. But even with the warning, there were still things that went wrong, including infrastructure damage preventing transportation and travel.

One significant point of this report is to simplify how a major hurricane affected transportation in Louisiana and the region. The information from this report communicates the real problems a traveler should be cautious about. This can be useful to know when on a future trip to Louisiana and the surrounding area. As a result of Hurricane Katrina there was no reliable transportation in the city and around it. Everything was flooded. Flooding prevented any way to travel other than swim, raft, boat, or on foot. That type of travel was dangerous and life threatening and is not recommended. Prevent a trip from ending up in a dangerous situation like a hurricane.

The struggle of survival that occurred with Hurricane Katrina is good to know. This gives real proof of what to avoid when becoming near a similar situation of severe weather. When living and traveling on a coast affected by hurricanes, the issue of reducing the amount of travel should be planned for in advance. This should be decided when there is a weather warning released by the National Weather Service/NOAA and in the news. Evacuating an area due to a hurricane is the best alternative. Instead of planning on remaining in an area threatened by a large hurricane or other severe storms, make a plan to avoid it. Hurricanes are not something a traveler should try to seek, and many do deliberately avoid them. There are some, though, that see themselves as adventurers and survivors and intentionally place themselves in preventable disasters. It is recommended to avoid that kind of behavior and evacuate.

One main reason to avoid a hurricane like Katrina is that there were over 900 deaths and tens of thousands injured. Thousands evacuated, while the residents that stayed became trapped. These residents possibly were forced to stay due to a lack of planning and ability to evacuate but this led to becoming immobilized from doing any recovery, because of flooding. As a result there was a lack of supplies coming into the affected area. The flooding also delayed the repairs on the infrastructure. When the recovery could not be made the stranded population panicked. In summary, avoiding the area during and after a hurricane needed to be a priority. Evacuating after the storm, while being trapped with no incoming supplies is something some residents did not expect. In the hours and days after a disaster there is a vulnerability that exists in the affected area and in the more unpredictable after events more damage, injury, and fatalities occur.

Natural disasters are expected to occur as was Hurricane Katrina once there is a warning, so be aware of warnings and the weather. Avoid traveling near the area in the days after a storm to avoid delays and the aftermath of a disaster. Disasters can be prepared for, but it is recommended to avoid having to be there in the first place. There is the reality that even though there are warnings not everyone is able to have the same resources and information at the right time to evacuate. Also, the local residents and businesses can only prepare so much, which should be noted to those who plan to wait out a storm that might trap survivors. As a result of a lack of disaster prevention by the local, state, and federal government before Hurricane Katrina, the fatalities and injuries after the storm passed continued to rise. Overall, there was a high rate of preventable fatalities, injuries, and damage, which usually is claimed to be caused by residents that did not evacuate, but in reality there were deaths and injuries in tax paying areas and the government could have managed this particular disaster better. Some events in a disaster are unpredictable, and blaming the government when it is too late is not going to help.

Airports Were Closed

As far as the air service, meaning the ability to get on a flight in or out of the New Orleans area, the Louis Armstrong, New Orleans International Airport, was closed for a few days. This airport is in the city of Kenner, bordering New Orleans on the west. Even though it is not in New Orleans it is very close. During the hurricane and afterwards, the airport was used as an evacuation point. Commercial flights did not resume until a couple weeks after the storm. One reason is the airport needed repairs. It also was in need of being cleaned up due to the large amount of evacuees. Another issue was that the airport had been turned into a makeshift hospital during and after the hurricane. The airport's staff had to convert it back into a functioning airport and do maintenance on it, bringing it back into operating as an airport.

The Lakefront Airport in the city of New Orleans is a smaller size facility and the general aviation airport. Some private charter flights fly out of there. That facility is outside the levee system, so the storm surge destroyed all the buildings there. The control tower was damaged, and they had to build a new control tower after the storm. That is the secondary airport for New Orleans. Both airports were shut down for the most part. They were just not running flights. The whole city and even the surrounding area of New Orleans could not really travel using an airliner or the interstate. The only way to travel was on foot.

Airports on Gulf Coast Shutdown for Hurricanes, like Katrina

Property of *Crash Lane News*

Vehicle Traffic Disruptions

The storm surge affected traveling with automobiles, preventing any travel in New Orleans, while causing delays surrounding the city. Travelers driving could go across the causeway bridge, which goes across the middle of Lake Pontchartrain. That was also damaged at some stops. The storm surge was one of the biggest things that affected interstate traffic, as well as affecting the local transportation.

NOAA stated that Hurricane Katrina greatly affected the transportation infrastructure and travel in the area. Interstate 10 is the main highway that runs along the southern part of Louisiana from Texas east to Alabama. A section of Interstate 10 goes over Lake Pontchartrain, and was destroyed by the storm surge and wake. This main interstate was unusable for a few months. Interstate 10 is one of the main interstate highways out of New Orleans. Travelers that were driving had to use Highway 11, which has a bridge. The hurricane had also damaged Highway 11 but it was still usable.

Property of *Crash Lane News*

Travel from downtown New Orleans to the suburbs of Metairie was not possible. The interstate was the normal route for this and was underwater in that area until they drained the city. This drainage took about a month. After that the suburbs on that side of town could get to the interstate to Baton Rouge, there was so much traffic that there were continuous traffic jams on the interstate. The transportation for the area was basically overloaded for the areas where people had evacuated to. There were serious transportation issues across the whole region for a while.

In Slidell, where the NOAA office is located, there was flooding on the south side of town. It was hard to get to the office from that side of town. Interstate 12 was basically shut down for several weeks after the storm. Many people had relocated to Slidell while the city was still flooded.

The city of La Place area, 25 miles west of New Orleans, has a low spot on Interstate 10 as well. That section flooded for a period of time. To the north on Interstate 55, lies the city of Ponchatoula, LA, where flooding obstructed travel on the northwest side of Lake Pontchartrain. There are plans to raise the highways in those areas so flooding will not happen again.

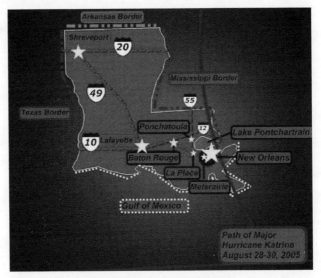

Property of *Crash Lane News*

The below chart mentions Hurricane Katrina was the 11th storm, occurring August 23–30, 2005. The chart also mentions there were winds at 150 Kt. This was considered a major hurricane in the days leading up to the its arrival on August 29, and during its path through Louisiana marked in purple.

Compared to Hurricane Katrina, Hurricane Isaac was smaller and caused much less damage. Hurricane Isaac was a minimal hurricane. That hurricane did have a pressing surge that went into Lake Pontchartrain. The western side of the lake had that affect occurring the most. That was due to a continuous period of easterly winds. The storm slowed down so much it basically stopped off along the coast of Louisiana and drifted for a while. Winds were piling water into the lake, and we did have some issues infrastructure wise. The below chart shows Hurricane Isaac is the 9th storm, categorized as a hurricane, with winds at 70 Kt, August 21 to September 1, 2012. The chart shows that the day before the center of the storm hit Louisiana was on the 28 of August, and the storm was considered a hurricane, marked in red. The day the center of the storm was in Louisiana was on the 29th and had lowered to a tropical storm, marked in yellow.

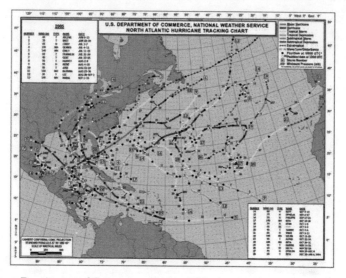

From Department of Commerce, National Weather Service. Public Domain.

Communication Blackout

Not only was the transportation locked up, pretty much all the communications were knocked out as well, due to the flooding. The flooding and later communication blackout impacted things greatly. To make a phone call people had to go over to Baton Rouge, which is eight miles away. Land line telecommunications were knocked out completely. The only way NOAA was communicating was by satellite phone or by 800 MHz, radio system. NOAA was fortunate to get a satellite phone because of the federal government.

Hurricane Katrina's Predictability

The warning for Hurricane Katrina came out on the Friday before. The storm made landfall Sunday night and Monday morning. There was about 72 hours, 48 to 72 hour range there, about three days, of advanced warning. The warnings have gotten better and better since 2005. In 2013, NOAA considered that advance time of warning for Hurricane Katrina to be below average. Back in 2005, that would be considered average, especially for the New Orleans and Gulf Coast area. The reason there is predictability is that storms fire up in the Western Caribbean and the Gulf of Mexico, but that area is still close enough to the Gulf Coast states to be a surprise. Sometimes the states in the path of the hurricane, like Louisiana, would only have a day or so to get ready, meaning evacuate or make some kind of preparedness plan, so with the ability to improve predictions of most storms, there is still that struggle of proximity to where the storm started limiting the warning to the public.

FEMA

There are many critical points of view on what occurred during a major hurricane. One area is the use of a disastrous event being used as a political tool for one side to bad mouth an opponent. This discussion and report is not to take sides on the political issues that may have occurred during and after Hurricane Katrina. A discussion about this disaster includes a brief point of view on what can be stated to have happened without taking political sides. Another issue is the public's perception and critical view about their situation being worsened by a lack of disaster preparedness. This report is not to say that things went wrong, but it is widely known things could have been better as of 2014.

Prior to Hurricane Katrina, many believe that nobody could have predicted the levees would have failed as badly as they did. Given the situation that had occurred in 2005 and the fact that the city's transportation was basically cut off, some have said that FEMA did as good a job as they could when they got in there. Given the circumstances of a flooded out city that lasted for weeks, and the situation of travel being blocked, FEMA did the best they could. The situation eventually got better and improved. That is one of the more positive ways of describing what occurred. Many survivors know that in a disaster the size Hurricane Katrina, the local, state, and federal government really needed to have more of a leadership presence. The leadership claimed to be available in an election speech and while things are going well in the city, state, or country while in office, may not be there in a disaster. In a perfect government, if there are first responders and emergency preparedness in a government's budget there need to be some signs of that service being available during a later disaster.

Many citizens that were trapped in the floods would state that planning did not occur at all, as a result of the failed levees. As a result of that point, any reader should be able to agree that something failed. From the residents' point of view the blame pointed at the government's control of the infrastructure and the levees. With these criticisms come the fact that FEMA did arrive and did provide relief and recovery to one of the biggest weather disasters in New Orleans' and Louisiana's history.

Hurricane Isaac

Property of *Crash Lane News*

Isaac was a Category 1 hurricane occurring in 2012. There were some transportation issues with Isaac that had interstate closures occurring. The interstates definitely got closed during Isaac. Interstate 10 and Interstate 55 were closed for a period of time, estimated at a day to a day and a half. The storm surge was lingering on the west side of the lake. Once the surge drained out, the interstates were able to open up again. It was a small section that was closed and there were other routes that people could take that were open. In summary for Hurricane Isaac there were sections closed on Interstates 10 and 55 that did flood. NOAA provided the public a long warning time before Hurricane Isaac arrived. It was a slow-moving system. The New Orleans area had five to six days of lead time before the system came in. There were some evacuations for communities outside of the levees, and they were smaller populations. The major part of New Orleans did not evacuate for the Isaac storm.

Travelers Caught in Major Hurricanes

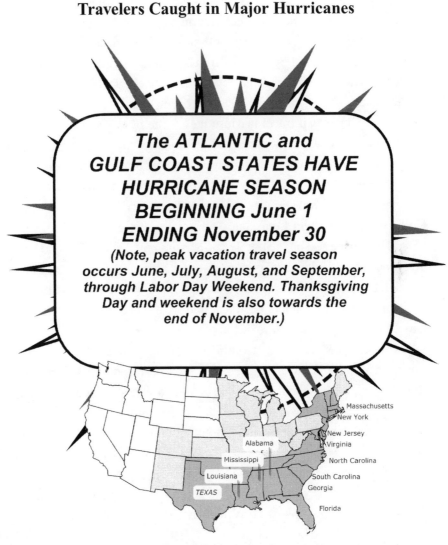

Property of *Crash Lane News*

Hurricane advice for travelers can begin in knowing what occurred with Hurricane Katrina. For Katrina there were people who were visiting New Orleans at the time of the hurricane. As the transportation infrastructure flooded, these same visitors and vacationers were stuck. The airport and the airlines look at the weather and see the storms coming, canceling flights about a day before the storm hits. There are some people on a trip that do get stranded temporarily. For Katrina they had to later be evacuated. There were also people stranded for Isaac as well. Isaac was not nearly as bad and actually during Isaac the hotel section maintained power, which was good, unlike Katrina. There are people stranded as a result of hurricanes. If a person is traveling by their own vehicle and there is an evacuation due to a hurricane coming, some hotels will basically force their guests to leave because of possible risks that may occur later when the storm hits. These individuals can travel because they came by car and it is not that bad for them because they get out of the area, saving their vehicle from becoming flooded as well as suffering any injuries or worse. An evacuation from the area ahead of time is something to think about when traveling. A suggestion for a traveler is to be aware of the hurricane threat if on the Gulf Coast, not only in Louisiana. Some states that people may travel to around hurricane season include Texas, Mississippi, Alabama, and Florida. The procedures the local areas businesses take are also good to know for a traveler, to be aware of what occurs, and how it affects transportation after it hits as a result. Travelers should watch weather forecasts for inbound hurricanes.

Watching the weather is recommended, especially during the tropical storm season here. Travelers going to the Gulf Coast from July to September should be aware of the weather advisories and the hurricane threat. The peak times of travel risk are from July to September. Once we head to October and November it is usually a time of a lower risk. Those months are not as active for hurricanes. Keep your eye on the weather forecasts, making sure there is nothing coming. If you see a potential hurricane or storm, the best course of action would be to plan ahead and postpone the trip, or change travel plans. Travelers should do this instead of getting caught in the middle of the storm.

Mardi Gras Weather

Mardi Gras attracts people across the United States every year for reasons that there is usually better weather down South at that time of year in February. Most of the states north of Louisiana get snow, which is also why it is a popular destination and celebration.

With the chance of having some warmer weather Mardi Gras season is considered to take place during a severe weather period, because Mardi Gras falls in February or March. New Orleans and Louisiana can get severe thunderstorms, lighting, heavy rainfall, tornadoes, and strong winds, all during that time of year. Hail is not a big threat, and is a rare event. The tornado threat and the strong wind threats are going to be the biggest concern during Mardi Gras. Then of course in February New Orleans occasionally could get snow. Snow is a very rare event, but it does occasionally happen. The snow melts pretty quickly because of the milder climate and location near the Gulf.

Besides the tornadoes, the bigger weather threat is the risk of severe thunderstorms. Some years there are some severe thunderstorms that roll through the area during the Mardi Gras weekend. When this occurs the option to postpone the parade to another day is a possibility.

Biggest Travel Concern

HINT: WATCH FOR FOG
November, December,
January, February, March
REDUCE SPEED OR PULL
OFF ROAD AT REST AREA
UNTIL FOG CLEARS

Property of *Crash Lane News*

The biggest weather threat as far as car accidents go is fog. New Orleans has sea fog oftentimes in the cool season months. Sea fog can be dense, reducing visibility to a few feet. There have been several deadly car accidents and multiple vehicle pileups during fog events. The fog and accidents is the biggest concern for drivers and forecasters. The cool season is from November through March. November can sometimes catch some off guard with the fog as well as the later months of January and February, where a driver may have become complacent to the effects of the weather.

Some outsiders might think traveling in or around a hurricane would be the biggest problem. But hurricane warnings gets the message out and do not affect travel while driving as much. For driving crashes and wrecks, the fog is the biggest threat. Nobody is out driving in a hurricane. They are either in their house hanging out or they evacuated. The New Orleans NOAA office has many fog advisories in winter. These advisories help to communicate if visibility is going to be less than a quarter of a mile. If there are low visibility warnings, slow down, and use extra caution. With advisories put in place there are still accidents as a result of the fog. People sometimes are just driving too fast at the wrong place and time when it comes to fog. The low visibility, combined with the problem that some drivers do not adjust the speed of their vehicle to hazardous weather conditions, is what causes accidents.

In Summary

A solution is to regularly check the weather threats when traveling to Louisiana and in the region. Check the NOAA alerts at www.spc.noaa.gov, or check the local news channel like CBS, ABC, and NBC, on television for weather advisories, or a cable news channel like the Weather Channel, CNN, and Fox News. In addition to having the news and advisories from NOAA, have a smartphone that is capable of the Wireless Emergency Alerts. Smartphone applications can give some added weather awareness and warnings directly from the government. A traveler can postpone and reschedule a trip or route, should there be the forecast of a hurricane. As for the fog a traveler should try to monitor the local NOAA offices' fog reports and try to drive when the sun is up.

Two Hurricanes, Iselle, then Julio, both headed towards Hawaii. The good thing is that their size, and category, reduces once arriving closer to the Hawaiian Islands. Nasa.gov image in Public Domain. From http://eoimages.gsfc.nasa.gov/images/imagerecords/84000/84145/eastpacific_vir_2014217_lrg.jpg

Honolulu, Hawaii NOAA/NWS Interview August 2014
Introduction to Traveling the Hawaiian Islands

The Hawaii National Weather Service office in Honolulu is very helpful. Crash Lane News spoke to their meteorologist about the weather in Hawaii, learning some travel tips. One example learned is the best time to travel to the Islands for a cruise, when is it best to get beach side hotel, and go camping. It was specifically asked, when is it best to travel to Hawaii? The answer from the meteorologist was positive, and slightly surprising. The reason the response about the weather was received as a positive, is the moderate weather Hawaii has year round, when later compared to the rest of the United States.

Hawaii is popular for tourist from the continental United States because of the weather, and because it is a comfortable tropical paradise. Tourists like the feeling the Islands give of being far from the regularly frequented tourist hotspots back in the United States. Many travel agencies like AAA work with cruises, resorts, hotels, and golf courses on the islands year round. Due to moderate weather, Hawaii is continuously a popular tourist destination. The summer, like the rest of the United States is the big time for tourism. It is also popular during the months leading up into winter, and even during winter. For residents in the continental United States facing the winter blizzards, and winter's extremely low temperatures, Hawaii is a popular tourist destination. For example, in November the prices might be lower due to the tourist off season, adding another perk to travel to the Islands. It is really one of the few places in the United States that is a year round destination for tourists. The more than perfect weather year round on the islands is very convincing to vacationers to take a trip there. The region's climate is attractive drawing many to the Hawaiian Islands, but with that good news traveling safe is still an important thing to focus on.

A traveler should know the weather, time of year, the pattern of El Nino, and geography, are the most important considerations in choosing a safe time to travel anywhere in Hawaii. It is important to know the weather patters, year to year. The yearly weather pattern can contribute the greatest amount of a weather forecast, as to when it is best to travel to Hawaii. A trip also depends on that specific time of year, meaning the months. Hawaii's year includes the seasons of spring, summer, fall, and winter, and choosing a trip during the best season is important, even though the weather is mild. The geography of each island and each geographical area's weather is also important to know. There is still a diverse climate, even though it is considered mild weather year round. The western and southern ends of the islands are a tropical rainforest. Due to the right conditions for the tropical rainforest this same windward area gets a lot of rain. At the same time there are tropical areas, each island also has some less tropical dry areas. The weather is going to fluctuate across the different areas on each Island as well as fluctuate across each Island.

CYCLONE's From the East and
NWS Area of Responsibility

The direction of severe weather towards Hawaii is important for residents, businesses, and especially those traveling. Most storms develop in the east Pacific, by Mexico, or further to the west than that. The term tropical cyclone is used by the NOAA/NWS website. The tropical cyclone term encompasses depressions, storms, tropical storms, and hurricanes. Tropical Cyclone is a generic name, used to describe any storm. The weather discussion will get more specific when there are detailed references about a storm system. Some specific names used to describe a storm include depressions, tropical storms, and hurricanes.

Hawaii can have a storm develop right in the basin. The basin is a shared area monitored for severe weather. This basin includes an area covered by the national hurricane center. The Honolulu NWS/NOAA office and the National Hurricane Center share an imaginary border at 140 west. The different areas of responsibility are important to know about. This is important because it allows the public to know what office is watching what geographic area's weather. The public can then follow that specific office's weather warnings, and other weather news. Knowing about the weather forecast is where preparedness begins for the public.

When significant weather like a hurricane develops in the area, the National Hurricane Center puts out an advisory. When the weather event is west of the 140, the meteorologist at the NWS Hawaii office begins to track the storm.

In addition to the area east of the Hawaiian Islands, the NWS/NOAA office is watching the whole Pacific for storm activity. The storms of the most concern are the ones developing east of the Hawaiian Islands. The office does not focus on what is referred to as west movers (these are storms coming east). The storms coming from west of the Hawaiian Islands, from the area around of the Philippines, or somewhere around there, is not going to later affect Hawaii. More attention is placed on the storms coming from the eastern area of the Islands. As a result, the weather near Central America, the Caribbean, and anywhere west of the continent is watched by NOAA/NWS Hawaii.

2014 is an EL NINO YEAR

El Nino affects Hawaii. El Nino affects almost everywhere. 2014 is an El Nino year. El Nino makes the Pacific more active in the Hawaiian Islands area than it would normally be. In the Atlantic Ocean it is less active, when it is an El Nino year. The Pacific Islands and the Hawaiian Islands get more activity. This year we have had quite a bit more storms in the Pacific region than the Atlantic region. More about El Nino is available online at www. elnino.noaa.gov.

Some recent hurricane activity, as of August 2014, has been reported by Nasa.gov.

In early August 2014, not one but two hurricanes were headed for the Hawaiian Islands. Storms arriving from the east are a relative rarity, and landfalling storms are also pretty infrequent.

The Moderate Resolution Imaging Spectroradiometer (MODIS) on NASA's Terra satellite captured this natural-color image of Hurricane Iselle over the Pacific Ocean at 10:40 a.m. Hawaiian time (1940 Universal Time) on August 4, 2014. Shortly after the image was acquired, the U.S. Joint Typhoon Warning Center reported that Iselle was a category 4 hurricane with sustained winds at 120 knots (140 miles or 220 kilometers per hour) and centered at 16.10° north latitude, 137.40° west longitude.

The MODIS image shows a nearly cloud-free eye in the center of a symmetrical storm; there is solid ring of clouds around the center rather than intermittent, spiral bands. Iselle was at its peak intensity at the time and it was likely an annular hurricane. Atmospheric researchers also detected signs of mesovortices near the eyewall. The smaller, tighter rotating structures within the larger storm are often associated with tornadoes on land.

Forecasters from the Central Pacific Hurricane Center predicted on August 6 that Iselle would make landfall on the island of Hawaii as a strong tropical storm or a category 1 hurricane late on August 7. Wind damage and heavy surf are likely, but heavy rainfall, flash floods, and landslides were the greatest concern as Iselle approached.

On August 5, the Visible Infrared Imaging Radiometer Suite (VIIRS) sensor on Suomi-NPP captured natural-color images of both Iselle and Hurricane Julio en route to Hawaii. The image below is a composite of three satellite passes over the tropical Pacific Ocean in the early afternoon. Note that Iselle's eyewall had grown less distinct; the storm had descreased to category 2 intensity. The bright shading toward the center-left of the image is sunglint, the reflection of sunlight off the water and directly back at the satellite sensor.

As of midday on August 6, Hurricane Julio was a category 1 storm, but it is expected to weaken to tropical storm force in the coming days. Forecasts suggest that the eye will pass north of the Hawaiian Islands on August 10, but it is possible that there will be some effects on land.

References and Related Reading

Dr. Jeff Masters WunderBlog, via Weather Underground (2014, August 6) Rare Twin Hurricanes Headed Towards Hawaii. Accessed August 6, 2014.

Dr. Jeff Masters WunderBlog, via Weather Underground (2014, August 4) Hurricane Iselle Headed Towards Hawaii. Accessed August 6, 2014.

NASA Earth Observatory (2013, March 5) In a Warming World, Storms May Be Fewer but Stronger.

NOAA Central Pacific Hurricane Center (2014, August 6) Hurricane Iselle. Accessed August 6, 2014.

NOAA National Hurricane Center (2014, August 6) Hurricane Julio. Accessed August 6, 2014.

Unisys Weather (2014) Iselle Tracking Information. Accessed August 6, 2014.

The Vane, via Gawker (2014, August 6) This Week's Buzzword: 'Annular Hurricane.' Accessed August 6, 2014.

The Hawaiian Islands Biggest Cyclone/ Hurricane was Hurricane Iniki

One of biggest cyclones/hurricanes that hit the Hawaiian Islands was Hurricane Iniki. This storm's event reached the islands September 11, 1992. The scale of damage or the degree of damage made this storm famous. At that time, the damage caused to the Islands infrastructure, residential areas, and businesses, was the most expensive event in Hawaii. It was also very expensive when compared to the hurricanes at that time that were occurring back in the gulf coast and the Atlantic coastal areas. In terms of damages it was the most expensive at that time. Since then, Iniki's damage has been surpassed with larger storms in the continental United States. It was scaled as a category 4 Hurricane. According to the Saffir-Simpson

Hurricane Wind scales a category 4 is stated to have winds of 130-156 mph, 113-136 kt, 209-251 km/h. These conditions cause catastrophic damage.

The NOAA website describes a Category 4 catastrophe as, "Well-built framed homes can sustain severe damage with loss of most of the roof structure and/or some exterior walls. Most trees will be snapped or uprooted and power poles downed. Fallen trees and power poles will isolate residential areas. Power outages will last weeks to possibly months. Most of the area will be uninhabitable for weeks or months." Information about the Hurricane scales in detail is available to the public at http://www.nhc.noaa.gov/aboutsshws.php.

The NOAA website has a summary of Hurricane Iniki. This is at the beginning of a Natural Disaster survey Report for Hurricane Iniki September 6-13, 1992. This report included a large amount of weather event information and is important for the public to know about.

"On the afternoon of September 11, 1992, a small but intense Hurricane Iniki struck Hawaii across the Island of Kauai. With damage estimates of $1.8 billion, this was one of the most destructive hurricanes on record anywhere in the United States. Seven persons died and about 100 were injured because of Iniki. However, because of the in-place warning system and the response of the populace, a greater human tragedy was averted.

Overcoming limitations in satellite coverage and with negligible surface observations, CPHC forecasters alerted the populace of Hawaii a day in advance that the storm would hit the state. The state and local emergency services organizations, the media, and the populace all responded quickly and appropriately. In short, the system worked.

Although hurricanes are common in the eastern Pacific Ocean, and not uncommon in central Pacific Ocean, they usually either remain well east of or cross south of the Hawaiian Islands. This was only the fourth time in the past 40 years that the state has been hit by such a storm. Despite the relative rarity, all involved were generally well prepared for the event."

Sometimes the weather is not severe, being mild for an entire year. Then some years Hawaii will get 6 or 7 of these storms. Cyclones skip a year sometimes, but then return. The milder years are more frequent, and it is something good to look forward to. With that kind of pattern it sounds like Hawaii is a mild climate, compared to the rest of the United States.

Hawaii does not get hit given their proximity to the paths of Cyclones, compared to other areas like the Philippines, Taiwan, Japan, and South Korea. The area the islands are in tend to get the atmospheric conditions known to have cyclones. Although, these same conditions are not very conducive for Hawaii to get the more severe scaled storms. One of the draw backs to good weather is complacency of preparedness. As a result, some areas on the islands are not as prepared, when compared to areas back in the continental United States.

Seasonal Weather

Seasonal weather is important to know. It can provide an estimate of when severe weather may be a threat. Seasonal weather awareness is also good when choosing a trip to the different geographic areas on each island. Generally, the summer season has the rare threat of Cyclones/Hurricanes, starting in June, with an increase of storms after the 4th of July. Then, the fall season, and the month of November, is the start of the rainy season, and winter.

During the summer months the Islands do not get too hot, being usually warm. Hawaii's weather during summer is more moderate than the rest of the United States. It is constantly cooled by the Pacific Ocean. The summer's day time highs are typically around 89 degrees F, in Honolulu.

The climate of O'ahu and Maui vary. The main difference depends on a geographic location. The main city's weather on Maui, is similar to Honolulu, O'ahu weather. The similarity is that the windward side of O'ahu and Maui get a lot more rain, when compared to the western side of those same islands.

According to the NWS/NOAA in Hawaii there are no other major weather concerns in Hawaii other than Hurricanes during the summer. Hawaii also faces winter weather that consists of some strong thunderstorms. Winter storms are short in duration. These short lived storms are spread out across the winter months. The total amount of days for winter storms are three to four, very mild for winter. During November through February these storms occur. These systems are described as not being that severe. With the milder weather, there are still issues of flooding. Floods regularly occur during these short and rainy bursts. As a result of some severe storms on an island the streams and waterways rise and fall quickly, but usually under heavier rain falls.

Weather Warnings

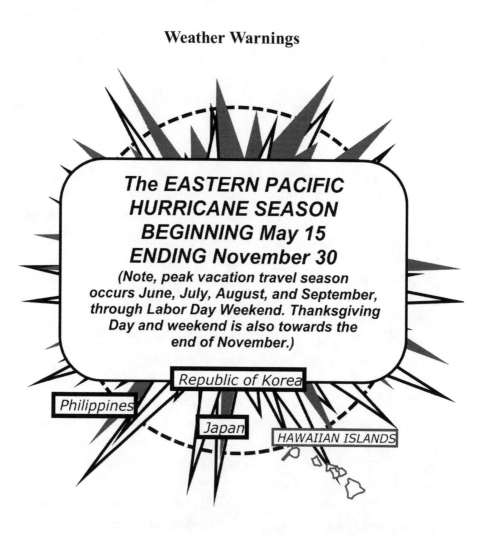

The EASTERN PACIFIC
HURRICANE SEASON
BEGINNING May 15
ENDING November 30
(Note, peak vacation travel season
occurs June, July, August, and September,
through Labor Day Weekend. Thanksgiving
Day and weekend is also towards the
end of November.)

Republic of Korea

Philippines

Japan

HAWAIIAN ISLANDS

Warnings and weather history are a big part of preparedness. This information is really the most important to know about. A particular weather season's threats are also very important to know about. Prior records help process what warning is needed to be anticipated to possibly occur. There may be a certain type of storm able to be predicted, and that can get prepared for if known about in advance. An example of this in

Hawaii is that a Hurricane warning for the Islands is 48 hours. When the NWS office has a track window when they expect a Hurricane or tropical storm for the islands a warning is issued at that time. Once the Hurricane is seen on the radar, the office issues the warning. When they spot a possible weather event that looks threatening a warning is communicated to the public. A forecast is also released to the public to convey these potential weather threats ahead of time.

As far as predicting a specific area that is going to get hit the hardest, a lot of times that is hard to do anywhere. The reason is some storm events sort of pop up unpredictably, and sort of go on random paths. Random storm destinations are difficult to warn the public about. The meteorologists look at the general lines, and big picture. For example, they can say Kauai and Oahu is the biggest threatened islands for a particular identified storm seen on the radar. The warning would mention that these areas will have the severest weather events. But there are limits to accurate predictions. As far as pin pointing an exact time when there will be a severe thunderstorm cell after seeing the weather develop a day in advance is impossible.

The best way to get information about the weather, climatology, and alerts while traveling around the Hawaiian Islands is to check the NWS/ NOAA website, and to have a weather radio. The radio broadcast is 24/7, of a voice recording of the forecast, from our office.

It is easy to get a NOAA radio signal if on land and near to the tower, which is good to know about. But what about when traveling at sea? Cruises are one of the most popular methods of travel and knowing about the weather at sea is always a concern even in a mild region. According to the NWS office a cruise ship will get the NOAA radio signal, assuming that they use the Radio. But, the big Cruise Liners are advanced enough that they have internet service on the boat. Access like that allows them to look the weather up live stream. Some Cruise Liners contract a private company to do the company's weather forecast. Many companies invest in ways to get accurate weather forecast for their ship, and this information helps manage their routes.

FOG

Hawaii will rarely get fog. FOG needs calm winds, and the winds are usually blowing so there is no fog. These same winds are also part of the reason VOG is not a daily sight in the sky because it keeps things cleared out with a constant blowing.

TORNADOES

There have been tornadoes on Hawaii, but a big tornado that causes damage is a rare weather event. For preparedness, the islands can get tornados, but they are not as anticipated to be a significant regularly. Tornadoes are pretty rare. The last warning the office issued for a tornado was December 13, 2008, for Kauai. Kauai is the furthest west island away from Oahu.

VOG/Volcano Affects on Climatology and Meteorology

To get a comprehensive view about the weather and Hawaii there is a certain point where its mild climate is also affected by some of the natural hazards like Volcanos. The NOAA/NWS office is not monitoring the volcanos directly. Volcanos do affect some things that have to do with the weather.

The big island, Hawai'i's active volcano is named Kilauea. Kilauea has been at a constant state of eruption since 1983. The sulfur smell is also at a constant state due to the lava's burning. A constant venting of carbon dioxide gas has slightly affected the weather. This activity plays a role when it blows over the more densely populated areas. With a south east wind this gas/smoke blows over the rest of the western islands. This incoming gas cloud is called VOG. People that have asthma and allergies, or have breathing problems have said they have been affected, and/or bothered by it. VOG's affects are not an everyday event, but it does occur periodically throughout the year. The affect it has on the islands is limited in that many times the VOG blows eastwards out sea, away from the westward islands. This eastward direction may be because the elevation of the mountains and dormant volcanos are blocking some of the winds blowing west. This also occurs because the volcano is on an island surrounded by different winds created, and constant due to the Pacific Ocean. Many of the populated areas really do not see VOG, unless they travel near the volcano.

VOG is something of a concern of course but does not black the sun out like a total eclipse. VOG is a haze, just like how the sky tends to appear in or around an area with wildfires. Smoke like a wildfire is the best way to describe VOG's appearance.

More information about this volcano is available at http://hvo.wr.usgs.gov/kilauea/

A Special Note and Hint by Crash Lane News

Crash Lane News would like to finish the section about the weather with Hawaii's Noaa office with another thanks for the NWS/NOAA advice and current information. Remember the important lessons about the weather. It is important to have weather history and forecasting. This is true even when living in a moderate climate that rarely has Hurricanes, Tornados, and Severe Thunderstorms. Be prepared for weather disasters no matter where, when traveling. When living in a mild climate, or tropical paradise, being complacent to the possibility there are storms is self defeating. There are many beautiful places throughout the United States like the example of Hawaii, that also have weather threats that disrupt travel. A lesson for all the United States and all U.S. Citizens is to respect the weather ahead of the trip, and avoid situations, people, and businesses, forcing a situation involving the weather. Traveling in a weather disaster is preventable.

7

Know About Tornadoes: 10 May 2008 Tornado Outbreak Weather and Travel Report

Includes Eyewitness Accounts of Tornadoes
<u>OKLAHOMA 10 May 2008 Tornado</u>

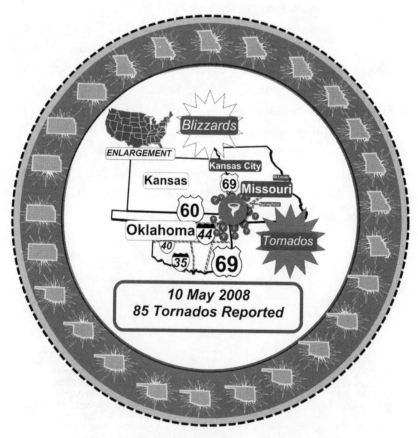

Property of *Crash Lane News*

The May 10, 2008 supercell tornado caused so much damage that it was considered one of the biggest storms of the century. The widespread destruction on the ground is still shocking to see in some of the pictures. The accumulative damage was very large. When compared to other storms known before about 2008 its damage was bigger than other severe storms. The damage is still bigger than the severe storms occurring more recently as of 2014. The travelers who witnessed the storm had little warning at the exact spot where the storm would occur, but there were some good advisories mentioned ahead of time. It is always a risk to drive when there are reports on the weather radio channels, but some travelers do it anyway due to the issues of reaching an appointment on time or because they have scheduled other time off from work. For this storm, there was a traveler who spotted the storm chasers from the Discovery Channel show, and later this storm was, in fact, on one of their shows. It was a big deal to have gotten that close to the tornado that caused that much damage and survive. The travelers that planned to head on through the storm took the risks and were lucky to survive.

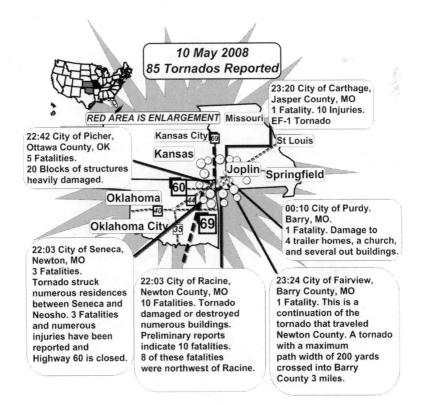

The part below does not describe the total destruction perfectly. It is here to summarize some of the more important parts mentioned by www.NOAA.gov about this storm. There was a significant amount of road debris reported because of this storm, but Highway 69 was unaffected.

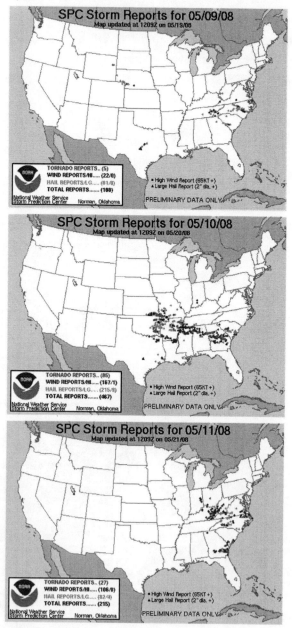

May 8, 2008 0100 UTC Day 1 Convective Outlook
Updated: Thu May 8 01:04:18 UTC 2008
Probabilistic to Categorical Outlook Conversion
Table (Effective Feb 14, 2006).
Public Severe Weather Outlook
The SPC is forecasting ...severe thunderstorms
expected over parts of the southern plains this
afternoon and tonight.... Please read the latest
public statement about this event.

CATEGORICAL GRAPH

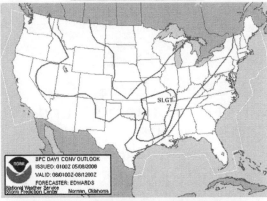

PROBABILISTIC TORNADO GRAPHIC

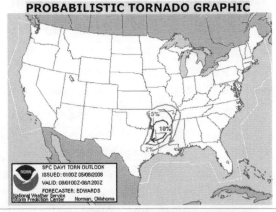

ISSUED: 05/08/2008
Probability of a tornado within 25 miles of a point.
Hatched Area:10% or greater probability of
EF2-EF5 tornadoes within 25 miles of a point.

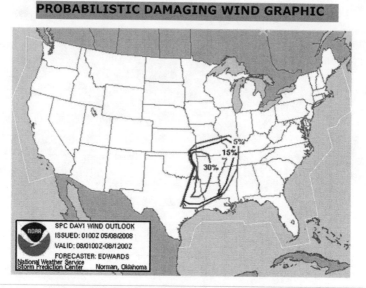

ISSUED: 05/08/2008
Probability of damaging thunderstorm winds or wind gusts of 50 knots or higher within 24 miles of a point. Hatched Area: 10% or greater probability of wind gusts 65 knots or greater within 25 miles of a point.

Storm reports and convective outlooks tell the full story of a tornadic weather event. The traveler that was heading through the tornado outbreak on May 10, 2008 knew about tornado alley prior to the trip to a certain point. It is obvious with all the news and warnings the public should know that during tornado season there may end up being a tornado if in tornado alley. For this storm, the day before the weather and sky were somewhat clear. South of Oklahoma in Texas it was not raining heavily prior to the trip up through Oklahoma. There was cloud coverage but it was still a bright day. The point of mentioning this is there were not many signs of an incoming storm that would cause a tornado affecting travel. The National Weather Service/NOAA report about the incoming weather was the best predictor of what later occurred. One piece of advice learned is other areas with severe weather in the United States might have a more gradual build up of storm activity that only the local population will be aware of and notice.

In the days prior to this tornado outbreak the weather seemed almost totally clear of severe weather on May 8, and 9, 2008. It was even described as somewhat clear during May 10, 2008 through Oklahoma, and into Kansas, other than some thick cloud coverage where the storm report mentioned there to be activity. The noticeable build up of a storm by the local population is more detectably visible for hurricanes, blizzards, and severe thunderstorms. In tornado alley that noticeable build up is faster that a bigger storm, and better monitored using the NWS/NOAA data. The confusion comes when the day before is clear, or with very bright clouds, creating a false feeling of safe weather to drive or travel in. A bright sky with some clouds or a thin layer of clouds causes some doubt that the following day will have a tornadic storm drop in suddenly. This doubt sometimes takes the traveling public's preparedness by surprise if the weather forecast is not checked. The good thing is that this storm was predicted by the NWS a couple days in advance. Convective outlooks are considered one of the best ways to see an advanced prediction about the weather.

Unfortunately, the public tends to remain complacent even with weather warnings and weather advisories. This complacency can be greater for those not familiar with the areas seasonal storms. One reason there is some complacency for those that live in tornado alley is that a direct hit by a tornado on populated area is still considered rare. This rare occurrence of direct hits is true even in tornado alley, and high winds from the entire storm system usually cause all the storms reportable damage. This particular storm caused numerous severe injuries across a few states, and caused many fatalities. This May 10, 2008 storm also caused multiple disaster areas lasting months across a few states and region. Travelers and residents should know that these outbreaks are difficult to pin point in advanced. They are difficult because even when there is the NWS convective outlook, the specific prediction on which interstates, highways, streets, counties, and cities that will be directly affected are unforeseeable, unpredictable, and unable to be pin pointed in the weather forecast.

Model weather data cannot plot points on a map ahead of the storm predicting which exact area or address will be affected. Model weather data is only a summarized version or what may occur, but it is also better than nothing. Because of the existing unpredictability, a word of advice for travelers is to understand before a trip that severe weather events like a tornado outbreak, and their storms aftermath, are a real danger. A trip through tornado alley from March through July every year should anticipate these severe weather outbreaks. If something is in the forecast make a plan to avoid traveling through the outbreak. This region on the United States in the spring time is a real hazard to drivers. This tornado outbreak hazard affects travel. These severe storms create real driving hazards occurring every year, and some storms cause accidents. Remember, when compared to the winter blizzards, the path of the tornado on the ground is far less predictable. These storms that cause a tornado can be forecasted a week or more in advance but there is still no certainty that a tornado will touch down.

CrashLaneNews.com would like to include that when a tornado touches down and the public is traveling near the tornado's area it is beyond too late to avoid the entire storm system. Weather events will definitely occur and be experienced by those same travelers. A good thing is that it is possible for these same travelers to get the current weather warnings if experiencing these conditions, and then make changes to the direction of travel to avoid the path of any tornados on the ground. The following is a NWS message from May 10, 2008. This is only part of what travelers and the local public heard over their NOAA/NWS weather radios. This is included because it could help the public to know what to do and expect to hear when a tornado is on the ground or right after one was on the ground. NWS broadcasted this according to CrashLaneNews.com, "A LARGE AND EXTREMELY DANGEROUS TORNADO WAS ON THE GROUND. THIS IS A THREATENING SITUATION. IF YOU ARE IN THE PATH OF THIS TORNADO TAKE COVER IMMEDIATELY. IF NO UNDERGROUND SHELTER IS AVAILABLE MOVE TO THE LOW LEVEL OF THE INTERIOR. ALL VEHICLES SHOULD BE ABANDONED FOR A MORE SUBSTANTIAL SHELTER."

The traveler that heard this mentioned that there were also specific cities and counties being mentioned in the message. The traveler also mentioned that the interstates and roads were not filled with traffic that day. There was traffic when going through a city but it was at a noticeable reduced amount and the speed was much slower. There will always be traffic moving during these storms from locals trying to seek shelter, travelers passing through the region, emergency responders, and storm chasers like from the Discovery Channel or from local news agencies. The overall reduced amount of local traffic was due to the advanced warning about the tornado. Most of the local residents, and storm chasers, received this information about this storm days in advance from the local emergency management agencies, weather forecasters, and the NOAA/NWS information being out of the path of the storm. As for travelers focused on commercial transportation issues the weather was a real concern. That time of year's weather was known about by every one in advance but there are some trips that end up too close to the storm. 2008 was a busy year for the weather in tornado alley. Before the May 10, 2008 storm there were storms and some smaller tornado outbreaks to include: 1. 03/02/2008-03/03/2008, 2. 03/12/2008-03/13/2008, 3. 03/17/2008-03/18/2008, 4. 03/26/2008-03/27/2008, 5. 03/29/2008-03/31/2008, 6. 04/03/2008-04/042008, and 7. 04/07/2008-04/09/2008. 2008 was a busy year for emergency managers, storm chasers, and a challenging year for travelers to be safe. By the time the month of May arrived some might not have expected it to include a disastrous tornado directly traveling through a city.

Below is the convective outlook for May 07, 2008. Note the below is from NOAA/NWS, and was helpful in forecasting that there could be a possible severe thunderstorms with tornados as early as three days before the big May 10, 2008 tornado outbreak. It is a good thing to know there is this summarized predictability, and it can allow a traveler to prevent a trip through the area once a weather report like this is made. The closer time to the more severe expected weather event the more accurate the NOAA/NWS weather outlook has been described.

SPC AC 080100

DAY 1 CONVECTIVE OUTLOOK

NWS STORM PREDICTION CENTER NORMAN OK

0800 PM CDT WED MAY 07 2008

VALID 080100Z - 081200Z

...THERE IS A SLGT RISK OF SVR TSTMS PORTIONS ERN TX/ERN OK TO LOWER

MS VALLEY...

...SYNOPSIS...

PROGRESSIVE MID/UPPER LEVEL PATTERN FEATURES PRONOUNCED LOW OVER CENTRAL OK...AND SHORTWAVE TROUGH FROM NRN ROCKIES SSWWD ACROSS SIERRA NV RANGE AND COASTAL SRN CA. SRN PLAINS CYCLONE ALOFT IS FCST TO CONTINUE EJECTING ENEWD ACROSS MUCH OF OZARKS REGION OVERNIGHT...ITS CENTER ALMOST VERTICALLY COLOCATED WITH SFC CYCLONE. SFC COLD FRONT -- INITIALLY ANALYZED FROM NERN OK LOW SWWD ACROSS W-CENTRAL TX...IS FCST TO OVERTAKE DRYLINE FROM N-S AND MOVE SEWD OVER MUCH OF TX..ERN OK AND WRN AR.

MEANWHILE...POSITIVELY TILTED MIDLEVEL WAVE OVER INTERMOUNTAIN W WILL MOVE GENERALLY ESEWD AS UPPER LOW DIGS SSEWD ACROSS BC. FOREGOING LARGE SCALE ASCENT AND RELATED DESTABILIZATION WILL OVERSPREAD AT LEAST MRGL LOW LEVEL THETAE TO CONTRIBUTE TO GEN THUNDER POTENTIAL OVER BROAD AREA...CONVECTION BECOMING MORE SPORADIC WITH TIME. ALTHOUGH A FEW TSTMS MAY PRODUCE HAIL/GUSTS APCHG SVR LEVELS...PRIND

SVR POTENTIAL HAS ECOME TOO LOW FOR REMAINDER PERIOD TO INTRODUCE PROBABILITIES ATTM.

...ERN PORTIONS TX/OK TO LOWER/MID MS VALLEY... SEVERAL LINES AND CLUSTERS OF TSTMS WILL CONTINUE TO MOVE EWD TO NEWD ACROSS THIS REGION THROUGH REMAINDER EVENING...WITH DAMAGING WIND AND OCCASIONAL LARGE HAIL POSSIBLE. A FEW SHORT-LIVED TORNADOES ARE POSSIBLE WITH BOW/LEWP CIRCULATIONS AS WELL. HAIL SIZES AND TORNADO POTENTIAL EACH SHOULD BE LARGEST IN ASSOCIATED WITH SUPERCELLS...ESPECIALLY ANY RELATIVELY DISCRETE/SUSTAINED STORMS. REF WWS 274-275 AND RELATED MESOSCALE DISCUSSIONS FOR INFO ON NEAR-TERM SVR THREATS.

POTENTIAL FOR SUPERCELLS OVERNIGHT WILL BE GREATER WITH SWD EXTENT FROM OZARKS INTO ARKLATEX REGION... HENCE RELATIVELY MAXIMIZED TORNADO PROBABILITIES FROM SE OK ACROSS SRN AR...EXTREME NE TX AND NRN LA. ALTHOUGH UNMODIFIED LZK/SHV RAOBS SUGGEST RELATIVELY WEAK LAPSE RATES ALOFT AND MODEST CAPE...VERY STG LOW LEVEL SHEAR AND SFC-BASED EFFECTIVE INFLOW PARCELS SHOULD BE MAINTAINED BENEATH 50-60 KT LLJ. COLDER MIDLEVEL AIR MASS ALSO WILL OVERSPREAD WRN PORTION OF MOIST SECTOR...COMBINING WITH RELATIVELY RICH SFC THETAE TO MAINTAIN BUOYANCY AOA THAT SAMPLED BY THOSE RAOBS.

FARTHER SW...A FEW TORNADOES ARE STILL POSSIBLE FROM TSTMS WITHIN THAT PORTION OF PREVIOUS MDT RISK AREA STILL AHEAD OF DRYLINE. HOWEVER...TRENDS IN CONVECTIVE MODES/COVERAGE...AND LOSS OF GREATEST SFC HEATING/BUOYANCY SUGGESTS POTENTIAL WILL SHIFT E OF THAT AREA INTO SOMEWHAT LESS UNSTABLE AIR MASS WITHIN NEXT 1-2 HOURS.

..EDWARDS.. 05/08/2008

Despite the fact that some vehicles had been damaged from the high winds, Highway 69 remained open as far as a traveler knows who had parked at a truck stop off of it the night of the storm. The damage was bad in that there were about 21 deaths total, hundreds of injuries, and millions of dollars in damage. The NOAA/National Weather Service reported many events for May 10, 2008. The following is only a few of the larger tornado events and what they caused.

The entire storm system is hard to describe but NOAA is able to include many details, all in the public domain, and useful later to look up to understand severe weather. The total event is stated to of had 85 tornados. There were reports of EF 4, EF3, EF2, and EF1 tornados during and after this storm system. 22:03 City of Seneca, Newton, MO. 3 Fatalities. Tornado struck numerous residences between Seneca and Neosho. 3 Fatalities and numerous injuries have been reported and Highway 60 is closed. 22:03 City of Racine, Newton County, MO. 10 Fatalities. Tornado damaged or destroyed numerous buildings. Preliminary reports indicate 10 fatalities. 8 of these fatalities were northwest of Racine. 23:20 City of Carthage, Jasper County, MO. 1 Fatality. 10 Injuries. EF-1 Tornado touched down on the northeast side of Carthage as Ivy St. and 90T. 23:24 City of Fairview, Barry County, MO. 1 Fatality. This is a continuation of the tornado that traveled Newton County. A tornado with a maximum path width of 200 yards crossed into Barry County 3 miles. 22:42 City of Picher, Ottawa County, OK. 5 Fatalities. 20 Blocks of structures heavily damaged. 00:10 City of Purdy. Barry, MO. 1 Fatality. Damage to 4 trailer homes, a church, and several other buildings. These larger reported events should also be known to have occurred while highway 69 was in use, making travel in a safe way complicated and risk.

Leading up to the May 10, 2008, tornado in Oklahoma, Kansas, and Missouri there had a few other severe storms in that area. This area and year became a reminder as to its disastrous events and the need for disaster preparedness and disaster relief. The solution is to know about weather warnings from NOAA/The National Weather Service and the News. This area is not called Tornado Alley for nothing, in that the tornado in Joplin, MO was also considered the storm of the century a few years later in 2011.

8

Interview with Dodge City, Kansas NWS/NOAA Office Covering the Greensburg Tornado, Travel in Tornado Alley, and the famous Storm Chaser Tim Samaras

<u>KANSAS 4-5 May 2007</u>

CRASHLANENEWS.com

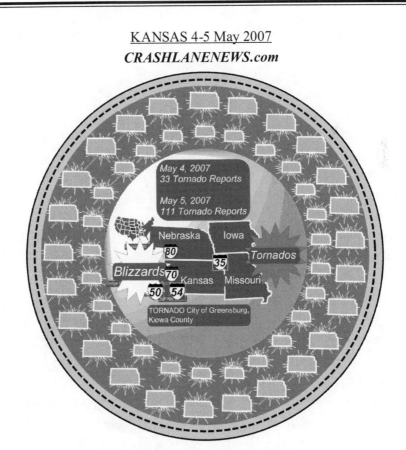

May 4, 2007
33 Tornado Reports

May 5, 2007
111 Tornado Reports

Nebraska   Iowa

Blizzards   *Tornados*

Kansas   Missouri

TORNADO City of Greensburg,
Kiowa County

Interview with Dodge City NOAA
Office, Kansas, October 2013

When speaking to Dodge City, Kansas NOAA forecast office in October 2013, an interview was made available with expert and veteran meteorologist, Larry Ruthi. The Dodge City, KA Office through Ruthi was extremely helpful. NOAA's ability to employ Ruthi to speak about the weather is an example of how this particular NOAA office has excellent public relation skills, benefiting the local and regional public in the area.

The Greensburg, KA tornado event on May 4, 2007 was the main topic in the discussion. The reason this storm was chosen was it was a high profile example of a tornado that occurred in southern Kansas. This storm was also a very large system affecting many people in the area to include people traveling. A traveler's eyewitness account for May 5 is also included along with the information made available by NOAA. The traveler was not in Kansas at the time of the Greensburg tornado but was near the area of the end of the tornado as it was dissipating way north on the Interstate 80 in Iowa and Nebraska. The combined May 4 and 5 was a huge storm system, with a large amounts of damage in Kansas, which also affected the entire region. Traffic in Nebraska and Iowa was affected severely on May 5.

This weather event is interesting because it was so large, and, as a result weather radio alerts were sent out to many counties in a few states. The included accounts by Ruthi and eyewitnesses also include information a traveler can apply into their own plan. Many people in the area of the time of this storm system, and the traveling public in the area, became an eyewitness. This information can be added into travel plans for next time. A good plan when traveling in Kansas is to keep things simple and start the planning of a trip knowing the weather forecast. A traveler should also learn how far in advance the Storm Prediction Center warning system puts out alerts for severe weather. Another issue is to know what type of severe weather can affect travel in Kansas, which includes blizzards, severe thunderstorms, and tornadoes.

Kansas is a part of the infamous Tornado Alley. This area is made up of the central states, from Texas, and Arkansas, going north, to Iowa and Nebraska. Kansas is like many other states when it comes to traveling issues mostly being caused from traffic accidents, but the weather there is something to watch from March to June as a result of the history of the tornado damage. Also note there are more accidents during winter for many commercial carriers, so the blizzards that cause low visibility and icy roads are also something to be on the look out for. Note here that with the publicity these storms have gotten in popular culture traveling in Kansas is rarely from an actual tornado. There are more severe storm warnings regarding thunderstorms across the state that can reduce visibility of the road, which is something to keep in mind. In addition to that Kansas annually experiences bad weather in winter, resulting in low visibility, in blizzards and the aftereffects of icy roads which will affect all types of transportation. The point of mentioning this up front is so that a traveler can keep the basic suggestions about the weather in check with reality of what goes on. Also, any storm being a tornado, severe thunderstorm, blizzard, or another type of weather that reduces visibility is going to endanger the regular flow of traffic and lead to a possible accident. Each state's location and geographical features are going to affect a traveler's perspective on the ground to a certain point, as a result. The ability to travel on a level interstate or road can affect a traveler's ability to see at increased distances or decreased distances. When the roads have hills the elevation reduces the distances available to the eyes that can prevent an accident.

Kansas has level ground, increasing visibility. Any increase in visibility is a good thing for travelers. Having a clear view to look out at the weather from a distance is a perk when traveling there. This can increase the last minute decision to pull off at a rest area or travel plaza in order to check the weather and take a break before going further. Kansas's level ground is also a good thing by allowing travelers to view road hazards further on ahead. An accident farther ahead on the road that might have been caused by the weather can be seen far in advance when the ground is flat. That is good because it can help a driver be safe and make a lane change to give the disabled vehicle room. Extra time can also be used to gradually reduce speed knowing there may be ice, or debris in the road, causing the disabled vehicle's accident.

Some storms may leave a path of destruction and when viewed from a distance can also be an indicator of the direction of the storm and if the storm has dissipated. If there is damage the common sense thing most would assume is that the storm is over. This is correct in the majority of events other than tornadoes, which makes traveling in Kansas sometimes unpredictable. With some large storm systems there can be multiple tornadoes; this fact is true in many other states also. So even if the weather is calm after the first day for a while, the next day could have even more tornadoes. This is exactly what occurred on May 4 and 5, 2007.

Greensburg tornado event information according to the National Weather Service/NOAA reports. These events were reported to have occurred May 4-5 2007. This is a brief summary of the storm, and is followed with a detailed discussion with the NWS/NOAA office in Dodge City, KS.

MAY 5. TIME 22:55. A tornado caused 11 injuries when it touched down. MINOR DAMAGE REPORTED. City of Osborne, Osborne County, Kansas. May 5 Tornado 04:40. In the City of Bennington, Ottawa County there were 4 people injured, and 5 homes damaged. Power lines were downed, causing power outages and transportation hazards on the ground. MAY 5. TIME 04:40. A tornado caused 4 injuries, damage to homes, power lines downed, in the City of Ottawa, Ottawa County, Kansas. MAY 4. TIME 03:33. A tornado caused one fatality, and one injury, two houses were destroyed. This event was in the City of Hopesville, Pratt County. MAY 4. TIME 255. A TORNADO CAUSED 12 FATALITIES, 63 PEOPLE WERE INJURED, DAMAGE TO MANY HOMES AND BUSINESSES, IN THE City of Greensburg, Kiowa County, KS. MAY 4. TIME 02:08. Tornado debris cloud reported 9 miles northwest of City of Coldwater, Comanche County.

Popular culture has used tornadoes as a background to the story including the *OZ the Great and Powerful,* of 2013. Tornadoes are one of the types of severe weather that has been reflected in movies, television shows, literature, and other media, as a result of the spontaneous timing and ability to cause the destruction they do. A traveler should not read too deeply into the fact about tornadoes in popular culture, in that there are many other things that need to be known to be safe. An interesting thing in the popularity of tornadoes is that it is more spontaneous and a surprise. It is true that Kansas is in Tornado Alley, but be aware of the other weather updates for that area. The fact that there have not been as many big budget movies about blizzards and icy roads does not mean they are less dangerous. A solution is for some movies to be made about those winter storms which can really add to the existing awareness of public safety. With the unpredictable nature of tornadoes in Kansas, the state is still safe to travel in. The actual chances of being hit directly by a tornado are very low. Remember that the storm system can sometimes be a bigger threat causing severe wind and rain, and this surrounds the actual cone of the tornadoes that touch down. Someone not familiar with this kind of weather may expect to see a tornado but will only see the rain and clouds from a distance. The reality is severe storm systems are something to be observant of. Make sure to change and make adjustments to survive the entirety of the storm. This is a good thing to remember when applying this information into a personal trip. The objective is to increase the awareness of the seriousness of tornadoes but to also learn about the effectiveness of having NOAA weather information available.

A traveler passing through the area did not witness these events. Many travelers knew the storm was being reported at that time through the NOAA weather radio and the news. One specific traveler was able to survive the storm on the Interstate 80 on May 5-6 while traveling west through Iowa and Nebraska headed to Colorado. Later the chaos of what happened in the area traveled was learned about. More and more news came out about this event in Kansas, Nebraska, and Iowa. After a few days the driver was routed back east on the Interstate 80, but was hearing about the size, and damage of the storm while passing east through Nebraska and Iowa. The interstate was not damaged and open during this event even though there was a report of damaged vehicles, and a truck blown off the road in Iowa during the storm previously. The traveler survived traveling west through the storm, and later survived going east through its aftermath. This traveler made it to two different destinations under disastrous conditions, without accident, and injury. Once arriving out at the final destination far from the area of the tornado he realized this was a national news story. People along the route taken, and on the east coast, as far east as Long Island, New York, where the trip's destination was, had heard about this severe tornado event. The traveler had doubts, considering there was suppose to be more communication to prevent disasters in the post 9/11 era, and post Hurricane Katrina era, the traveler was surprised to have ended up going through that size of a storm driving west, and surprised when sent through it's disaster area the second time going east. During the second trip there was even more of a surprise to be headed to the state of New York, knowing the traffic density there. It seemed dangerous then to be forced into that kind of weather, and aftermath, then heading through a very dense area in New York City, out to Long Island, NY. This trip still seems risky when thought about today in 2014. It also seems frustrating because there is little credit given to those surviving these types of work conditions. It is amazing to be forced into disasters repeatedly for work, surviving their obstacles. To top of those frustration travelers that survive might later get unsafe driving violations when not paying attention to the signs on the side of the road, being turned out to be unsafe when really they have survived driving through some of the biggest, and most dangerous weather events in the world. As the result, many travelers know that they get mostly negative credit for being unsafe, without getting any recognition to be safe when they were placed in a preventable situation like a disaster. It is not them that is unsafe even though they may fall into a speed trap later on. To this day in 2014 there is a traffic enforcement system that is unsafe because it allows the road to remain open, when they could be closed for a brief period of time.

The Greensburg, KA Tornado Predictability

NOAA's Larry Ruthi is a very knowledgeable source of information regarding weather forecasting/predictability in Kansas. The Greensburg tornado warning that went out May 4, 2007, was about a half hour before the tornado hit. Tornadoes are identified by details that lead NOAA to believe there is a tornado. With the warning for a specific tornado like that NOAA typically issues alerts 20 minutes to as much as 40 minutes before it hits a particular location. The size of the tornado can be a factor in the amount of lead-time, which is the amount of time there is a spotted tornado headed to a city that is being warned. For big tornadoes, the probability is very high that there will be a long warning for the event.

Crash Lane News believes the fact that a EF5 tornado compared to a EF3 gives a larger lead-time sometimes is a good thing in a way. The damage an EF5 causes will be much more threatening and affect a broader/wider area. In summary an EF5 will be more visible, resulting in more weather reports being made and more information. In the event it is night time the radar is going to be the best tool to help predict the path and lead-time of a tornado. A smaller tornado can be overlooked and can sneak its way through radar and other storm spotters, preventing the longer lead-time warnings while being just as dangerous.

A good discussion to start with is with the difficulty in the screening of which thunderstorms will end up as tornadoes. Severe thunderstorms are able to be predicted.

Ruthi emphasized the problem is predicting which ones will eventually be a tornado. The seasonal tornado can be the best way to try to predict which severe thunderstorms will turn into a tornado, but that is not enough either. In the particular case of something like Greensburg and knowing what the environment/situation looks like they will try to get a warning out before the tornado develops and touches down. In a large supercell opening environment they will try to get a warning out 10 or 15 minutes before there is any report of a tornado by spotters.

Another example of a huge and deadly tornado would be the Joplin tornado. There was a warning out for that super cone three years ago, about 25 minutes before the tornado formed. They typically base a warning on the conditions and observations of the character of a thunderstorm, and based on spotter reports, and any other conditions that they can incorporate into the warning process. Usually for a big tornado they will have it significantly tied and have a report out before anything is on the ground.

Travel Was Affected for a Couple of Days, May 4 and 5, across Kansas and Region

A traveler mentioned to NOAA they had been driving in Iowa, far north above Kansas where the tornado had hit on May 5. The traveler was crossing into Nebraska when the very end of the storm was seen. The warning on the radio repeated a message that there was an EF5 tornado on the ground in the area. This was a frightening message to get. Many travelers had been pulling off the road as a result of the warning and the weather. Visibility was bad, to the point that traffic on the interstate was slowed to 20 mph and then would go up to 40 mph. Many vehicles slowed due to the storm's wind and heavy rainfall. The storm was so intense, as a result some vehicles pulled over on the side of the interstate. This particular storm was a big concern for travel in the entire region at the time. Trips that were routed through Tornado Alley during this storm became a nightmare.

NOAA stated the thunderstorm that spawned the Greensburg tornado May 4, was responsible for creating another tornado that killed a sheriff's deputy. This occurred on Highway 50, up in Macksville, Stafford County. The storm system had multiple tornadoes touching down across the state of Kansas. A cyclic supercell will produce multiple tornadoes. The Sheriff drove into low visibility. He never saw the tornado as a result of the heavy rain and wind. His cruiser was blown off the road a quarter mile. He subsequently expired from his injuries. Crossing paths of a tornado while being unaware of the surroundings is a real danger. Traveling at night when we are not going to see signs of tornadoes and other hazardous things is something to try to avoid. We are dependent upon on the warnings that are put out. A traveler on the Interstate 80 in Nebraska May 5 and 6 heard about the devastation of the EF5 in Kansas, and knew he was lucky to have survived that size of a storm that made EF5 tornadoes two days in a row.

Know the Importance of Being Able to Receive Tornado Warnings

Travelers should carry a weather radio with them. Weather radios scan for a particular frequency depending on what alert service is in the area. Travelers are most likely to get a weather warning that way.

There are services that you are probably familiar with that will monitor a location's cell phones through GPS. The location information is matched with the weather alerts and then the company will send a customer a notification by phone or text. When customers move into an area covered with a warning polygon as a result of a tornado, an alert will be sent to the customer. The service provider will send a notification when you move out of the warning area. That is a very good way for a traveler to get useful information. When traveling through an unfamiliar area and where the county lines are unseen this service may also be very informative. The warnings are by county. Sometimes a traveler will not know what county he or she is in. This can be confusing when receiving a warning on the radio, so if a warning is heard they may not be able to have the awareness of the approximate location of a tornado threat. If they have a smartphone the GPS and alert are going to narrow and reduce a certain amount of confusion. This is a very beneficial thing the public should remember about the smartphone.

Storm Predictability

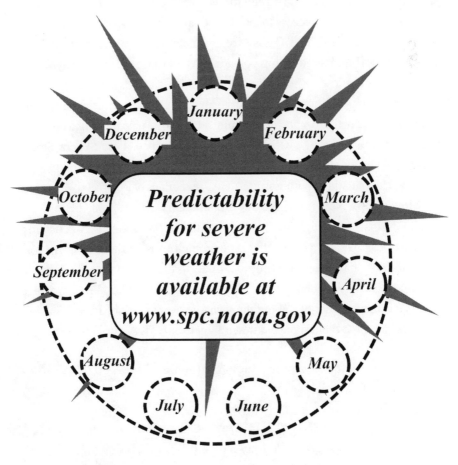

There are certain ways the public can identify if a possible tornado is coming ahead of time. The Storm Prediction Center out of Norman, OK, has a website available to the public at www.spc.noaa.gov. All of the NOAA weather offices have a link to the Storm Prediction Center convective outlooks. Convective outlooks provide an area that will most likely have severe thunderstorms and tornadoes. The outlook area gets a little bit better detailed when you get closer to the time of the event. The day 3, day 2, and day 1 before a storm are mentioned. The outlooks are very detailed. The storm prediction center will provide a multimedia briefing that will discuss the nature of the threat. Each of the forecast offices also do a multimedia briefing with the most detailed hazardous weather outlooks. The different NOAA weather offices are at weather.gov. Individual weather offices can be looked up to give more specifics for the area and the timing for the evolution of the convective event.

The public also has access to the watches and warnings. The warnings are available on our web pages. Those are available on the applications and the private vendors and the warning polygons. All of those options are available to start planning a week in advance based on hazardous weather outlooks from the storm prediction center. The storm prediction center at spc.noaa.gov is a really good place to start for planning a trip while also making a decision to avoid traveling through extreme weather in advance. Type SPC or Storm Prediction Center at a search engine, and it will send you to the right place.

Travelers should know about the NOAA examples of a convective outlook for May 3, 2007. Note this is the day 2 predictions which should be for May 5, 2007. This is actually the days before the big tornado in Greensburg, KA picture of what was expected. The amount of time that the storm was predicted may have been a few days similar to that of the tornado down in the southeastern states November 2006. Below is the link to the main page on the convective outlooks about the tornadic event that occurred May 4-5, 2007. In this time the famously known Greensburg, KA, tornado occurred.

http://www.spc.noaa.gov/products/outlook/archive/2007/day1otlk_ 20070503_0100.html

May 3, 2007 0100 UTC Day 1 Convective Outlook
Updated: Thu May 3 00:40:19 UTC 2007

Probabilistic to Categorical Outlook Conversion Table (Effective Feb 14, 2006).

Categorical Graphic

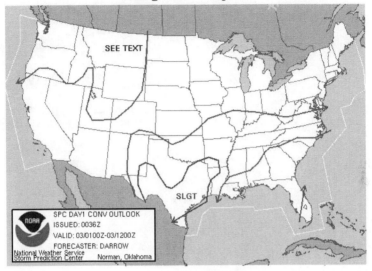

From www.noaa.gov Public Domain

Probabilistic Tornado Graphic

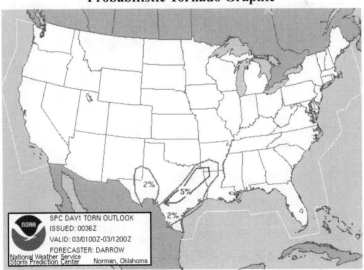

From www.noaa.gov Public Domain

Probabilistic Damaging Wind Graphic

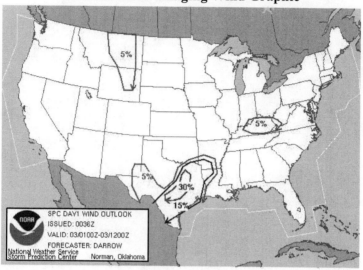

Public Domain

Probabilistic Large Hail Graphic

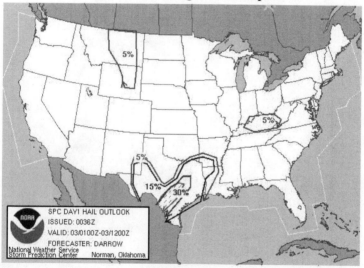

Public Domain

SPC AC 030036

DAY 1 CONVECTIVE OUTLOOK
NWS STORM PREDICTION CENTER NORMAN OK
0736 PM CDT WED MAY 02 2007

VALID 030100Z - 031200Z

...THERE IS A SLGT RISK OF SVR TSTMS ACROSS MUCH OF TX...

...TEXAS..

WELL ORGANIZED...LONG LIVED MCS CONTINUES ITS PROGRESSION ACROSS NCNTRL TX THIS EVENING. FORWARD PROPAGATION IS ROUGHLY 35-40 KT WHICH PLACES LEADING EDGE OF STRONGEST ACTIVITY NEAR THE LA/TX BORDER BY 03Z. THERE IS SOME QUESTION WHETHER ITS SPEED WILL BE MAINTAINED OR BEGIN TO SLOW SOMEWHAT AS DIURNAL INFLUENCES BEGIN TO WEAKEN INSTABILITY DOWNSTREAM. ONE THING IN ITS FAVOR FOR CONTINUING DOWNSTREAM INTO THE ARKLATEX IS THE EXPANSIVE PRECIPITATION SHIELD AND LOCAL COLD POOL IN ITS WAKE. DAMAGING WINDS AND LARGE HAIL SHOULD ACCOMPANY THIS MCS.. ESPECIALLY ALONG THE LEADING EDGE INTO THE MID-LATE EVENING HOURS.

FARTHER SOUTHWEST...AIRMASS IS QUITE UNSTABLE ACROSS THE HILL COUNTY INTO NERN MEXICO. ALTHOUGH DRT IS UNCAPPED WITH ROUGHLY 3000 J/KG...DOWNSTREAM SOUNDING AT CRP CLEARLY DISPLAYS A LAYER OF INHIBITION THAT SHOULD LIMIT SRN EXTENT OF DEVELOPMENT UNTIL DEEP LAYER FLOW BEGINS TO VEER LATE IN THE PERIOD. LATEST THINKING IS BOW-TYPE FEATURE OVER BURNET/ BLANCO COUNTIES WNW OF AUSTIN METRO AREA WILL RACE NEWD ALONG TRAILING BOUNDARY FROM NCNTRL TX MCS.

THIS FEATURE WILL PRODUCE DAMAGING WINDS AND POSSIBLY VERY LARGE HAIL. LARGE HAIL MAY ALSO ACCOMPANY MORE ISOLATED SUPERCELLS FARTHER SW INTO THE VALLEY REGION...ALONG WITH PERHAPS A TORNADO.

ONGOING THUNDERSTORM ACTIVITY BENEATH THE UPPER TROUGH ACROSS SERN NM INTO WEST TX WILL GRADUALLY WEAKEN WITH LOSS OF DAYTIME HEATING THIS EVENING. UNTIL THEN...STRONG STORMS SHOULD PROPAGATE SEWD WITH A THREAT OF MAINLY LARGE HAIL.

...NRN HIGH PLAINS..

EXIT REGION OF UPPER JET AXIS WILL SHIFT EAST ACROSS THE NRN ROCKIES TOWARD THE NRN HIGH PLAINS LATER TONIGHT. THIS LARGE SCALE SUPPORT WILL LIKELY MAINTAIN DEEP CONVECTIVE THREAT ACROSS PORTIONS OF MT INTO WY. IN THE SHORT TERM...THUNDERSTORMS THAT DEVELOPED OFF THE HIGHER TERRAIN EARLY THIS AFTERNOON HAVE PROGRESSED RAPIDLY TOWARD THE ALBERTA/SASKATCHEWAN/MT BORDER...WITH OTHER ISOLATED STRONG STORMS NOW INTO SERN MT AND NERN WY. UNTIL BOUNDARY LAYER LAPSE RATES WEAKEN OVER THIS REGION IT APPEARS GUSTY WINDS AND SOME HAIL MAY BE OBSERVED.

...KY...

CONVECTION THAT DEVELOPED ALONG E-W FRONTAL BOUNDARY FROM KY INTO VA IS IN THE PROCESS OF WEAKENING THIS EVENING. MORE ORGANIZED CLUSTERS OVER KY COULD LINGER FOR A FEW HOURS POSING A THREAT FOR MARGINALLY SEVERE WIND AND SMALL HAIL BEFORE INSTABILITY IS OVERTURNED.

http://www.spc.noaa.gov/cgi-bin-spc/getac1.pl

May 3, 2007 0800 UTC Day 2 Convective Outlook
Updated: Thu May 3 05:59:38 UTC 2007

Probabilistic to Categorical Outlook Conversion Table (Effective Feb 14, 2006).

Categorical Graphic

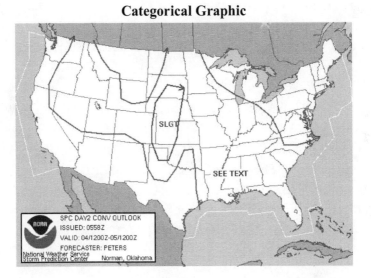

Probabilistic Graphic

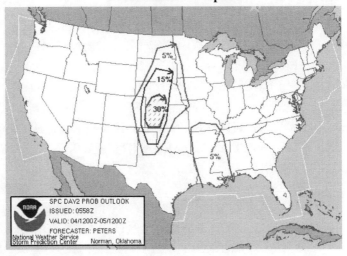

SPC AC 0305581

DAY 2 CONVECTIVE OUTLOOK
NWS STORM PREDICTION CENTER NORMAN OK
1258 AM CDT THU MAY 03 2007

VALID 041200Z - 051200Z

...THERE IS A SLGT RISK OF SVR TSTMS ACROSS THE CENTRAL PLAINS..
...CENTRAL PLAINS..
PACIFIC SHORT WAVE TROUGH EXPECTED TO DIG SE TOWARD THE GREAT BASIN SHOULD EVOLVE INTO CLOSED LOW BY 12Z SATURDAY OVER UT IN BASE OF WRN U.S. LONGWAVE TROUGH. A LEAD SHORT WAVE TROUGH/SPEED MAX PROGGED TO BE OVER THE FOUR CORNERS REGION AT 12Z FRIDAY WILL MOVE NEWD INTO THE CENTRAL PLAINS BY LATE FRIDAY AFTERNOON/EARLY EVENING...AND THEN TRACK NWD TO THE NRN PLAINS FRIDAY NIGHT.

MODELS CONTINUE TO SUGGEST DRY LINE MIXING EWD INTO CENTRAL PARTS OF THE PLAINS FRIDAY AFTERNOON. HOWEVER...GIVEN LIKELIHOOD FOR MID/UPPER LEVEL FLOW ACROSS THE PLAINS TO BECOME MERIDIONAL BY LATE IN FORECAST PERIOD ALONG ERN PERIPHERY OF WRN STATES TROUGH...DRY LINE SHOULD NOT MIX TOO FAR EWD OF THE HIGH PLAINS. SURFACE LOW OVER SERN CO IS EXPECTED TO DEEPEN THROUGH THE PERIOD WITH APPROACH OF FOUR CORNERS MID LEVEL IMPULSE...AND TRACK NNE TOWARD NERN CO/NWRN KS.

AT 12Z FRIDAY...A CLUSTER OF TSTMS IS EXPECTED TO BE ONGOING ACROSS PARTS OF WRN NEB IN WAA REGIME ALONG NOSE OF SLY LLJ. THIS ACTIVITY WILL TEND TO DIMINISH IN INTENSITY FRIDAY MORNING AS THE NOCTURNAL LLJ WEAKENS. SLY LOW LEVEL FLOW EAST OF THE DRY LINE WILL

ADVECT MOISTURE NWD WITH SURFACE DEWPOINTS IN THE MID 60S LIKELY REACHING THE KS/NEB BORDER BY LATE FRIDAY AFTERNOON WITH UPPER 60S TO THE OK/KS BORDER. PLUME OF STEEP LAPSE RATES EXTENDING EWD ATOP THE MOISTURE RETURN IS PROGGED TO RESULT IN A MODERATE TO VERY UNSTABLE AIR MASS.

SURFACE HEATING AND INCREASING ASCENT SPREADING NEWD WITH FOUR CORNERS IMPULSE SHOULD WEAKEN THE CAP OVER THE PLAINS FOR TSTM DEVELOPMENT ALONG THE DRY LINE IN WRN KS BY MID-LATE FRIDAY AFTERNOON. ADDITIONAL DEVELOPMENT WILL BE POSSIBLE NNEWD ALONG ANOTHER BOUNDARY EXTENDING INTO CENTRAL NEB...AND ALSO SWD ALONG DRY LINE INTO OK/TX PANHANDLES. DEEP LAYER SHEAR VECTORS CROSSING THE DRY LINE FROM WRN KS TO TX PANHANDLE WILL FAVOR SUPERCELLS.. WHILE FARTHER N INTO CENTRAL NEB...SHEAR VECTORS ORIENTED ALONG THAT BOUNDARY WILL TEND TO RESULT IN LINE SEGMENTS. TORNADOES AND VERY LARGE HAIL WILL BE POSSIBLE...ESPECIALLY ACROSS WRN KS. A CLUSTER OF TSTMS..POTENTIAL MCS DEVELOPMENT...IS EXPECTED FRIDAY NIGHT ACROSS THE CENTRAL PLAINS AS THE LLJ RE-STRENGTHENS.

...OZARKS/LOWER MS AND TN VALLEYS TO CENTRAL GULF COAST STATES..
MODELS ARE IN GENERAL AGREEMENT INDICATING SRN STREAM SHORT WAVE TROUGH...NOW LOCATED OVER THE SRN HIGH PLAINS OF W TX...WILL DE-AMPLIFY ON FRIDAY ACROSS THE LOWER/MID MS VALLEY. DEEP LAYER ASCENT AHEAD OF THIS WEAKENING AND SLOW MOVING TROUGH AND IN WEAKLY CAPPED MOIST AIR MASS IS EXPECTED TO PROMOTE TSTM DEVELOPMENT ON FRIDAY FROM THE LA/MS COAST NWD TO THE MID MS/OH VALLEYS.

ALTHOUGH INSTABILITY SHOULD BE GENERALLY WEAK ACROSS MUCH OF THIS REGION DUE TO WEAK LAPSE RATES..30 KT OF NWLY MID LEVEL FLOW ALONG WRN EXTENT OF DE-AMPLIFYING TROUGH IS EXPECTED TO RESULT IN EFFECTIVE BULK SHEAR /AROUND 30 KT/. THIS MAY SUPPORT A FEW SEVERE STORMS PRIMARILY FROM SRN MO SSEWD THROUGH THE LOWER MS VALLEY.

..PETERS. 05/03/2007

CLICK TO GET WUUS02 PTSDY2 PRODUCT

NOTE: THE NEXT DAY 2 OUTLOOK IS SCHEDULED BY 1730Z

Below shows the day after the 4–5 May 2007 Tornado event.

http://www.spc.noaa.gov/products/outlook/archive/2007/day3otlk_20070503_1100.html

Categorical Graphic

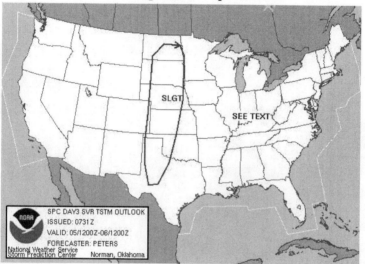

Probabilistic Graphic

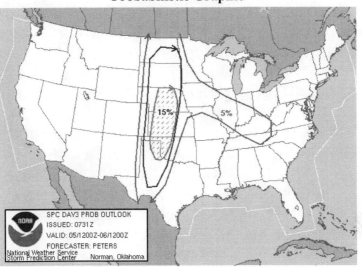

SPC AC 030731

DAY 3 CONVECTIVE OUTLOOK
NWS STORM PREDICTION CENTER NORMAN OK
0231 AM CDT THU MAY 03 2007

VALID 051200Z - 061200Z

...THERE IS A SLGT RISK OF SVR TSTMS ACROSS THE PLAINS
STATES..

...PLAINS STATES..
MODELS ARE IN GENERAL AGREEMENT DURING DAY 3
FORECAST PERIOD INDICATING LITTLE EWD MOVEMENT OF
WRN STATES LONGWAVE TROUGH AS DOWNSTREAM RIDGE
STRENGTHENS AND BUILDS NWD ALONG THE MS RIVER
VALLEY AND ACROSS THE GREAT LAKES REGION TO HUDSON
BAY. A SHORT WAVE TROUGH IS EXPECTED TO TRACK NNEWD
ACROSS THE CENTRAL PLAINS TO THE NRN PLAINS AND
ADJACENT PORTION OF SRN CANADA ON SATURDAY/ SATURDAY
NIGHT IN NEARLY MERIDIONAL MID/UPPER LEVEL FLOW. IN

THE LOW LEVELS..A SSW-NNE ORIENTED SURFACE BOUNDARY IS EXPECTED TO EXTEND FROM THE SRN HIGH PLAINS TO THE CENTRAL DAKOTAS AND WILL BE THE PRIMARY FOCUS FOR TSTM DEVELOPMENT ON SATURDAY.

SLY LOW LEVEL WINDS WILL MAINTAIN MOISTURE RETURN ACROSS THE CENTRAL U.S. ALONG/E OF SURFACE TROUGH/ DRY LINE...WITH SURFACE DEWPOINTS IN THE MID-UPPER 60S EXPECTED TO REACH NWD INTO PARTS OF THE DAKOTAS AND WRN/SRN MN SATURDAY AFTERNOON. STEEP MID LEVEL LAPSE RATES EXPECTED ACROSS THE PLAINS STATES ATOP THE RICH LOW LEVEL MOISTURE WILL RESULT IN A VERY UNSTABLE AIR MASS.. ESPECIALLY FROM NEB/KS SWD ALONG/E OF DRY LINE WHERE SURFACE HEATING WILL BE GREATEST.

TSTMS SHOULD BE ONGOING AT 12Z SATURDAY ACROSS PARTS OF NEB/SD IN WAA REGIME ALONG NOSE OF LLJ. NEW TSTM INITIATION IS EXPECTED ALONG THE EXTENT OF THE SURFACE TROUGH FROM THE DAKOTAS SWD TO THE TX PANHANDLE SATURDAY AFTERNOON. A BAND OF SSWLY MID LEVEL WINDS AT 50-70 KT EXTENDING SSW-NNE ACROSS THE PLAINS STATES WILL RESULT IN 40-50 KT OF DEEP LAYER SHEAR FOR ORGANIZED STORMS.

THE GREATEST POTENTIAL FOR SIGNIFICANT SEVERE INCLUDING VERY LARGE HAIL AND TORNADOES SHOULD BE LOCATED FROM CENTRAL PARTS OF NEB/KS INTO WRN OK/TX PANHANDLE WHERE GREATEST INSTABILITY WILL COEXIST WITH STRONG DEEP LAYER SHEAR CROSSING THE SURFACE BOUNDARY.

...IA SEWD THROUGH LOWER OH VALLEY TO KY/ERN TN... MODELS INDICATE TSTM DEVELOPMENT IS POSSIBLE ALONG WARM FRONT EXPECTED TO EXTEND SEWD FROM IA THROUGH CENTRAL IL TO KY/ERN TN. MODERATE INSTABILITY SHOULD

DEVELOP ALONG THE IA/IL PORTION OF THE WARM FRONT WHILE INSTABILITY SHOULD TEND TO DECREASE WITH SEWD EXTENT INTO KY/TN. EFFECTIVE BULK SHEAR VALUES ALONG THE WARM FRONT SUGGEST POTENTIAL FOR ORGANIZED STORMS. HOWEVER...GIVEN LACK OF DISCERNABLE MID LEVEL FEATURE FOCUSING CONVECTIVE DEVELOPMENT... THIS OUTLOOK WILL INTRODUCE LOW SEVERE PROBABILITIES ALONG EXTENT OF WARM FRONT.

NOAA's Description on How Greensburg, Kansas, Tornado Affected Travel

It is obvious that the EF5 tornado weather caused disasters affecting travel. The Greensburg, KA, tornado is a good example of how a large tornado affected travel in a rural area and a small city. Each tornado is going to impact an area differently. Emergency management at the federal, state, and local level worked like it was supposed to.

There was debris blown from the tornado across the highway 54, closing it down. The highway was closed for a number of days after the storm. Traffic through Greensburg was routed west of town to the north around where the path of the tornado had caused damage and created debris roadblocks. The main road through Greensburg was closed for a few weeks while debris removal occurred.

While these roads were closed the access to the area was also closed, so the area could be searched for survivors while preventing people from going back into the area and causing the possible need for them to be rescued if they became trapped or stuck under debris. For about two to three days after the tornado hit, there were the search and rescues taking place. The emergency management personnel of the town were managing access to the public and residents. This brought some control and knowledge as to if everyone missing has been accounted for, while preventing further issues. Emergency responders were shutting everything down and preventing anyone from getting into or out of the area so that the search and rescues were done thoroughly.

NOAA also mentioned the city of Greensburg after the storm did not have a problem with looters. This part of the world has a very dim view of the protection of looters. There is nothing to be aware of specifically in that event.

The disaster relief and assistance also moved into the city. Some organizations such as the Red Cross, Salvation Army, local churches, and other charity organizations helped with the recovery. These groups also helped the rebuilding process. FEMA and other federal agencies provided assistance.

A FEMA report also went into detail about the switching of scales titled, *Tornado Damage Investigation Greensburg, Kansas 1699 DR-KS October 12 2007.*

The purpose of this report is two-fold: to provide a preliminary "ground-truth" of the new Enhanced Fujita (EF) Scale wind speed classification system1 and to document the damage caused by the tornado. The tornado that struck Greensburg was one of the first tornado occurrences since the EF Scale was developed and thus provided an opportunity to compare the wind speeds derived through use of the EF Scale (observed damage) with wind speed calculated through material failure analysis. The EF Scale uses observed Degrees of Damage (DOD) to derive wind speed ranges, which are then used to classify tornadoes.

More about tornado scales are available at www.spc.noaa.gov/efscale/.

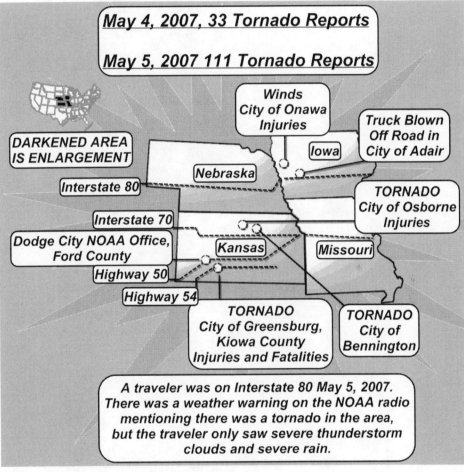

May 4, 2007, 33 Tornado Reports

May 5, 2007 111 Tornado Reports

DARKENED AREA IS ENLARGEMENT

Interstate 80

Interstate 70

Dodge City NOAA Office, Ford County

Highway 50

Highway 54

Winds City of Onawa Injuries

Truck Blown Off Road in City of Adair

Iowa

Nebraska

TORNADO City of Osborne Injuries

Kansas

Missouri

TORNADO City of Greensburg, Kiowa County Injuries and Fatalities

TORNADO City of Bennington

A traveler was on Interstate 80 May 5, 2007. There was a weather warning on the NOAA radio mentioning there was a tornado in the area, but the traveler only saw severe thunderstorm clouds and severe rain.

Property of *Crash Lane News*

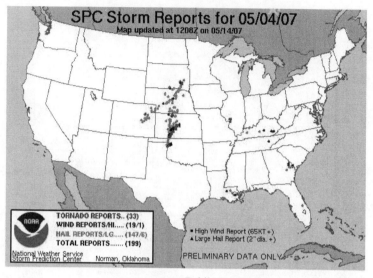

www.noaa.gov. Public Domain.

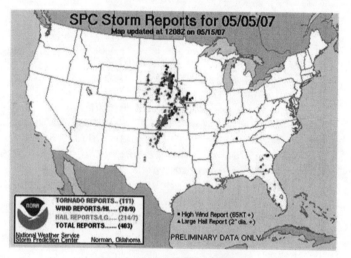

www.noaa.gov. Public Domain.

The above map shows the area in the United States where this storm occurred on May 4, 2007. The upper left-hand corner shows the region the storm affected travel due to low visibility. The below map is the state of Kansas and some of the significant events that occurred according to NOAA.

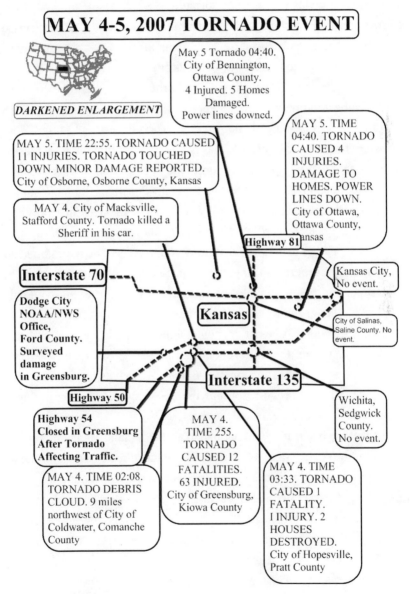

MAY 4-5, 2007 TORNADO EVENT

DARKENED ENLARGEMENT

May 5 Tornado 04:40. City of Bennington, Ottawa County. 4 Injured. 5 Homes Damaged. Power lines downed.

MAY 5. TIME 04:40. TORNADO CAUSED 4 INJURIES. DAMAGE TO HOMES. POWER LINES DOWN. City of Ottawa, Ottawa County, Kansas

MAY 5. TIME 22:55. TORNADO CAUSED 11 INJURIES. TORNADO TOUCHED DOWN. MINOR DAMAGE REPORTED. City of Osborne, Osborne County, Kansas

MAY 4. City of Macksville, Stafford County. Tornado killed a Sheriff in his car.

Highway 81

Interstate 70

Kansas City, No event.

Dodge City NOAA/NWS Office, Ford County. Surveyed damage in Greensburg.

Kansas

City of Salinas, Saline County. No event.

Interstate 135

Highway 50

Wichita, Sedgwick County. No event.

Highway 54 Closed in Greensburg After Tornado Affecting Traffic.

MAY 4. TIME 255. TORNADO CAUSED 12 FATALITIES. 63 INJURED. City of Greensburg, Kiowa County

MAY 4. TIME 03:33. TORNADO CAUSED 1 FATALITY. 1 INJURY. 2 HOUSES DESTROYED. City of Hopesville, Pratt County

MAY 4. TIME 02:08. TORNADO DEBRIS CLOUD. 9 miles northwest of City of Coldwater, Comanche County

NOAA's Weather Forecast Continuity

There are challenges any local area faces when already suffering the damage from a disaster. One can be for a response to have the ability to continue its repairs. Another challenge is to have NOAA make sure to warn the area if there is another repeated weather threat in the days after the storm. There was the El Reno tornado in 2013. Then some days later the same area had another tornado warning and a tornado. That surprised everyone on the outside, because Oklahoma already had a huge tornado and now all of a sudden there was another one.

The day after the Greensburg tornado the area had another round of severe weather outbreaks. There was lots of hail, and while NOAA was surveying the Greensburg damage they observed a tornado touch down just west of the city. This tornado was not as threatening, but it did destroy a barn. Their warning operations continued because the threat continued. After the Greensburg event, they had a team out doing damage surveys and had the normal forecast warning team back in the office providing the warning service regardless to the fact there was a tornado disaster. Every day's weather is new and different. NOAA has to be maintained and alert to the atmosphere as things develop. Everybody was very busy, put in overtime, and put a whole lot of extra effort into surveying while also keeping watch over the weather. There were all kinds of press interviews, and all kinds of other types of excitement about the big tornado outbreak. NOAA tried to keep up with everything that had already happened with the tremendous storm system and its damage, as well as for future storms. They managed our human resources the best they could, keeping up on weather verifications.

With all the bad things that happened as the damage, injuries, fatalities, and other issues there was a large amount of data collected about tornadoes. The overall destruction caused by severe weather, and tornadoes, is always unfortunate. Anyone that survives an EF5 tornado storm is lucky to have survived. On the positive side, the data collected was good and can help predict and add to the other information about tornadoes in Kansas.

NOAA doesn't sit back and let things go once there is a disastrous severe weather event. During the cleanup there was a potential threat of more subsequent weather. There was a meteorologist to help onsite for briefings and provide help to the emergency management people involved in operations. The service they provided for the cleanup operation went on for several weeks after the tornado. The Dodge City NOAA/National Weather Service's continuity of providing weather warnings was excellent. A disastrous aftermath can be shocking and relief is sometimes forgotten about. This offices ability to watch for another severe weather tornadic event provided a more comprehensive way to manage a disaster and its aftermath.

Building Codes

The relief and the response were ongoing for a long time. With the large amount of damage, injuries, and fatalities, as a result of the storm there can be some suggestions made into having a building code require structures to have a safe room.

NOAA mentioned the building codes that are current now are the same that have been in place for a while. There has not been much change or tightening to the building codes in the local city area after Greensburg, KA. After the 1999 tornadoes, there was not much change in regard to building codes and structural requirements. There were a number of buildings reconstructed from subsequent damage from the 1999 tornadoes. One challenge that occurred at that time was rebuilding without using the right code and requirements. There were mistakes that were made. Builders cut corners and sometimes make honest mistakes when not following the codes that exist.

For the May 5, 2007, tornado rebuilding process the city tried to go with a green building design, good for the environment, while conserving energy. These houses are very secure and are well above code requirements. There has not been the tightening of codes because there is an event like this. It is a very isolated event in a way. The existing codes adequately cover most of what happens. There are tornadoes that will destroy everything unless you have a concrete reinforced bunker. In that scenario where a tornado hits a house directly, that is about the only thing that will survive. The current buildings are as good as possible, but the fact of a threat from tornadoes remains, which can lead someone to build with concrete reinforcing materials.

Part of that problem in having all homes built out of solid concrete is the cost. It costs more to build a bank vault type of house than it does to build a regular 2X4 wood construction house. Building materials required for that safe room the size of a house design would be a big price. A home does have the option to build one concrete reinforced safe room, which would be much lower on the budget scale. A safe room is encouraged and most of the people back in Greensburg have a safe room built into their house, or have an outside safe room in the ground away from the gas, electric, and flammable materials.

There are a number of companies that offer safe rooms that are a steel structure buried into the ground. These are very good storm shelters. They are very high quality, and are not terribly expensive for the safety and security they provide. They are also a very good buy and investment, and certainly have a widespread use in areas hit by tornadoes.

Traffic Enforcement in a Tornado

Travel regulations put in place by the local, state, and federal traffic enforcers always place the driver at the center of the cause of an accident or a violation. With last year's El Reno tornado accident involving Tim Samaras, it looked like his death was not the normal outcome for storm chasing activity. Most storm chasers distance themselves enough from the storm and are safe. With his death, there is extra awareness as to what safety precautions are required when traveling. Storm chasers are following many safety regulations, but they are putting themselves out in the storm's hazards to study these events. It is heroic in a way but can also be seen as public endangerment and endangering themselves when the outcome is fatal. Law enforcement is unable to control weather and the disaster area very well when there is a big tornado touching down. Based on that incident law enforcement's ability to close roads where a tornado is passing though is very limited. There are no traffic control officers available to follow tornado disasters close enough while also keeping themselves alive as well as preventing the public from becoming injured; it is all too spontaneous and unpredictable. When it comes to disasters there may also be a decision from law enforcement to avoid becoming a casualty of the storm, reasoning an issue of officer safety is at hand. The main point is handing out tickets may not be safe while in an area where a tornado is blowing, and law enforcement knows that. This is something that the public should also know in that law enforcement might not be trying to be in the area of the path of the storm.

NOAA stated if anybody violated the traffic laws, such as blocking emergency vehicles, law enforcement can take action. Storm chasers have clogged the roads and made it difficult for emergency vehicles to get where they need to go. There are some chasers who make it difficult and those people have been ticketed. And there are a number of law enforcement agencies out there that have a very dim view of chasers because of the irresponsible actions of a few. There are different classes of chasers. There are really good ones that share information about the weather that they collect. And then there are others that are out there for the adrenaline rush and care nothing about the welfare of the people they are endangering, trying to get the pictures that they can sell. Those people are a problem for the law enforcement community, and the health and safety of the communities that they are traveling through. There are two different kinds of storm chasers. A traffic ticket is one way to deal with them.

Crash Lane News believes that if a ticket is going to save a life many would agree with it being written. Unfortunately, the timing of a ticket at the right place and time when it actually prevents an accident is a hard reality. It is difficult to see the benefit of traffic tickets when there are accidents anyway and when there are accidents because the roads are not closed in severe weather. Accidents continually happen anyway. In many areas where there is a strong enforcement presence alternatives to handing out tickets are recommended to increase public safety. Storm chasers and the rest of the public have to use good judgment that is going to protect them and avoid unsafe driving violations.

When someone does not know there is going to be a storm and they are not chasing it and they are just traveling through, it would appear to be frustrating to get ticketed at that time. Violations and tickets given out in a crisis like severe weather, and tornadoes, would seem excessive and cause further questions about safety. Another problem is when someone ends up in the storm and law enforcement and the Department of Transportation did not close the roads, or their road condition warnings were not being communicated.

NOAA mentioned if that kind of thing happens, it is not under their control. It is an act of God at that point. Law enforcement cannot ticket a traveler for not being intimately aware of their surroundings. If someone violates a traffic law or violates a command from a traffic management officer, no one is going to get ticketed if they just get blown off the road.

NOAA encourages people to subscribe to a private service or carry a weather radio that gets NOAA warnings along for the trip. That is probably the best way to know where the warnings are. NOAA offers training sessions for anyone who wants to learn about the formation of clouds that they can watch and get a feel of what the weather is doing. One thing to watch is when a thunderstorm appears it could go tornadic. There are indications that can be taught of what formations to be on the lookout for. The weather training service offers spotter training sessions in each one of our counties. Most offices in the Central Plains do provide spotter training sessions.

Tim Samaras and Storm Chasing

Property of *Crash Lane News*

In the *National Geographic* magazine of November 2013 the front page has the storm mentioned from last May 2013 in Oklahoma in El Reno. The cover is with a picture of the storm chaser Tim Samaras covering a past tornado storm from a few years ago prior to 2013. Tim Samaras died while chasing the El Reno tornado when his car was crumpled up from the wind blowing it off the road, and while blowing debris made contact with it at speeds of over a couple hundred miles an hour and more. The car looked like a little ball of white tinfoil and the make and model was unrecognizable without the emblems. Tim Samaras was well known in popular culture, known by many meteorologists and the public where he traveled to collect data about the storms that affected their areas. He was particularly famous in a role on the Discovery Channel's *Storm Chasers* program starting up in 2008. That was a cable television program that covered some storm chasing activities in Tornado Alley. In addition Tim Samaras worked on National Geographic's *Disaster Lab*, 2008, and *Master of Disaster*, 2009, and was a National Geographic Grantee. Tim Samaras also authored a book, *Tornado Hunter: Getting Inside the Most Violent Storms on Earth, 2009.*

Now that Tim Samaras has passed there may be some additional concern regarding traveling in the storm chasing community and also by the public following these programs. These programs sell because there is a public demand about the topic of weather due to the risk of living in areas that may be affected by severe weather.

The public also gets curious about the more tragic stories like this, where there is a fatality and may want to know more about him, such as what was he like? Was he sometimes an extreme storm chaser by putting himself in danger? Or do you think the storm got lucky? NOAA mentions Tim was a very good chaser and very competent. Tim could find tornadoes while also not putting himself in danger. He was not one of the more extreme chasers that are sometimes shown on television stations. Tim ended up being at the wrong place at the wrong time, making an unfortunate mistake that was fatal.

This tragedy can also be a life lesson learned by those who live and travel near tornadoes. NOAA encourages people not to ride out tornadoes inside their vehicles. For instance, Tim should have put himself in a safer location than where he was. Part of the problem may have been the traffic around the metropolitan area. That was in the evening when there was a high density level of traffic on the I40 in Oklahoma City, OK. Tim may have gotten caught in that. As a result of traffic, the vehicle could not get away from the tornado. When a traveler gets caught in a situation like that there is no good solution; it is too late. The preventive step if there were a next time would have been not to have been chasing the storm from an angle where the tornado could end of cutting off a safety route.

The best preventive solution is to track the tornado from the behind. Unfortunately, many chasers get caught in the path of the storm after dropping their probes along the predicted path of the tornado right before it arrives in that location. On the high plains on the open roads, chasers can track a tornado from the rear but sometimes are trying to probe the path.

If someone is caught in the path of the storm without an exit, the recommendation from NOAA is to get out of the vehicle in a low-lying area, in a ditch or culvert. A low area will provide some protection, as opposed to getting hit head on in a vehicle while stuck in traffic. A reality check to this suggestion is if someone is in a shallow ditch they may still get hit by debris, so the ditch should be of some depth. Another problem when being out of the shelter of the car and in a low spot on the ground is the risk of getting hit by large hail. There is golf ball size hail that may also be blowing at wind speeds about 100 miles an hour. This hail can cause damage, injuries, and even fatalities. There is also a potential for flash flooding when in a low lying area. There was flash flooding subsequently for that El Reno tornado. In the scenario of exiting a vehicle to seek shelter in a low area as a culvert, someone could have drowned from flooding. As a result of the risk of the weather in a low lying area out of a vehicle, it can be seen that there was not really a good place to go that particular day and for other tornadoes. A risk is being killed by one of the threats posed by severe weather like tornadoes that may be occurring aside from the threat of getting killed by the tornado's wind speed and debris. In summary, if someone is caught in traffic and unable to go anywhere and if there are no structures nearby, take shelter in a ditch or culvert, so as much wind will pass over. There is still a recognizable safety risk there. It is also not a good solution if being in there is avoidable. Seek a storm shelter ahead of time and make use of weather updates. The chances a person has come in contact with a tornado like that one is extremely low and can also be avoided through the news reports, making the chances even lower.

The challenge is there is a certain fear that exists. People that are in the middle of a trip are too scared to get out of their vehicles. They also don't want to get wet or muddy and would rather risk staying inside the vehicle's protective shell. Travelers do not want to go down into a ditch but when it comes to survival they should just do it if you absolutely get caught in traffic and something really bad happens. It is kind of a toss-up. You have to pick your chances in your vehicle, knowing you and it might be blown away, and then crushed. Take shelter in a nearby ditch or any kind of a structure. You are better off there than being inside your vehicle.

It sounded like Tim was trying to probe the storm with equipment. The public follows these chasers out of a curiosity as to the events and data they collect but also for some of the technologies that are collecting information about tornadoes. The movie named *Twister* had a story line that included the chasing and the probing of a tornado similar to some of the current shows out there about tornadoes. Some chasers have probes that seem more believable and collect more data now. The little probes they set out in *Twister* are very much Hollywood. Tim set out turtle probes, which were sensors that he would place in the path of the tornado on the road. There was at least one he was able to get probes into the circulation of the tornado. He would get information from the probe in the center of the tornado. It had a video camera that would look up inside the funnel, and a side camera that would watch the debris flying around. That same turtle probe survived the tornado, and it is a really neat video. Tim was really good with media. He was also doing lightning research. Really good high quality stuff. NOAA will miss Tim in the scientific world. His death in 2013 was shocking. It is too bad he got a little too close to the storm; he was out of luck.

Comprehensive Summary

Some major points to remember and summarize is that there are ways a traveler can try to predict the weather tornadoes may be in.

One suggested solution is to follow the severe weather predictions by NOAA at the storm prediction center, www.spc.noaa.gov. That might be one of the more important things mentioned to add to a trip's plan. Another is to have a weather radio to get warnings while traveling, and also to have the Smartphone Wireless Emergency Alerts.

Another problem is the fact of how dangerous it is to travel through Tornado Alley during April, May, and June. If there is a warning take notice of it and make changes in order to avoid becoming a statistic. Some states known to have weather during that time include Texas, Oklahoma, Kansas, Nebraska, Iowa, Missouri, Arkansas, and additional states from the surrounding region. One of the most dangerous times of the year to travel through Kansas is tornado season because there are also many severe storm systems that can reduce visibility. Another dangerous time in Kansas is the winter months because of the icy roads and a blizzard's poor visibility.

Traveling through Tornado Alley may occur for business and may not be able to be avoided. The news about the storm chasers becoming a part of the storms' fatalities should be an additional warning and reason to drive defensively while in poor conditions. The chance of seeing a storm and then also driving along storm chasers is very low, unless a company is based out of the state in Tornado Alley. With the yearly weather storms the chance a traveler runs into an EF5 is unrealistic. A traveler should know that it is a very low chance they will ever be traveling in that kind of weather and hopefully will be able to avoid a trip or be more prepared for it by following the weather forecast. Also note that the predictability of a tornado is still being researched and tornadoes are still considered unpredictable, while the severe thunderstorms that cause a tornado are studied more and watched with new technologies.

9

Interview with the Boston/Taunton NWS/NOAA Office About the Weather and Travel in Massachusetts/ New England, Connecticut, and the North Eastern United States

Massachusetts

Property of *Crash Lane News*

National Weather Service – Boston/ Taunton, Massachusetts Interview

Massachusetts faces natural disasters from the weather like all the United States, making an interview with NOAA very informative for a traveler. An interview with Warning Coordination Meteorologist Glenn Field is included. Knowing the point of view of a professional weather forecaster like Glenn provides some good solutions that may help travel in Massachusetts. These solutions can also help in other surrounding states in the New England and the Northeast region, like New York. There is also some current information about the latest Smartphone Wireless Emergency Alert warnings and some reasons why they have become a necessity to improve traveling. Smartphone users have the opportunity to have a higher level of awareness for where they are located. A traveler should also know there are ways to schedule a trip to avoid bad weather, and there are suggestions about predictability of tornadoes, hurricanes, and blizzards, included in the following report.

Hurricanes that threaten New England can be spotted many days in advance up to and over a week. The last hurricane that officially hit New England was Hurricane Bob back in 1991. New England has not been hit directly by a hurricane in 22 years. There have been tropical storms that have been pretty bad as Irene. And recently Hurricane Sandy sideswiped the area. Sandy mostly went into New York and New Jersey. Sandy was not even a hurricane technically when it arrived because it had weakened.

The last major hurricane that hit was in 1954 Hurricane Carol. That was a category 3. The average return period/time for major hurricanes is 59 years. Coincidentally it has been 59 years. Right now is right at the average for a major hurricane. It does not mean that New England is going to get hit this year or the year after, but that average return period of a major hurricane could occur sometime soon.

About the hurricane image: Some major storms sometimes have a star shape in the center of the system, which is why it is added here. Not many symbols that represent a hurricane will have this form included at its center.

Property of *Crash Lane News*

Springfield Tornado and Helpful Tornado Information

A major tornado can be expected every 10 to 15 years. A major hurricane comes roughly every 50 to 60 years, meaning a category 3 or more.

Massachusetts recently had an EF3. This is the new tornado ranking. It used to be the F scale (Fujita scale), now it is the EF Scale (Enhanced Fujita Scale). This recent EF 3 tornado went through a few cities to include Westfield and Springfield, Massachusetts. The tornado also traveled east from there to a town called Monson. It was on the ground for 38 miles. This was on June 1, 2011. The tornado's wind and debris killed a total of three people along its route. It was very, very, lucky that many more lives were not lost. It was actually in the city of Springfield, a larger city in Massachusetts, it crossed the river, and where it crossed was far enough from where there was a whole row of cars at rush hour at a bridge. Had it been just south it could have sucked all those cars into the river. That would have been pretty bad. It is very fortunate actually, of where the tornado went. It was not like the Midwest where you can see a tornado coming from miles and miles and get a half an hour lead-time warning. But this storm out in the Springfield area developed just west of there. There was no warning time when the tornado was in Springfield. When it got out to the city of Monson they had 45 minutes of warning time. The people in Monson and Brimfield had some extra advance warning time. They could also see it on television before it reached them, and most had gotten the warning on the weather radio, or off any of the news stations. They had a total of 45 minutes to evacuate to a storm shelter.

Property of *Crash Lane News*

Historically, tornadoes have been remembered and recorded by the National Weather Service – Boston/Taunton, Massachusetts. Back in the

1950s was the famous Worcester tornado. At that time, tornadoes were on the F scale, and that one was an F4 tornado. The Worcester tornado killed 94 people, injuring 1,226 people. That was before weather radar took effect. But the point is that really disastrous tornadoes happen in New England, enough to be a public and traveling issue and concern.

Blizzard Warnings

Winter storms happen every winter in New England. Big blizzards are modeled to occur every three to five years. A traveler should know how much of a warning is available for blizzards. Compared to tornadoes, hurricanes and blizzards both have a different type of warning. These warnings will usually start out with a watch, which is two to three days ahead of the estimated time of arrival of the storm. It is upgraded to a warning 24 to 36 hours ahead of the storm's estimated arrival time. The media are all over that, as well. Winter weather can be pretty bad, we had the blizzard of 1978. We had a blizzard of 2013 in February. This region can get 30 inches in one big dumping. Blizzards have some pretty bad winds obstructing visibility as well.

Know the Time of Year to Watch for
Possible Severe Weather Threats

If you are traveling in the late summer or early fall, particularly watch for hurricanes if you are out on Cape Cod, which is a famous tourist destination. Also watch for a hurricane warning if on Martha's Vineyard and Nantucket. Be aware that for certain popular tourist destinations there are also certain issues in those areas that a visitor may not be aware of but are a concern. This is something to know in order to plan and make sure to evacuate at the right time. For that area visitors are dependent upon ferries for transportation from the island to the mainland. Make sure to avoid being stranded, because a hurricane for that time of year is a possibility.

Recommended Ways to get Weather Information

Wireless Emergency Alerts

The new nationwide weather communication method is the Wireless Emergency Alerts, or WEA. The WEA is communicated on smartphones to the user. It is automatically programmed as a function on a smartphone. A smartphone user does not have to do anything to sign up for the alert; it is automatically enabled and is not an application a user would have to find. Wireless Emergency Alerts are on the phone from time of purchase. The alerts will stay on the phone as long as the phone is used in a safe and secure way.

Wireless Emergency Alerts communicate a few of the more unpredictable weather threats once they are confirmed to be occurring. Tornado and flash flood warnings automatically appear on phones. Some types of weather will not be communicated, for example, the many severe thunderstorms nationwide. There are so many thunderstorms that management of what to communicate and not to communicate has narrowed down the alerts. Tornado warnings and flash flood warnings will automatically appear.

In New England, an alert was communicated in 2013. There was a weak tornado in Connecticut. NOAA issued the WEA for a tornado. The use of the WEA here was a great success story. Two managers of a sports athletic dome got the WEA tornado message on their cell phones two minutes before the tornado. The managers saved 29 children and three adults, evacuating them to a place of safety. This all happened two minutes before the roof of the dome flew off and was blown across Interstate 91. The evacuation would have never happened if it were not for the Wireless Emergency Alert. The ability to communicate the current weather conditions and threats like this example can prevent damage, injury, and fatalities. That is one of the advantages of the new smartphone, communicating the wireless alerts about the weather. What happens is if you are moving into an area with a warning polygon. A traveler will know if he or she is in an area near a cell phone tower, that cell phone tower will broadcast a warning message every five minutes.

When someone new is driving into the severe weather area, they will get that message every five minutes. If you acknowledge it once on your phone you will not get it again if you are in the same area for the same warning. The advantage is more precise alerting, as a result of a person's exact proximity to the storm. They have it for drivers who are driving through severe weather.

NOAA Websites

There is a webpage you can check: it is Weather.gov/Boston, which covers southern New England to include Massachusetts, Rhode Island, and most of Connecticut.

The broader source of NOAA weather news is at Weather.gov. Weather. gov has a map of the whole country, and you can click on any state you want and it will take you there to view that area's weather forecast information. The forecast office with responsibility in that area will pop up and then a viewer can go to that individual website. Individual weather websites tend to have more area specific content that may be useful.

NOAA Radio

Another good thing especially if you are traveling is to have a weather radio. If you find the weather broadcast on the scanner you can pick it up. Or you can buy a separate radio from your favorite electronics outlet. The National Weather Service broadcasts on several different frequencies. Broadcast range from 162.4 to 162.55 MHz, and it is a 24-hour broadcast. Wherever travelers are in New England there is bound to be a weather broadcast.

Cars and Weather Radios

Only a few automotive manufacturers in the industry have weather radios installed and ready for use at the time of purchase. With all the possible violations and security requirements, travelers are not really required to know anything about the weather unless being informed during a specific event at a checkpoint controlled by law enforcement or the Department of

Transportation. A mandatory weather radio would be a great thing to have in addition to a smartphone. A weather radio in your car when traveling in the region of a storm can communicate the level of a storm's severity. BMW, Subaru, Mercedes, Range Rover, and SAAB have weather radios in their cars. A weather radio is also easy to have installed in a car that does not have one. For the cars that do not have a radio it is kind of a thing of the past with the new smartphone, but a portable radio can be the solution if one is required. A weather radio is better than nothing, and does provide another layer to a trip's security.

Summary

With the bad weather that exists in the New England area travelers should watch weather news forecasts. In addition to the many travelers that face the regular weather threats throughout the rest of the country they should consider themselves lucky if they are never caught in a New England blizzard, hurricane, or severe thunderstorm. It should be noted that it is an area that suffers from these major storm systems annually and continually. Compared to other areas this is one that faces those three major severe weather systems. It is an area that gets more of the extreme winter storms compared to the rest of the United States. A traveler's point of view on this area may usually not associate that the area is threatened by these storms. Many other areas in the United States usually face maybe two of the three. For example, having tornadoes or blizzards, but not three combined. Also not all occur all in the same month in hurricane outbreak in November, with a separate severe thunderstorm with tornadoes, and then a blizzard. The change of seasons spreads these out and it is important for travelers to use a calendar to cross reference the weather and storm patterns.

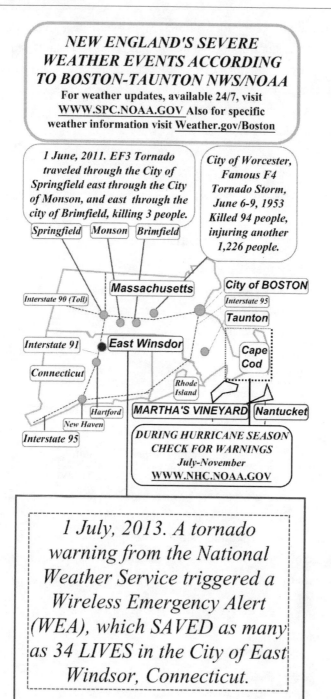

NEW ENGLAND'S SEVERE WEATHER EVENTS ACCORDING TO BOSTON-TAUNTON NWS/NOAA
For weather updates, available 24/7, visit WWW.SPC.NOAA.GOV Also for specific weather information visit Weather.gov/Boston

1 June, 2011. EF3 Tornado traveled through the City of Springfield east through the City of Monson, and east through the city of Brimfield, killing 3 people.

Springfield | Monson | Brimfield

City of Worcester, Famous F4 Tornado Storm, June 6-9, 1953 Killed 94 people, injuring another 1,226 people.

Massachusetts

Interstate 90 (Toll)

City of BOSTON
Interstate 95
Taunton

Interstate 91 | **East Winsdor**

Connecticut

Cape Cod

Rhode Island

Hartford
New Haven
Interstate 95

MARTHA'S VINEYARD | **Nantucket**

DURING HURRICANE SEASON CHECK FOR WARNINGS July-November WWW.NHC.NOAA.GOV

1 July, 2013. A tornado warning from the National Weather Service triggered a Wireless Emergency Alert (WEA), which SAVED as many as 34 LIVES in the City of East Windsor, Connecticut.

New England Weather Event Map Property of Crash Lane News

A tornado warning from the National Weather Service triggered a Wireless Emergency Alert (WEA) which saved as many as 34 lives in East Windsor, Connecticut. Five adults and 29 children were in the Sports World Complex soccer dome when the manager received the WEA on her Iphone. She immediately evacuated everyone to an adjoining building. Within two minutes of evacuating everybody a tornado hit the dome, sending it flying across the interstate. The children and adults were safe, thanks to the warning issued by the National Weather Service Weather Forecast Office at Taunton, Massachusetts. For more information check out www.nws.noaa.gov/weatherreadynation/wea.html

(Crash Lane News, knows the great benefit of there being a WEA for floods, tornados, and warnings for blizzards, and hurricanes. With that awareness, the public still needs to have a personal plan to evacuate the threatened area ahead of time. Know where a severe weather shelter is at all times. Then, avoid traveling around the area where the storm recently occurred. A weather disaster's aftermath may end up lasting months. When the WEA warnings have stopped, be aware the area will likely still have numerous traveling hazards. Some of these are unreported, and can cause traffic accidents. Debris left from a storm on the road, for example the Sports Dome Complex's roof, or fallen trees, fallen power lines, and damage from houses blown into the middle of the road. Debris also includes elements of the storm like ice, and water from rain, and the later flooding. Debris on the road can last days to weeks, and even years. Some less traveled roads are neglected and big disasters cause there to be debris to be there longer. This all leads into the issue that some disasters, and their aftermaths, have caused severe civil unrest. Unfortunately, it is usually the challenges of something like a disaster that tests humanity, through torturing a city's population, and finding if there is any lasting internal strength of survival. Most areas within the United States usually fail that test for the bigger sized disasters no matter what kind of preparedness is taking place. The type of relief that arrives being local relief groups, state emergency management, or FEMA, also does not make an immediate difference during the aftermath and civil unrest. Because of those important points, avoiding those areas before, during, and after, can save a trip from becoming the cause of a casualty. Note, remember that failures within emergency management exist. Know that some failures are expected by the government for the larger sized disasters, and asking for transparency at that point is too late. A traveler can avoid all of this with a weather forecast and some common sense.)

10

Interview with the NWS North Carolina about the Weather and Travel

North Carolina

Tornado Outbreak 14–16 November 2006 in North Carolina Riegelwood, NC Tornado

The Riegelwood tornado occurred in North Carolina on 16 November 2006. This tornado was a supercell that started out over the water. It was pretty strong and it came across Broonsborough. The tornado went between Myrtle Beach and Wilmington, intensifying. And it went up to 74 and 76 and then it went 10 or 15 miles north, and dissipated. This tornado did a lot of damage. The category was an EF Scale, the Fujita scale, EF3. Winds approaching were about 200 miles per hour. The tornado killed eight people that included two children, and hit a mobile home park where twenty people were injured. The tornado was part of the three-day outbreak in the southern states from Louisiana all the way east to North Carolina.

This tornado was not on the interstate. It was by the 74 and 76, which was a rural area. If you look at the map 500 yards on either side of that it would not hit anything. It was bad luck. Intensity-wise it was one of the stronger ones North Carolina had. Sizewise, we don't have pictures because it was dark so we could not know what we needed to see. It was about a seven mile long path of damage, about a hundred yards wide. It was really rated an EF1 for most of the area until it picked up near Riegelwood; it was a mile long there. And then the path became 300 yards wide. When comparing the Riegelwood tornado to the one in El Reno, OK, the El Reno tornado was much larger. The main difference is that it was described as being over a mile wide.

Predictability

There was a tornado warning out about 8 to 10 minutes. It was early in the morning, at 6:21 a.m. People were still asleep or just getting up for work. Unless they had a weather radio on and were able to be awake to hear it and they were watching TV, they would not have known it was coming. It is dark at that time in the morning so even with the warning the tornado would not be seen in order to avoid its path while driving or even to report its location.

Those overnight late tornadoes are extremely dangerous. That is why there is an emphasis on having a weather radio. It would have given you eight minutes' time if you had an evacuation planned. The trailer park did not have a storm shelter and if it did it was so early the storm was more of a surprise. That kind of morning arrival time for a tornado is unfortunate.

For travelers, some advice would be to have some access to the news about the weather. A satellite radio that has weather channel stuff would be a good thing. The actual weather channel is not on there anymore. You just have to be weatherwise. Also have a weather radio—they are mobile—with 5 or 6 frequencies. With a weather radio, a user may have to change back and forth between frequencies to find the closest weather warning.

Smartphone applications are more reliable because they know your ZIP code. Some applications are available that track different weather storms. The challenge is that some states may use them more than others, so when traveling in a region it is kind of difficult to know how each state's alerts are going to work.

It is not unusual to get a tornado in November in North Carolina. Climatology mentions North Carolina has a secondary tornado season in November. The primary season for tornadoes is in the spring like most areas threatened by that type disaster. In the South, there is a secondary system and stream. North Carolina can have a tornado in November. It is with the rapid moving cold fronts, as the colder air will try to penetrate when winter is setting in. We have a few of these cold fronts every year.

They are not producing tornadoes or wind damage now, and this year has been relatively weak.

North Carolina had another tornado in November in the late 1990s. In Orange County that was an EF3 and an EF4. That tornado happened in the middle of the day, differing from the Riegelwood tornado occurring in the morning. So it was a strong squall line that came through. Tornadoes do not happen every year in North Carolina, but they can happen every five to ten years.

The EF3 is one of the stronger tornadoes for North Carolina. That is not normal for the area, for tornadoes to get that strong. EF3s are more common in the Midwest, and Oklahoma, Texas, and the rest of the states in Tornado Alley. The EF3s are also more common in Alabama, Mississippi, and parts of Georgia, when compared to North Carolina.

Hurricanes are more of a threat than tornadoes in North Carolina. The southeast side of North Carolina list hurricanes as the number one expected weather disaster. Hurricanes make the biggest impact. With that issue the state gets tornadoes produced off of those hurricanes. These tornadoes are usually small and short lived.

Storm Chasers

The El Reno one was pretty intense and the media and people are still talking about the events. That was one of the most photographed, observed, and giant tornadoes on record. That tornado was for Norman, Oklahoma; it is tornado central. It is where the national research lab is setup. Oklahoma is really into the weather compared to other states that face the same amount of weather issues. It is amazing how much focus and resources they have. There are also chasers around that area and can be seen when driving.

Tim Samaras was a borderline storm chaser and more of a research guy. Sometimes people will get money in advance and go out and take pictures and videos, which is nice. But they are not taking any measurements. Many in the weather business do not put Tim Samaras in the class of the thrill seeker. The problem is now that you are getting way too many of these thrill seekers. The problem is that thrill seekers get in the way of the regular traffic trying to evacuate or meteorologists studying the storm or first responders. Storm chasers in it for the thrill are actually dangerous. Their unsafe driving can lead to a big collision. There are just so many people out there chasing, period. It can be a traffic issue. A lot of the current public interest in thrill seeking has to do with television and cable.

NOAA's Website about Riegelwood, NC, Tornado

For information from the local NOAA office about the Riegelwood, NC, tornado go to weather.gov/ilm/significantlocalevents. Then go down to 2006. There is an official report of what happened, which is public information. There is an explanation of reflectivity and velocity. It has a good map of the path and area of the event, showing the location of a tornado to the highway and other landmarks. There are some radar and velocity if you want to see what the outlook looked like on radar. There are some other severe events there, including tornadoes.

Reflectivity

Reflectivity is the radar, just like the radar images that are provided on television or on the computer. That is just coming back showing the intensity of the rain droplets. The black balloons on that are just clouds or sprinkles. The red gets more intense. The velocity is the red and greens. The way you read that image is that inbound data are coming in from the south of the coast. The reds are away because there are some rain issues because the winds are so strong.

We have an enhanced EF scale, which is the only way to estimate winds to see what the destructive force is. This can be done by observing what damage it did. Now the problem with the Riegelwood storm was that we only had buildings where we could only go as high in the rating as an EF3, because they were trailer homes. When a trailer gets destroyed the storms power only goes so many miles an hour due to the construction being able to be blown away. Now if we had a building that is on a foundation with reinforced rebar rod, beams, with brick walls, the tornado could get a higher rating. That would allow the scale to show that higher winds had blown into and through the area. The enhanced Fujita Scale bases a tornado rating off those types of observations and facts about durable construction.

You can see down below, the enhanced F scale indicators. Small barns and buildings when destroyed have a certain rating.

There is a table for rating the size of storms. One example is a small barn or outbuilding with a typical construction, and a size less than 2,500 square feet. It tells how it has wood or metal posts built up construction. It has what kind of construction with a large door. They would go through and say the doors are closed. We do have walls. They would go from top to bottom. If you have a collapsed door on a small barn would be 83 miles an hour. The lower would be 68 and the upper would be 102. That gives the winds a range, helping to gauge a storm. If it is a brand new barn with metal construction, all that good stuff, then it would be rate on the stronger end of the scale. If it is an older barn, 30 or 40 years old, you can estimate what it is made of in a picture. And seeing what the construction is like, you can go to the lower bounds, which is 68. Now they had one barn there and one house. Going back to that table if you can go back to the enhanced Fujita scale events indicator, and go down a little farther there is one that is actually the masonry apartment or motel, which is number 7. And you can see, here is how the construction is if it is less than 4. It is very detailed how you go through. If you have collapsed three-story walls on an apartment or motel, between 115–150, and the average is going to be 133 miles per hour. So it looks like we got that and you plug in the 133. Then plug that into the table at the bottom and it is running close to an EF4 and EF3. That is how wind speeds and scales get determined, based on damage. There are also some blank spots that arise when trying to size up a tornado. Riegelwood was just at the very end of the storm. The storm was possibly bigger than an EF3 but there were no buildings to base that off of being a rural area and coming out of the water. The existing description of the Riegelwood, NC is as detailed as possible by using the mentioned information to identify the EF rating, but note the ratings may not always be 100% accurate.

The NOAA office did an objective analysis of the damage. If there was an anemometer there that was still working we would go with that. Most places base information off wind equipment, but even with the private stuff the equipment does not work in making a rating reliable and accurate. The work NOAA does is forensic meteorology, with the challenges of technical and equipment failures.

Hearing an EF5 on a Radio

The public that is lucky enough to be aware of the tornado makes a radio a good thing to have. Not many people will ever be in the exact same area where a tornado is. The low chance of this is also a good thing to know and not have to worry about. So combining the awareness the radio provides with the probability of being right where a tornado is can give some time to prepare and seek some shelter.

Some of the traveling public are rarely exposed near EF5 storm systems. When the radio mentions EF5 the public might be even luckier. If the public will know the size and possibly the direction, it can avoid the area it was spotted and reported. Things do not always get called in fast enough though. Note that it is usually the bigger storm systems that get spotted ahead of time while some of the smaller ones tend to catch some off guard and take the public in the area by surprise even with the warnings.

The interesting issue is that there are warnings that go out about the strength of the storm in the surrounding areas in the following hours. These messages have been stating that there was a set size storm as an EF5 in the area. Some messages on the weather radio also mention that there was an EF5 in the area that can literally mean a few states. There can be confusion when hearing these warnings in that the information may not be specific to each person's location. A traveler should use common sense and prevent from going out into any spotted tornado and even into the area where severe thunderstorms are predicted that may cause a tornado. The best thing is to avoid travel if there are EF5 warnings.

NOAA does not know how strong they were until after the storm and they do their assessment. A storm may also last a few hours, leaving one state and heading north to the next area. It can be rated more accurately once NOAA goes out to see. NOAA has some hints on radar that most of the public do not know about.

Tornado Caused Debris Ball

The Riegelwood tornado winds were pretty strong and the only thing we can do is to word it that this is an especially dangerous storm, if you have that confidence. Now with polarization with radar installed you can actually see some of the debris balls. A debris ball could be leaves, straw, one of the best reflectors they say is water coated housing insulation. When a house gets destroyed from a tornado the insulation gets thrown up in the air. The debris has to be high at several thousand feet to make it on the radar. The tornado has to be strong and pumped up to get that debris up that high, where the debris is tens of miles or 70 miles away. When a debris ball is identified on the radar, a tornado warning goes out. A debris ball can help add to a warning being made that there is in fact a tornado.

Recommendations for Travelers

The above included some recommendations for a traveler going through North Carolina during severe weather. There were also many areas and a great deal of information on weather forecasting.

Some travelers had been traveling across the region during this storm that lasted a few days. Traveling in poor and hazardous conditions are in many examples not from choice. The result of being in a severe storm is from being assigned or choosing a route along or near the path of where a storm develops while already in route. In Georgia on the 15th and 16th, that was the closest call for some travelers. The mentioned fatalities in the early morning in the tornado in North Carolina was also a deadly result of this storm. Travelers who survived and were able to witness the path of the storm headed north on the interstate originating from Louisiana, Alabama, Georgia, into South Carolina, North Carolina, and continuing north on a trip up to the northern states. Knowing there is a storm system but also having an appointment to make on time, there are some things that can be requested and some that cannot from the employees' point of view and ability to make requests. Also, there are many unknowns where travelers may not know the severity of the forecasts and the storm as it is ongoing around them. The best recommendation is to know how to get the local weather news. Know how to replan and manage a trip to go along with the fact that things like the weather may change. When a trip is scheduled months and weeks in advance it is tempting to just go even though there is severe weather like a thunderstorm or hurricane but it is something a traveler can prevent and change to be safer.

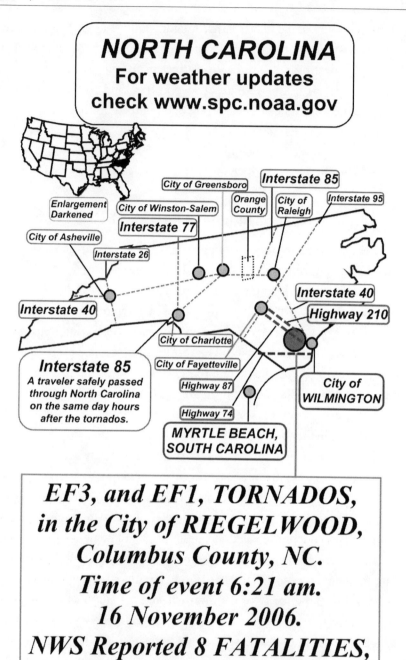

NORTH CAROLINA
For weather updates
check www.spc.noaa.gov

Enlargement
Darkened

City of Greensboro

Interstate 85

Orange County

City of Raleigh

Interstate 95

City of Winston-Salem

Interstate 77

City of Asheville

Interstate 26

Interstate 40

Interstate 40

Highway 210

City of Charlotte

Interstate 85
A traveler safely passed
through North Carolina
on the same day hours
after the tornados.

City of Fayetteville

Highway 87

City of
WILMINGTON

Highway 74

MYRTLE BEACH,
SOUTH CAROLINA

*EF3, and EF1, TORNADOS,
in the City of RIEGELWOOD,
Columbus County, NC.
Time of event 6:21 am.
16 November 2006.
NWS Reported 8 FATALITIES,
with Damage to Property*

City of RIEGELWOOD, Columbus County, 6:21 am. 16 November 2006, Tornado Activity
stated by NWS/NOAA

F3 Tornado

Several trailer homes were lifted from their foundation and broken apart, with debris scattered for several hundred yards. Many cars and trucks were lifted and thrown. One house was wiped completely from its foundation. A few brick homes on the north side of Highway 87 suffered major damage. Tornado caused 8 fatalities, and many more injuries.

F1 Tornado

A few dozen trees (12-18 inch diameter) snapped. Tractor and trailer rig flipped. Large wood-framed building with metal roof destroyed. Portion of roof lifted off house. Two large trees uprooted.

F1 Tornado

Once the tornado moved north of Hwy 87, it crossed mainly rural area wooded areas south of Highway 210. Most damage that occurred between highway 87 and highway 210 was to trees.

Crash Lane News' Report From a Traveler in the Mid November 2006 Storm

"A traveler passed through North Carolina 16 November 2006 after the Riegelwood tornado. The traveler's day started at 1200 pm in Byron, Georgia. The weather was somewhat clear so the trip continued heading north to make a stop in Atlanta, GA, but while there did notice the thinning of the violent storm system from the previous days. The traveler was in Atlanta until 600pm, then started traveling east. There was no road debris from the tornadic outbreak and storm earlier in the day. The reason there were no signs was it was a smaller size storm. The traveler was also lucky to be driving in areas of the southern states not directly hit with tornados. A good thing at this point was that the storm had already left heading north through North Carolina, Virginia, New Jersey, Maryland, and Pennsylvania, towards western New York. The route the traveler was on was an exact match to the path of the storm with both eventually ending

264 | Crash Lane News

up in New York, but the storm was moving much faster, leaving the driver back in Georgia. The traveler was glad to not be under this particular storm any longer, and was relieved. This traveler survived driving under this storm from Louisiana, Mississippi, Alabama, and to Georgia. Some advice for other travelers that might find themselves forced to drive during unpredictable events like a tornado outbreak is to reduce speed and use extra caution. According to this traveler, the interstates were never so open, while the weather over them was never as violent since that mid November 2006 storm.

A few days later this same traveler learned the details to the story of the tornado outbreak. Many travelers like this one are usually surprised to find out about these more serious stories. The news agencies in the local area can raise a great deal of awareness about the severity of a storm with a picture and a report. When the public sees it on television and in a newspaper it is more believable and becomes confirmed as to have really happening. With that later realization travelers know the weather forecast and severe weather warnings ahead of the later news reports, but it is unpredictable as to what ends up being a big news story. A traveler that drives always knows this reality about the weather. Drivers are the first ones to know the hazards each weather event creates. Unfortunately, these same drivers know this because they are pressured to travel in bad weather due to the roads being left open by the Department of Transportation and Law Enforcement. One remaining issue discovered is that the Department of Transportation has the option to leave the road open when the weather is forecasted as severe. The main reason is that a tornado outbreak in a specific area is still unpredictable so to close down an entire state's transportation would be viewed as too much work, and possibly excessive. The other side of it is that is the real issue of a failure to keep the public from harm. Most would agree that with all the weather radar and forecasting why are the roads left open in these events. This is especially true when the Department of Transportation and Law Enforcement write unsafe driving tickets throughout the area this trip went. With the money spent by a state to have traffic enforcement the rest of the time there should be more of a budget spent on communicating warnings to the public. Leaving the roads open while later playing the speed trap game when the weather is clear shows there is a definite fabrication of what is occurring.

One suggestion is to invest in electronically controlled signs. A sign can communicate a reduced speed limit, or to communicate a road closure, or the amount of traffic density ahead. With Wi-Fi technology updates can be controlled periodically from a remote office. Money should be spent on improving traffic enforcement signs to be more accurate to the changes of road conditions. An improvement like this could make signs more visible in a storm and at night while presenting information to the public that could prevent an accident with what is occurring on the road at that moment. A sign like this would be more accurate. The inclusion of a visible sign communicating the current weather in the county being traveled would go beyond the current NOAA/NWS weather warnings. A sign like that at each county line would possibly do more and communicate more than a weather radio or smartphone because it would eliminate the confusion of what county a storm is in. A sign with a detailed message about safety could make a huge difference in preventing accidents. Something like that would be a huge in improving communication at the right time, preventing huge pileups, preventing injuries, and preventing fatalities.

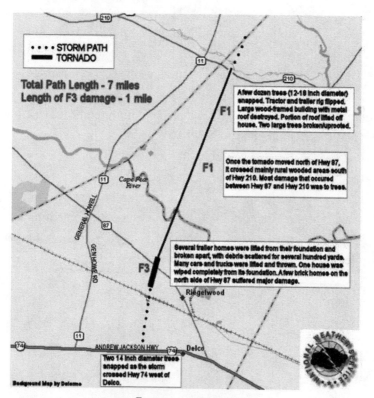

From www.noaa.gov

(The above map is from NOAA North Carolina and shows the tornado's path crossing some of the highways, which affected travel in the area.)

11

Interview with the Peach Tree, Georgia NWS/NOAA Office about the Weather and Travel

Georgia

Property of *Crash Lane News*

Know about the Tornado Threat in Southeastern United States in November

Introduction to 38 Tornadoes Outbreak across Southern States November 14–15–16, 2006

Includes public information and a meteorologist's point of view provided by the NOAA Peach Tree, GA Office

The following is a summary of real events that occurred back in November 2006. The purpose of this report is to give an added awareness of the reason a traveler needs to check the weather forecast. This report is also not to encourage someone to recreate a trip where they are faced with the threat of traveling near a tornado outbreak. All the encouragement or motivation gained from reading this is to give travelers the informational tools to identify a weather threat and then to adjust their trip planning so they can avoid real dangers that can occur when traveling in a storm.

The main research on the background of this storm can be found at the www.spc.noaa.gov website. There is historical information about the weather of previous storms that the public can look up. Also check the current weather forecast.

Tornado Outbreak in the South November 2006.

The following tornado events from the November 2006, are listed by NOAA/ National Weather Service. These are included to show the widespread damage and there were many more events mentioned to have occurred. 22 Tornados were reported on November 14, 2006, and 18 Tornados on 15-16 November. A TORNADO was reported to of happened at 1000 11/14/2006. 1 INJURY AND 4 TRUCKS OVERTURNED, IN CITY OF PALESTINE, Arkansas. A TORNADO was reported at 0750 11/14/2006. 1 FATALITY AND DAMAGE, IN CITY OF MONTPELIER, Louisiana. TORNADO 0805 11/14/2006. 2 INJURIES AND DAMAGE, IN CITY OF AMITE, Louisiana. TORNADO 0830 11/14/2006. 6 INJURIES AND 25 HOMES WITH HEAVY, DAMAGE IN CITY OF SUMRALL, Louisiana. TORNADO 1630 11/15/2006. 6 INJURED IN MONTGOMERY, Alabama. TORNADO 2205 11/15/2006. POWERLINES DOWN AND DAMAGE IN CITY OF HEADLAND, Alabama. TORNADO 2000 11/15/2006. 6 INJURED in the city of Columbus, Georgia.

These few examples show the devastation and damage occurring during severe weather. Many warnings were put in place for this event while some were unprepared. It is important to prevent the chance of being out on the road during a storm. But in the case that is your job, that prevention is not always possible so try to pick and choose the time to take a break and let a storm pass through. A traveler's story of survival is included in this report and it is important to mention that this same traveler ended up traveling along the path of this storm system as it moved east and north. So from Louisiana up to North Carolina the driver was on and off the road working. After the storm ended the driver traveled up north into western New York, with a new destination heading far out west. The overall weather faced in this few weeks of work out on the road included tornados, and ended with being in the aftermath of a blizzard. Ice was on the roads, and highways, on the west coast. Looking back on this trip it seemed risky and there was some luck factored into surviving every weather obstacle. In summary, the traveler had passed through the areas of Louisiana where Hurricane Katrina had hit a year earlier in 2005, then survived the tornados in the south, and also later passed through the western part of New York. It was basically an introduction to all the areas and disasters that had gone wrong on one trip. This made this November 2006 trip through the south unforgettable.

About the Peach Tree Office

The NOAA Peach Tree, Georgia office, is the main office in North and Central Georgia. The local NOAA office was friendly and willing to provide an interview and information about the November 2006 tornado outbreak. The office gave detailed answers for all questions regarding this particular storm. Their ability to communicate helpful information to the public is a great service.

The NOAA Peach Tree, GA office, was able to give some additional information regarding this storm from the traveling point of view and the NOAA weather rating system. This is reliable and relevant to a book about traveling safe in that it adds some real firsthand witness accounts from a government agency. NOAA's point of view is good to have along side of a traveler's point of view, which is also a part of the research on this November 2006 tornado.

Suggestions for Travelers

The introduction into this storm can be with the time it was first predicted. A traveler should make a note to remember the different storms' prediction times for their own travel planning. A section on predictability of possible storms and current conditions can give the needed time to change travel plans.

The November 15 to 16, 2006, tornado was predicted by the Storm Prediction Center, NOAA. A traveler's point of view is included; he was in the Columbus, Georgia area when this storm caused some serious and real damage. This tornado outbreak was interesting because of the widespread news reporting on it. Another reason it is interesting is it was a single storm system lasting a few days, and the threats it created to those that were traveling safely. When there is a large storm system being forecasted it is a good idea to continually get information about the storm if in the area.

After the storm is over there are also ways the public can find out how much warning time was made available by the government NOAA office. The Peach Tree NOAA office knows the amount of time the local area was warned. This also refers to the amount of time it took to send out a county warning on the weather radio frequency and to other sources. The ability to send an alert starts when a severe storm system is predicted to occur in the area. Storm prediction can occur days in advance. The point of time where a tornado has been spotted to have occurred out of the severe weather warning is a much shorter amount of time. In the minutes leading up to the actual tornadic event NOAA is watching radar images and data for signs of a tornado, NOAA also gets eye witnesses calling into report there is a tornado. Once there is confirmation, NOAA sends an announcement to the county area and warns the surrounding counties.

One issue the traveling public noticed is when moving from county to county the warnings may vary. Each county might be sending out warnings at different times. The ability to know what is being spotted can sometimes be a challenge to communicate in an organized and coherent way by NOAA across multiple counties or a region. When traveling through many counties where the weather warnings vary as well as the weather, from the severe thunderstorms to the more severe tornadoes, try to use the weather radio. Having the most recent and updated information requires travelers to leave their weather radio on. It is better to park and wait for a tornadic event to pass.

In mid-November 2006 people were traveling through that particular area and became caught in the middle of the tornado storm warnings. Most people caught in the tornadoes were stationary but there were also high winds that affected traffic. There was a lot happening that day. Some travelers and the local areas residents did get caught up in the elements of the storm.

One traveler, for example, stated they had never suffered damage and injury. In their experience with this storm they noticed the chaotic news of the tornado event occur when they were in the same area. The traveler was close enough to experience the fear the storm had on the local public. The public was more prepared and was engaged in the activities of closing businesses down and heading home to a shelter. The public was also vigilant for outsiders that may be looters at the time before the storm and after the storm. To the news it was an interesting weather and survival story to write about, read about, and share.

Do a Search on How Much of a Warning Was Made Available before the Storm Hit

One area to research is to find the amount of time the 38 tornado outbreak storm had been predicted and how much of a warning the public had. When looking up information about the storm the amount of time the Storm Prediction Center, www.spc.gov, may have issued a watch is a starting point to what the traveler was seeking. This is the amount of time stated in NOAA's hazardous weather outlook.

Another specific search is a look at the amount of time that any warnings may have been issued in a particular county. This is a locational way to look at the warning system. There are different alerts being sent out in one state like Alabama to the different counties and can be complicated if traveling during a storm.

The specific county is good to know when later looking up the storm. The traveler had been in Columbus, GA, overnight on the 14 of November according to the record of his trips and receipt information. Columbus is right on the border of Alabama and Georgia. Highway 80 runs through the city going east to Macon, Georgia, which is about 95 miles away. Also, the 80 goes West to Montgomery, Alabama, connecting to the 65, from Columbus, about 82 miles away.

When NOAA issues a warning for a particular county keeping a record of it, and also can later go back and see if severe weather occurred in that county. There can be a later determination about whether a warning had gone out ahead of time. Specific information about the county of where a person is searching about this time of the alert is required to match the best alert to the city. The county where one tornado was reported to have occurred was located where Fort Benning was located near Columbus, GA. Fort Benning covers portions of Muscogee County and Chattahoochee County. The main storm that had affected the state of Georgia occurred on the 15 of November 2006. There was a tornado at Fort Benning.

NOAA mentioned the path was half a mile long and a quarter mile wide. It damaged about 20 warehouses, and several houses in the Macdonald manor housing area. That tornado occurred at 3:15 pm Eastern Time and the tornado warning was issued at 2:59 p.m. Eastern Time in Muscogee and Chattahoochee counties. For people not familiar with U.S. time zones the storm can also be described to occur at 1915 Universal Coordinated Time, also known as Greenwich Meantime, and also known as ZULU time.

There was about a 16-minute lead-time on the tornado warning, as stated by the Peach Tree NOAA office. The NOAA link http://www.noaa.gov/features/protecting/tornadoes101.html mentions that the average tornado lead-time is 13 minutes. Compared to the average of 13 minutes, this office had identified it early to add an additional three minutes of lead-time to 16. The 16 minute lead-time is a good thing to know, while being able to look back on all that happened, knowing there was a warning that did get communicated to Chattahoochee County, Muskogee County, including Fort Benning, and the city of Columbus. Another good thing to know is that the traveler did hear the tornado sirens. The difficult thing to process out of all this is the traveler was unable to seek shelter due to him not being familiar with the weather and its alerting system. The sirens let him know there was some weather activity and when he looked up his position later on, he realized he was actually a good distance away from the area where the tornado caused the damage. The Peach Tree Office was on top of tracking weather that day. The public got an extra three minutes to the average warning time, notifying them to seek shelter.

The tornado at Fort Benning was the only tornado spotted and known to have caused damage at that time and place in those counties. That was a huge storm. The detailed information about individual storms is available to the public from NOAA. Past storm information can be good to have when looking to plan a future trip. The average survivor of that storm looking back might not remember how much of a warning they had if any was available where they were.

As for the traveler driving through Georgia that day, the warnings on the radio in different counties may added some confusion as to the actual location of the tornado in regard to their own, and how much time was given to alert the public. Past storm information can be a good thing for a traveler to add to their records or traveler log. Weather experiences should be summarized in the different locations, along with the time of year. For the record of what failed to work, which in this case was the fact the traveler was unable to get a warning as to where the threat was until it had occurred. A weather history can also help with future planning.

Suggestion for Travelers on How to Seek a Storm Shelter Based on This Tornado Outbreak

A witness to the severe thunderstorm, not the tornado, had left Columbus right before that tornado had touched down at Fort Benning, in Columbus, Chattahoochee County, GA. The traveler drove along the 80 going east. When driving he noticed the dark colored clouds, and the eerie light effect they had created in the afternoon. The sun was covered with clouds at the time this tornado had touched down, but it was still very bright out at times like there were pockets of thin clouds. Also the color of the light was different from the usual thunderstorm. The rain showers were short intervals of time but heavy. Overall the day the tornado occurred in Georgia was not filled with a massive thunderstorm lasting many continuous hours. The day's weather was cloudy and dry in the morning. The afternoon's weather had brief periods of bad weather of wind and rain, occurring around the time of the tornado. And the wind of the tornado sounded like a high pitch crumpling, bending, twisting, smashing, of metal. This sound was very brief, lasting only seconds and less. It was similar to the sound one would imagine with a large metal structure being destroyed, where a metal beam is bending or dragging during the demolition. This tornado was heard many miles away from the location of the tornado, and a sound wave traveled making the traveler think that it was a vehicle accident he heard, or some lightning and thunder a part of the brief winds and patches of bad weather.

When comparing the account of this tornado to the account of the Greensburg, KA, tornado in 2007 and the Picher, OK, tornado of 2008 it was actually a much milder storm the day of the tornado, but before had some signs of severe weather coming in similar to those larger tornadoes. The day of weather seemed a lot less mild and the fact there was a tornado was a surprise to the traveler, being that there seemed to be violent weather the night before compared to the day of. It is hard to think about the overall event using the logic of what occurred, based on only one person's point of view. These strange events and accounts of what happened also prove there is a need to have a local weather office such as NOAA to take weather reports from the public and use them to help send out warnings.

There were later reports of severe weather spread across the area, although most of the damage seemed to have occurred in the city of Columbus, resulting from the tornado being there. The traveler was far enough east in Macon, GA, and heard the tornado warning alerts going off. The public was very prepared and aware of this storm at the time, knowing a tornado was coming the day before.

The night before a traveler was asked by a truck stop cashier in Columbus if he was a looter. The traveler said no, being that he had a job and was on a business trip of his own. The traveler unknowingly was asked this, finding out that there was a severe thunderstorm warning out early. The person asking him this was trying to put their own version of reality together of who he was and what he was doing in an area that has a severe weather warning. The fact that there was a storm expected that might cause a tornado and disaster where looting is suspected to occur is not something someone wants to be accused of. It is scary not knowing about the forecast, and finding out about it when being asked if you are a looter. It was a threat arising from a false accusation and fabrication, while also having to worry about how to make a business appointment on time the next day.

A suggestion for someone ending up in an area that is unfamiliar while there is a tornado going on is to pull off the road to seek a storm shelter. If working an area that is unfamiliar facing threats and a tornado, call a supervisor or another contact in the area like a customer. They might be able to help in directing you to a storm shelter. If not working in the area an easy thing to do is to pull off to the next service station or business and ask if there is a storm shelter available to the public. You hope that they do not say that you're a looter, and if they ask make sure to reply that you are not a looter and passing through on business.

The news of this particular storm was common knowledge but if you are traveling, sometimes shelter may not be easily available. The time to seek shelter from a tornado after a warning is a very small amount of time. The ability to make a call, or pull over to ask for help, may not be possible. It does seem like a helpless situation, but the chances of traveling on the path of where the tornado will hit is also very low, and the chances you survive are high, even if in the same county where the tornado hits. A traveler will survive from a direct hit from a tornado in a majority of encounters. This is true if a traveler is even in the same county the tornado is reported and this is a good thing to know. With those mentioned points about how to seek shelter, there are additional hazards that tend to occur from severe weather that can be a threat to traveling safely.

Injuries and Damage Report

There were six injuries reported as a result of this particular tornado at the U.S. Army base Fort Benning, GA. They were described as minor injuries without details of their exact extent. The injuries occurred in the Macdonald Manor housing area, when six homes were destroyed.

After the tornado, NOAA's Peach Tree Office went down to Fort Benning to perform a survey on the damage caused from the storm. This can help identify the strength, size, location, and other data left from the storm. This information is kept with a record of the event, and can later be used to predict future storms. If one happened there is a probability that it could happen again. There were a few cars in the parking lot that got hit with significant debris. But it appears that there was no one outside in that general area when it hit, which was good. Some additional damaged included 20 warehouses built before World War II. The ends of two warehouses were blown off. Also, an 18-wheel truck was blown over, without a fatality, which was amazing and lucky for the driver.

The proof that the NOAA warnings and weather updates are good is when there are assessments to how significant some damage was, causing fatalities. It could also be viewed as a miracle by survivors knowing the full power of the storm. A truck weighing tens of thousands of pounds was tipped and blown over in the same tornado where only six injuries occurred was lucky. Anyone that survived that storm in the immediate area should consider themselves lucky. As for travelers who had left the area right before the tornado had touched down, they also should know they are extremely lucky.

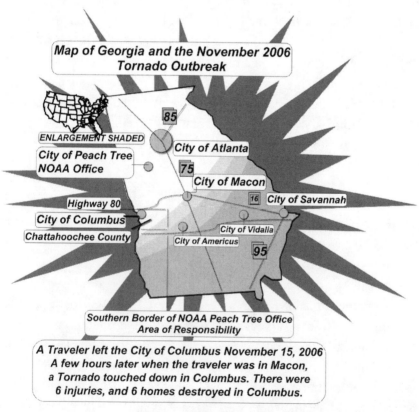

Map of Georgia and the November 2006 Tornado Outbreak

ENLARGEMENT SHADED

City of Peach Tree NOAA Office

City of Atlanta

City of Macon

Highway 80

City of Savannah

City of Columbus

Chattahoochee County

City of Vidalia

City of Americus

Southern Border of NOAA Peach Tree Office Area of Responsibility

A Traveler left the City of Columbus November 15, 2006 A few hours later when the traveler was in Macon, a Tornado touched down in Columbus. There were 6 injuries, and 6 homes destroyed in Columbus.

Know the Challenge of Traveling When Severe Weather Conditions Exist

As for future advice about traveling when severe weather has been expected or predicted, there are some questions a traveler should ask. One question is, what kind of recommendation can the NOAA office give to travelers who may not get a warning until it is too late. Some travelers cannot avoid a trip. Many trips will be exposed to a route threatened by severe thunderstorm conditions every year. The current problem is if someone knows there are tornadoes occurring around them and they are not familiar with the area they are driving in, pinpointing the threat may not be precise. The problem is that some travelers cover a lot of ground and cannot find the perfect time and place to pull off and seek shelter. The challenge for travelers is that many trips are going for the duration, for distance, for time, in order to increase their businesses profits. The safety issue of finding the threat from the weather is second to that profit. This problem is followed with a solution that is a recommendation directly from NOAA in Peach Tree, GA.

NOAA recommends the following if you do not know the exact location and the exact threat from the weather. Their solution is to have a map that has the county names. It is still legal to look at a map while driving. If the county being traveled is also being warned by NOAA, there can be some clarity as to the specific locations specific weather risk and threat. Most highway maps are not properly mapped by the name of the county. NOAA mentions the names of major cities that may be affected in addition to the counties. If you happen to be in a rural area, it would be a good idea to determine which county you are in.

Smartphone Applications about Severe Weather Warnings

There are also some cell phone apps able to track a GPS location, and are all provided by private companies. These applications track the GPS location of a cell phone, and will alert the owner if he or she happens to be inside the polygon of the actual warning. When NOAA issues the warning to go out to the smartphone, it is usually based on the four sided polygon. A polygon is a four sided shape of the actual area being warned. And so if a traveler with a smartphone is in that box they will receive an alert. Smartphone alerts can help keep a level of alertness as long as you have cell reception where located and while traveling.

There Is No Safe Vehicle to Be in during a Tornado

If talking about traveling in severe storms like a tornado there is no vehicle better than others. When traveling when there is a tornado there is a risk of being stuck in a vehicle being vulnerable to a real threat of debris and the wind. NOAA recommends that if you are in the area in a vehicle and a tornado is imminent and you cannot in any way avoid it, get out of the vehicle. Once out of the vehicle lie at a low spot, a roadside depression, or a ditch. If those low areas are not available, something low like the described is recommended. For a tornado, there is no vehicle safe, especially passenger vehicles. There are no vehicles safer than others.

This plan may not be seen as the best thing by travelers. Travelers who were driving trucks at the time may have been the only vehicles on the road due to the issue of appointments. For this storm, most of the vehicles had gotten a warning right away, possibly days before if local to the area. Anyone can still consider themselves lucky to have avoided the tornado at Fort Benning, GA.

Eyewitness Account of Their Vehicle's Performance the Night before the Tornado in Columbus

The traveler who was driving mentioned earlier did witness some of that stuff. There was a lot of pressure on the vehicle in the storm the night before. The night before on 14 November a truck driver felt like the whole truck was going to tip over. The light weight of the driver compartment blew and would shake with each wind stream's compression on the path the truck traveled. In summary, it felt like the wind blowing hard was just moving the cab of the truck. The movement was not affecting the steering wheel and the engine from traveling in a straight and steady line on the road. The engine and steering component of the truck is weighing over 12,000 lbs, just for the front of the vehicle. Trucks are so heavy they give a driver the impression they are protected as being anchored to the ground, more so than if driving a standard size passenger car. This can be a self-defeating feeling if travelers do not take weather warnings seriously, thinking the vehicle's weight will protect them, driving in a way like they are indestructible from the threats the weather poses with a tornado.

NOAA's review to the above statement is that the wind speed from a tornado can lift anything. The trucks out on the road often end up being damaged in tornadoes. The force the winds create can lift even a tractor trailer and cause severe injuries, fatalities, and damage.

NOAA Comment about Commercial Motor Vehicles Not Being Safe during a Tornado

NOAA mentions if talking about tornadic strength winds, while also talking about a much higher profile vehicle like a commercial vehicle, the wind effect on the side of the vehicle with a full trailer is actually going to be higher than a passenger car. When talking about tornadic winds over a hundred miles an hour, the wind pressure on the vehicle depends entirely on the strength of the tornado. Two or three years ago, a tornado went through the Dallas–Fort Worth area. It went right across the yard of one of the major trucking companies. In the video, several trailers are lifted well into the air. These trailers blew and then were deposited hundreds of yards outside of the main truck yard there. Those are pretty heavy trucks that could weigh up to 80,000 pounds fully loaded and as much as 30,000 empty, so lifting them up requires a lot of force form the wind. These trucks were at the company's yard so they might not have been full. They probably weighed less at the yard if parked and not being used. For Dallas, there are three main interstates running right through there which were affected. There was some pretty impressive video of the tornado event as a result of it being in a city. In a weaker tornado a commercial motor vehicle is probably heavy enough for it not to be lifted, but with that example there is really no safe vehicle to be in.

The traveler replied to NOAA stating that after seeing some of the other photos of tornado damage that are common in the news it is common sense that being in a vehicle is not a safe shelter. The debris could also just break the window of a vehicle too heavy for the storm to blow away, causing the driver to be injured and lose control of the vehicle.

Vehicles with Weather Radios Are Better than Not Having a Radio While in a Vehicle if Caught in a Storm

Being in a vehicle is not the best place for a tornado but if caught in a storm a vehicle that has a weather radio is going to have more of an advantage than one that does not. This is a small advantage, as a result in the challenge of getting the right frequency and knowing the county. But having a radio is better than nothing.

A traveler who was in the storm system had a weather radio in the vehicle and was able to switch to the NOAA weather warnings. One question that came to mind for NOAA was if cars were going to be required to have a weather radio. NOAA mentioned there are a few cars that have the weather band standard on their radio. They are usually some of the higher end car manufacturers, Mercedes for example, and Lincoln offered it for a while right in the standard radio equipment that came with the car. But it is very few. Some aftermarket car stereos have those. A traveler can always buy portable ones to carry with you. But if you are traveling out on the interstate those weather radio broadcasts are fairly low powered, so you might not always get a signal. Also, you can pickup more than one transmission and so if you are in an unfamiliar area you would not know what transmitted message you will have to be listening to. The weather radios have some usefulness on the road but not as high a usefulness compared to someone at a fixed area as a house or at work, knowing the county and surround counties. Your best bet is going to be having reception and getting alerts somewhere along the interstate. There will usually be good cell reception along the interstate corridors. Your best bet is going to be one of the phone apps, especially those that use the cell towers and GPS that is keeping track of where the phone is. And they have apps that will monitor the warnings that go out issued by the National Weather Service, and if it issues those warnings it will alert you on the phone.

Those alerts are a nice to have in the present time and would have been good if available in 2006, in the November outbreak. The probability that there was a device available to the public like the current smartphone at that time in 2006 is likely but was not yet available to the mass public. The Wireless Emergency Alerts were also not at the same level as the current system if there was a type of phone out there in 2006. There were some ways to get the warning using the regular mobile phone system like calling the Department of Transportation's road conditions or calling a weather service station, but it is not like the current system.

Some carriers are better than others when it comes to their reliability of making sure the user gets an alert. Smartphone users have to do some research on that.

The cell phone apps that track where your phone is at, track your location on the phone and then compare that to the warning polygons that go out. When traveling across an unknown area this warning is helpful. Many years ago they had the county names along the side of the road. Crossing into each county would be communicated to the driver through a sign. You just don't see those as often anymore. Some highways curve in and out of two, three, four or more counties, then back into the first county. It is one of those situations where you're literally behind the curve of information and lost. Even with a traveler aware and consciously trying to keep up with the name of the county you're in is kind of hard to know. Now once again, if you have a map you can approximate where you are along the interstate. You can see what county you're in. With the map, have the cell phone application that tells you if are falling into a warning area.

Unfortunately, because NOAA is a government agency they cannot recommend one commercial weather application over another or one smartphone over another. NOAA recommends that the public go on the Internet and research the National Weather Service or Severe Weather Warning application available online. Also research the other mobile applications regarding the weather. Research what features the applications have, finding the best one. That is the most comprehensive suggestion available a traveler can use to find a good smartphone device for now. The ability of an individual to get a warning once purchasing a smartphone and uploading a severe weather warning application depends on how good the coverage is out in the more rural areas. Most mobile phone service providers have better coverage in the interstate areas. For interstate travel, the smartphone is pretty good. If you start getting off the interstate on the state U.S. highways and smaller roads, the coverage can decrease in rural areas. With this challenge, having a smartphone is still one of the better ways to be connected to weather warnings and other alerts. The key is to stay aware of where you are at. And have a source of receiving that warning, whether it is a radio, or otherwise. Stay aware of where you are and where you will travel. It is tough traveling through the area you are completely unfamiliar with especially under the added stresses of a severe storm. In the case that there is the potential for bad weather, check the weather before you leave and see what areas have the potential. Make sure before you leave, have the weather conditions and forecast, providing you with the sure weather or possibilities of what you may be endure. Internet access allows a view at the large outlooks for regional areas, out of the Storm Prediction Center in Norman, Oklahoma. A traveler can check if NOAA is predicting a slight risk of severe weather or a moderate risk. Just knowing that you might be running into one of these issues beforehand is good to know. Once you are traveling into it and in it, it is too late. It can be difficult to figure out the severity of the storm when you are in it.

The Response and Recovery

The traveler researched the response for the 2006 Columbus tornado outbreak. The storm seemed like an F1 which is kind of small, but it must have still affected the area considering what was already mentioned.

NOAA said the tornado was small, but the storm it was a part of affected a very large area, including a few states. The tornado was confined onto the area of Fort Benning, in the boundaries of the base.

When discussing the FEMA response part of the recovery and rebuilding, the traveler asked if FEMA helped. NOAA said it probably comes out of the Department of Defense budget. The damage surveyors recorded that some warehouses were damaged, and most that were hit by the tornado were no longer in use. The warehouses were World War II era wooden warehouses and not in use anymore.

A couple of the housing areas got hit, and six houses were badly damaged or destroyed. This occurred at the housing subdivision on base.

They have several different areas of base housing. The response and recovery for them were to move a family from a damaged house into one that was empty and ready to be used. It is also possible that the families living in the damaged houses might have had to find housing off post if there was none available. The Department of Defense would have the budget on maintenance or replacement for that issue.

From www.noaa.gov Public Domain

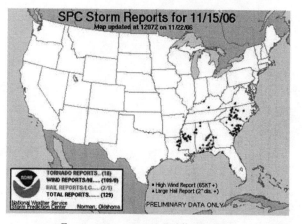

From www.noaa.gov Public Domain

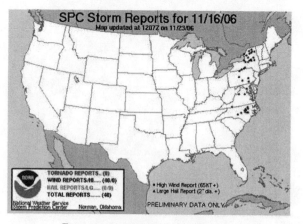

From www.noaa.gov Public Domain

Thankful and Lucky

Travelers know they are lucky to have survived the mentioned November 2006 tornadic storm. Being able to remember how dangerous it was is a good thing, in that the lessons learned can help deter a future trip from being taken obliviously to the weather predictions available from the NOAA and the news. Looking back on a bad and dangerous situation is a useful way of managing future travel plans in order to be safer. The hazards that were present back in November 2006 are still amazing when thinking that some traveled through on business while also being residents of the area.

One traveler never heard of so much bad weather in the form of a three-day storm across so many southern states in the middle of November. Being forced to travel through storms regularly occurs in order to make appointments as well as when living in the area of the storm. Because this storm lasted a few days, the hazardous conditions made a lasting impression on the locals as well, where some had become suspicious of travelers moving through the area during a time of crisis. Some locals sometimes see an outsider arriving at a time of crisis as a threat to possibly loot an area of a disaster. There are also many other concerns that the residents and businesses become worried about in the event of a disaster.

It was a surprise for some who traveled through that storm a few days and weeks later when watching the recovery on the news. It takes the images from news agencies for some to realize they had been right in the middle of a large tornadic outbreak. The images from the news, as well as the NOAA weather reports, are able to describe the few places that did get some direct tornado damage. These storms always do much more damage than what is described, in that the area's transportation delays are usually not reported as much as the injuries, fatalities, and property damage

The blowing of the commercial trucks really hard the night before on 14 November 2006 was just the beginning of this storm, which continued to cause damage later on the 15th as stated in the above, and then later in North Carolina. Without NOAA travelers and the public could think that cloud coverage could be just a little rainstorm. The November 2006, 38 tornado outbreak, was a very expansive story across the southern states at the time and still is in 2014, eight years later for the drivers that traveled through on business. Georgia suffered minimal damages and injuries despite the extensive area of the South damaged. The surrounding states were not as lucky, unfortunately, where eight fatalities were reported by NOAA to have occurred in Riegelwood, North Carolina.

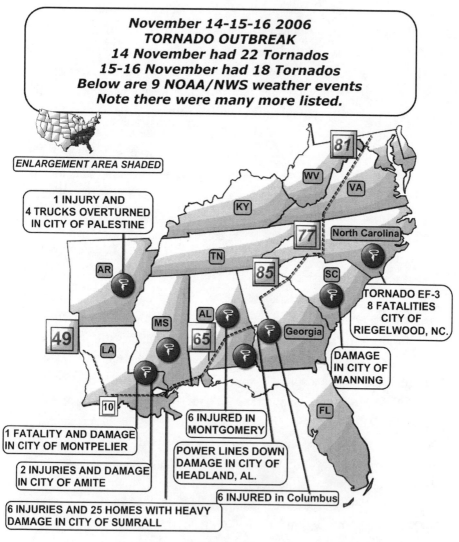

Public Domain

November 14–15–16 2006

Explanation of Map

The following is an explanation of the map labeled the 14–15–16 November 2006 Tornado map. Some suggestions are mentioned on how a traveler can read and follow the NOAA Storm Prediction Center at www.spc.noaa.gov. There are two good things that will be covered that should be remembered. The first is that a traveler should have a weather forecast for a trip and make the right decisions to stay safe should there be severe weather. The second is that a traveler can use the information from www.spc.noaa.gov to learn about the current warnings while also learning the after report of all that had occurred during the storm. This storm was seen to be predicted on the 14th, but there were still many travelers taken by surprise. In addition, the storm became very widespread across many states and the warning from NOAA did not mention the probability anywhere close to what had later occurred. NOAA is a good resource for travelers who want to know more about the weather, but they should also be realistic to the ability of NOAA to predict each area's severe weather down to the tornado.

The NOAA Weather Reports are in part made by the public and first responders about the event. These GREY boxes on the map include the reports. The reports mention some examples of where some of the injuries, fatalities, and damage occurred because a tornado touched down. Two important things can be shown in this map. The first being the need for a traveler to watch for severe weather through watching the local news or visiting the NOAA Storm Prediction Center website at www.spc.noaa.gov. Another thing is to remember a storm and study how it came close to your trip, route, and plan. This can be done by visiting the www.spc.noaa.gov/climo/reports, then map out where you were and where the storm reports mentioned there were fatalities and damage. This can help determine if further planning and management of safety need to occur. This is good information for the next trip. NOAA usually reports a large amount of data regarding injury and damage for a large storm. A traveler should put in some extra time and effort to study up on ways to use this public information to protect oneself and travel more safely.

The BLACK text boxes linked to the map below explain a traveler's story through the area on November 14–15–16, 2006. This traveler was driving through almost every state mentioned having severe weather and tornado outbreaks to include Louisiana, Mississippi, Alabama, Georgia, South Carolina, and North Carolina. The traveler's journey near and around the TORNADOES was lucky, as you can see. This does not mean that it is safe to traveler in severe weather but to be read as an advisory as to that things could have been much worse for the traveler. The route took narrowly dodged a total of 38 tornadoes when looking on a map. But when mapping the route and tornadoes to geographical proportions there are great distances between the tornadoes, reports, and the route. This 38 number is from all the public reports about tornadoes to NOAA during the storm and many may have been F1s similar to the Georgia example. The hype is real when it comes to the damage but the probability of being hit was low, reasoning to why the traveler was not injured, killed, or suffered vehicle damage. There are also more reports of damages not mentioned by NOAA not in the map, and the map was made to try to summarize how the storm was spread out. The map looks busier than the reality of what occurred but it is also proof as to what some travelers on business get forced into or end up being caught in.

The Usefulness of a Map Can Lead to Safer Driving

A traveler who is aware of the dangers of driving in a storm is beginning to having an understanding to safety. A traveler can survive a storm like this by using the following suggestions stated by the traveler who crossed all these areas and survived.

First the driver tried to make sure he had a radio working for any emergency warnings. The radio is very useful in that a tornado warning can be heard. A weather radio is now not the only source of warning information with the new use of mobile phone applications. Having information about warnings in advance from applications, the radio, and local people, can summarize what kind of level, size, and threat will be faced.

Another important thing is that the driver managed his ability to drive safely despite the conditions. Driving under severe weather is not always easy mainly because of a storm's reduction of visibility. When a severe thunderstorm floats over many states staying safe may not be possible, because there are conditions that make constant security issues. One problem worth repeating is that storms create low visibility. In this particular storm the night of the Fourth there was so much rain and wind that visibility was reduced. The ability to see while traveling in a storm at night can be one of the greatest challenges that a traveler will ever face. Strangely and confusingly, it is more about being able to see in your immediate area than the scenario of the surrounding 38 tornadoes. Staying parked and letting the storm pass is one suggestion. This cannot always work if there is no place to stay for as long as it may take. Also, if a storm was not known to be coming for that area staying parked through its time of low visibility cannot be prepared for.

Being caught in a storm also occurs because travelers are required to keep appointments, and keep a constant heading on a destination for business. Just because there is a severe thunderstorm warning ongoing in the southern states as was back in November 2006 does not mean that businesses elsewhere will temporarily delay all appointments. If the Department of Transportation does not officially close the roads or if the other transportation industries are not officially shut down like an airport, then the business will try to make their employees be at that appointment on time. Businesses are reasonable to a certain point when it comes to these situations but they may need convincing or proof. Communication by the traveler can help describe that the severe thunderstorm turned into 38 tornadoes and there may be a delay or the need to reschedule an appointment. As of 2014, it is not illegal for a business to knowingly send employees into severe weather, knowing they have higher chances of being involved in an accident, causing an injury, fatality, and property damage. Law enforcement at the federal, state, and local level allows people to travel through severe weather, knowing these travelers have a higher chance of having an accident, injury, or fatality. The winter weather is the biggest example of this regular occurrence of travel continuing under questionable safety conditions.

There are also other reasons like an emergency situation involving first responders, search and rescues, and other unmentioned situations the public may be in related to an emergency. Some weather warnings also do not describe everything that will occur and are estimates. This can lead to travelers having to decide how to travel in a way that will allow them to keep moving to survive the events. For this storm, surviving was an accomplishment. Considering the later found events, with 38 tornadoes reported, it can put the decision to keep traveling in a storm in a safer perspective. Sometimes it is not worth taking a chance like that. But if the decision is taken and a traveler survives, he or she will have similar words of advice.

Some advice to follow through with when deciding to drive in severe weather: Make sure to inspect the vehicle before leaving. There is no sense is driving through a storm without making sure all the tires are good and filled with the right amount of air pressure, and that the headlights and emergency lights work. There are many other components to a vehicle to inspect as well, before making a riskier type of trip into the weather. Also make sure the roads are open by checking with the Department of Transportation. Just because they were open an hour into a storm does will not mean they will be open forever, so make sure to pull off ahead of time to give yourself the time it takes to find a safe place to wait until the roads open up. Think ahead. The inspection of the vehicle is the most important thing to check even when the roads are closed temporarily. In the event the vehicle may not survive the weather conditions, requesting to delay due to vehicle maintenance, damages, or an inoperable vehicle should be made back to the business's office.

Another important word of advice is the ability of the driver to know the condition of his or her vehicle and how it performs in severe weather ahead of time. Does it provide the right amount of visibility once in a storm? Even though the lights work and the windshield wipers and defroster work, there are some other performance issues. Maintenance of a vehicle is important to a certain point but the driver's ability to perform is the last and final factor. What the vehicle's specifications are can be a focus area when coming down to the final decision to travel, but will a driver perform at the same level as the vehicle, preventing an accident at the right time? Those are the questions travelers need to ask themselves and it is kind of a luck issue as well as to what may occur as a obstacle even if they are on top of their ability to perform.

Check safety specifications. Make sure the vehicle has the basic features to handle the type of weather. One issue is visibility, which can mean two basic things. The first is how the driver can see the road, traffic, and the situation. The second is how the road, traffic, and the situation sees the vehicle. There is an interaction between the two.

Driver's Point of View and Visibility

The most important thing for all forms of transportation is that the vehicle allows the driver a good enough amount of visibility to see the road. What many cars and pickup truck drivers do not know is this fact. One point is that some vehicles can see the road better, and also give the driver a better situational awareness and view around the vehicle in relation to the road and the weather conditions. When most people test drive a car or vehicle they do not take it through a driving course that tests its ability to see in the nighttime storm, like the mentioned night before the extreme weather event of 38 tornadoes. What happens is that most people test the windshield wipers or lights and maybe read about the safety features when driving in storm conditions. Tire traction monitoring has become a popular security feature to check out or request. Also a road thermometer is popular, in order to know if there are icy roads. Why vehicles are not required to have a thermometer considering the high accidents in winter is a mystery. It seems that with all the hype about traffic enforcement, there should be a different system to decrease the number of violations and accidents.

Many issues and vehicle specifications will increase a driver's visibility while driving. One is the design of the vehicle being able to give the driver a clear and full view of the road. Vehicles lower to the ground have a reduced point of view of the road. The reason is the angle of view is reduced to a more linear alignment to the ground. The higher off the ground the more of an angle, while also seeing farther ahead and behind. A vehicle that can see farther away will have a longer time to react when it needs to adjust its speed or direction. This line of sight ability of specific vehicle is an important safety feature and specification to think about before deciding to drive when there is bad weather. If the only vehicle available is low to the ground a traveler should try to avoid driving in the more severe weather conditions. That extra three feet of view from off the ground adds enough time to slow down in any weather but is needed more in extreme weather.

Knowing how a vehicle's height adds to a traveler's ability to see more is something to also know when shopping for a vehicle.

Another thing related to visibility is the ability for a vehicle to react in any type of weather condition. A vehicle higher off the ground will have more maneuvering ability. Features like four wheel drive are recommended. This can be useful when driving into an area that may have debris and flooding of roads with mud. A vehicle that has four wheel drive is definitely recommended if heading into a severe storm. This feature can enhance the visibility of a driver, allowing the vehicle to be mobile and keeping the driver's view more under control.

One example of a vehicle that has a higher angle of view is the commercial motor vehicle. Because their angle of view on the road is higher above all cars, pickup trucks, and other vehicles on the road, it provides truck drivers a longer time to react and slow down, because they can see more and farther away. These trucks also sometimes have four wheel drives, allowing better traction if driving over an unstable road. The difference between what a regular car and pickup truck sees and what a commercial motor carrier sees is huge and the public should know about it for safety awareness and also to have some more common sense when making decisions on the road. This is not to recommend that commercial motor vehicles have better chance of survival in a big storm with tornadoes, but they will have a better view and more time to react.

The Road's, Traffic's, and Situation's Visibility of the Vehicle

When deciding to go into a severe storm the decision based on if a vehicle, traffic, and the situation from the outside will allow your car to be seen to prevent an accident is important. If you can see, great, you're halfway safe; now every other driver near your vehicle on the road is going to have to see your vehicle through the poor visibility. Not all severe storms are the same and traveler will need to know which has lower visibility than others. Winter blizzards should be remembered as causing the lowest visibility out of all others. One thing many have in common is the fact that there is low visibility. This can be a bad thing where other drivers may not see your car.

To make sure your car can be seen would be to make sure the lights work, and to also have them turned on during storm conditions. Lights are one of the most important ways to counter low visibility from other drivers' points of view. Some vehicles' rear signal, brake, and night time lights are more visible than others. Researching which vehicles perform the best in low visibility can be done when car shopping. Another way to boost visibility is to simply have a lighter colored car, or a car that might be easy to see against a commonly occurring type of storm condition. Some colors are better than others, and researching that when shopping for a car in your specific area can help you make a more thoughtful decision.

Another suggestion that can increase your visibility is to have a form of communication like a radio, mobile phone, or other communication device that can help communicate to others when in distress. If you are involved in an accident and your lights do not work to warn traffic to slow down, additional signaling should be attempted. Communication can really make a big difference in making something more visible. It there is very low visibility from the rain, snow, or wind, the communication of a location and what is going on can give some background information about a hazardous situation involving you or someone else's vehicle and how to avoid it. Visual signals only go so far, and with poor visibility a message over the CB radio or from the weather radio when heard can prevent accidents, injuries, fatalities, and more. The ability to use a CB radio to alert other travelers of a situation will be made clearer later when they are closer to the area while being more observant about the message they heard. The use of audio helps prevent injuries and fatalities. A description of what to see and hear and what to be on the look out for can map out what could be expected, and gives an additional sense of direction to an obstacle and/or road hazard.

An example is if a car is off the road and hidden by debris, describing the vegetation, the weather, the communication of a mile marker, GPS coordinates, and nearest city may allow a towing company/friend/family/ or as a last resort a first responder, to find and retrieve your car. Verbal communication adds to someone's ability to see and is still faster than all the hype of social media out on the road. In case there is a language barrier using common sense to survive and possibly trying to find someone who can communicate to help is a suggestion.

The November 2006 Storm Perspective from NOAA

The traveler asked NOAA their opinion of what is the largest storm that ever hit Georgia that you know of, that you saw with your own eyes, and compared to this one at Fort Benning? Was the November 2006 one of the biggest storms you ever heard of?

NOAA replied that one of the bigger outbreaks would be the late April 2011 tornado. That was the same outbreak that hit Tuscaloosa, Alabama. There were many deaths in Georgia as a result of that event, being a fairly large outbreak. There have been quite a few large tornadoes other than the November 2006 outbreak. There were several tornadoes across North and West Georgia during that 2011 outbreak. The 2011 storm system was bigger than the 2006 system.

These occurred in the NOAA Peach Tree office area of responsibility. Their area runs from the Georgia to the Tennessee line, and south to the city of Americus and the city of Vidalia, GA. Georgia only had one tornado in that whole outbreak in November 2006. Now there may have been 38 across the southeastern United States, but we only had one in the Peach Tree office's area. The November 2006 storm can be placed into some perspective with that. There may have been more measures across Alabama or Mississippi. It just was not that big of an event for Georgia.

12

The Future of Search and Rescue

This is the Earth on January 1, 2014 from the GOES Satellite, NASA.gov, Public Domain. Note that this satellite image shows clouds over North America, the cause of the clouds being that thick is from the winter season. Low visibility caused by similar clouds, and severe winter weather causes accidents. A picture like this confirms the need for preparedness at the right time and place.

NASA's public relations wrote an article, "NASA Develops Enhanced Search and Rescue Technologies," in 2010 about search and rescue. The article provided the public a brief glimpse into the future regarding search and rescue technology and improving its capabilities. The following is the complete and original article. The article is followed by some brief additional comments by NASA's writer Rani Gran about the article and writing it.

Greenbelt MD.-NASA which pioneered the technology used for the satellite-aided Search and Rescue capability that has saved more than 27,000 lives worldwide since its inception nearly three decades ago, has developed new technology that will more quickly identify the locations of people in distress and reduce the risk of Rescuers.

The Search and Rescue Mission Office at NASA's Goddard Space Flight Center in Greenbelt, Md. In collaboration with several agencies, has developed a next-generation Search and Rescue system, called the Distress Alerting Satellite System (DASS). NASA, the National Oceanic and Atmospheric (NOAA), the U.S. Air Force, the U.S. Coast Guard and other agencies, are now completing the development and testing of the new system and expect to make it operational in the coming years after a complete constellation of DASS-equipped satellites is launched.

When it goes online, DASS will be able to almost instantaneously detect and locate distress signals generated by 406 MHz beacons installed on aircraft and vessels or carried by individuals, greatly enhancing the international community's ability to rescue people in distress, said NASA Search and Rescue Mission Manager David Affens. This improved capability is made possible because the satellite-based instruments used to relay the emergency signals will be installed on the U.S. military's Global Position System (GPS), a constellation of 24 spacecraft operating in mid Earth orbit (MEO).

Under the current system, which first became operational in the mid-1980s as part of the international COSPASARSAT system, the so-called "repeaters" are placed on NOAA weather satellites operating in low-Earth (LEO) and geostationary orbits. Although it has proven its effectiveness, as evidenced by the number of persons rescued over the system's lifetime, the current capability does have limitations, Affens said.

The LEO spacecraft orbit the Earth 14 times a day and use the Doppler effect to help pinpoint the location of the signal. However, a satellite may not be in position to pick up a distress signal the moment a user activates the beacon.

NOAA's geosynchronous weather satellites, on the other hand, orbit above the Earth in a fixed location over the equator. Although they do provide continuous visibility of much of the Earth, they cannot independently locate a beacon unless it contains a navigation receiver that encodes and transmits its position. Emergency beacons are offered both with and without GPS location data. Furthermore, the beacon-to-satellite ink can be obstructed by terrain.

DASS overcomes these limitations, said Mickey Fitzmaurice, space systems engineer for the NOAA Search and Rescue Satellite-Aided Tracking (SARSAT) program, the organization that operates the U.S. component of the COSPAS-SARSAT system now comprised of 40 nations. "With a mid-Earth orbit Search and Rescue capability provided by GPS, one emergency signal to determine its precise location. Right now, it can take an hour or more before we can even act on a signal," he said.

Goddard began work on the new system in 2002, a few years after studies revealed that repeaters placed on a constellation of satellite operating in mid-Earth orbit would significantly enhance Search and Rescue efforts. With NASA funding, Goddard engineers developed a proof-of-concept instrument and worked with the Air Force to fly it on GPS satellites to demonstrate and evaluate its effectiveness. Currently, nine GPS satellites are flying the proof-of-concept technology and an additional 12 are planned. Goddard is using the testing to fine tune the technology before transitioning to a final system after 2015, which will be deployed on the Air Force's Block III GPD satellites.

As part of their research and development effort, Goddard engineers also designed and built a new ground-tracking station on the Goddard campus to receive, decode, and locate the 406 MHz distress beacons worldwide. NOAA plans to use the design when it begins constructing a DASS ground station in Hawaii next year and perhaps another in Florida in the future, Fiztmaurice said.

The U.S. will not be alone in using mid-earth orbiting spacecraft for its Search and Rescue instruments. Europe has begun development of a Search and Rescue capability on its Galileo system, Russia, its GLONASS system, and China, its compass system. All are modeled after the NASA developed DASS.

"DASS technology is the future of international satellite-aided Search and Rescue," Affens added. "A few years ago, we looked to see how we could improve the system and we concluded that the international Search and Rescue community would benefit from new technology installed on GPS. We would be able to identify distress signals faster and with a greater level of precision. In the end, this will save more lives, reduce risk to rescuers, and save money because less time will be spent searching."

NOAA, as the lead U.S. agency for the SARSAT program, maintains a national registration database of 406 MHz emergency beacons. "The database is a vital part of the SARSAT program and is used to expedite the Search process, especially if the location of the beacon is not immediately known," said Mickey Fitzmaurice, space systems engineer for the NOAA SARSAT program.

Should NOAA receive an alert, the agency can contact names listed on the database to validate the signal and get probable locations of the persons in distress. This enhances the overall rescue coordination process and prevents unneeded rescue attempts if the beacon is accidentally activated.

Although commercial vessel and aircraft operators are required by law to carry emergency beacons, recreational users are not. However, anyone who owns an emergency beacon is required to register their names, addresses, vessel, or aircraft information and emergency phone numbers with the registration database. Fitzmaurice encourages recreational boaters, aviators, and hikers to buy beacons and register their information to help assure rapid Rescue.

NASA's Rani Gran Interview

The following includes the discussion with NASA's Rani Gran. It is hard to really look into the future and accurately make predictions on what will occur when it comes to search and rescue technology. There have been some new improvements in the area tracking commercial airlines and vessels in the mentioned above article.

At the time NASA wrote the above article the DASS was still experimental. There were an estimated 12 to 20 GPS satellites launched with the DASS technology on them at that time. The goal was to have 20 and maybe more. There was a process of waiting for each of the GPS satellites going up and working. The development of the design and the technology being put into action took a few years. New satellites were built for the DASS program.

Prior to the DASS, there was a personal locator device that would cut down the time of finding a specific location. The time it took in finding someone was reduced from minutes to seconds. Sometimes if a traveler became stranded or in need of help in Northern latitude as Alaska this device could help, but had some delays. The information on the weaker areas the old beacon worked in and how well it worked is not currently available.

In order to know the beacon's locating signal to pinpoint the location there needed to be two satellites. The Geostationary Operational Environmental Satellites (GOES) satellite will pick up a location if it is in the United States. Then there is the need of another polar orbiting satellite to come over and get the signal's location. The beacon needs both those satellites to find the exact locational point. Sometimes the satellites get it in minutes if you are lucky. It may also take several hours for the right path to come.

The new DASS is going to make it faster to pinpoint a location. The GPS satellites that will be used will go in a lower orbit. There are multiple satellites that will be used, hoping to make finding the beacon more efficient and quicker.

There are beacons for hikers that are great. NOAA and search and rescue highly recommend beacons, also known as personal locator devices. Someone interested in learning more can go to a camping store or an outdoor store to find out if they sell them, or if they can refer them to a retailer that does.

There are also beacons that are attached to boats, ships, and cruise liners, as well as personal locator devices that someone can attach to themselves just in case they go overboard. These are good for vessels that may become threatened by storms that could become big enough to capsize the vessel. For that risk beacons are highly recommended.

In Alaska it is really tough when it comes to rural traveling combined with the weather, and then the low visibility when it becomes dark all day for a few months. As a result of the challenge and size of the state, Alaska has is own Red Cross that does all its search and rescue. A lot of their technology is finding a person from radio towers. That system takes longer to search and rescue. There are also more planes and vessels that end up in need of help. If the new DASS system is put in place and then these beacons get installed on the planes and vessels, it would greatly reduce the amount of time it takes to search and rescue someone.

A lot of people use aircraft to go from their homes to the nearest city. So a better search and rescue system is needed. Currently, anything that can get picked up if near a radio tower and if the signal and device work properly. Some advice now is if a traveler is in trouble, going towards a radio tower will help with the search and rescue process. The strategy is for travelers to hopefully take themselves into the signal area if their aircraft left them in a remote area.

The DASS and the satellites are definitely more reliable than radio towers. The main reason is a satellite can see more and will allow search and rescuers to be more responsive. A satellite signal from the ground is going to be picked up by 20 or more satellites constantly rotating around the earth, compared to a radio signal that may not have that angle from above in the sky a satellite has.

The personal locator device is one of those unsung heroes. It is sometimes kind of funny when it comes to the false alerts or when later looking back at how a device was able to become a hero in a rescue. There is a little bit of bureaucracy in the government in getting the perfect GPS system funded and also running. The GPS experiment started well before the 2010 story about the DASS. NASA was also committed to other technologies through the years which led to some of the delays in getting this new system being designed and tested, all on a budget.

The Future of Travel

Crash Lane News believes the future of travel with the above examples can be anticipated by travelers more. The future is able to be described in a basic, simplified, and understandable way. The difficulty is predicting exactly what is going to happen accurately. The following is an attempt to read into the existing issues. This is done to suggest and advise a way to plan a safer trip.

Some existing issues that affect travel the most include the ongoing struggle between civilization and nature, meaning mostly the weather and other natural disasters. It is a good idea to try to manage both disaster size threats and smaller size threats in a way to prevent injuries, fatalities, and property damage. Travelers can predict their own future based off of weather forecasting, Wireless Emergency Alerts, FEMA, NOAA/National Weather Service, and make a plan based on what they foresee.

Another way to look into the future is knowing the current legislation in the works, and laws. Government planning can affect the local, state, and federal government where the public travels. Knowing these laws will give a traveler the awareness to what the current travel procedures are and what is required to follow to avoid delays. Everyone can be a predictor of the future for themselves and it is good preparedness.

Popular Culture and the Future of Travel

The images of futuristic technologies and futuristic transportation systems is now and always be in the United States' popular culture. Some of these images are inspiring and do help developers get the inspiration to find some solutions.

Travelers use popular culture's view for their own travel plan. Some areas of popular culture past and present include: movies, music, television, newspapers, and magazines. The most significant popular culture to travelers of the past and present were and are books. There are many other forms of popular culture that contributed to how people decided to travel and how developers of transportation and technology created and built real designs. The imagination of the public based off of the current culture that includes fiction seems real, but never occurred, and has influenced many trips.

One example of a very influential, inspiring, interesting, refreshing, knowledgeable, and unique creator of popular culture is the author James Michener. Many countries and regions of the world are described in his fictional work. Some of his books are based on the real conditions at the time he wrote his books. His books still seem real. The stories seem to have been based of real situations and are educational to audiences. His ability to use popular culture and know the current times to build a possible reality that exists across many years has kept readers interested. Michener's ability to describe a story that spans many years or distances helped make a name for himself greater than many other artists and writers. His work is not considered travel books although many or almost all of his work has a different location. His stories give the audience a detailed description of a country that is similar to a travel book or travel magazine like *National Geographic*. With this description, Michener's style slightly compares to *National Geographic*. For that reason, a traveler should be realistic to popular culture's accurate description of a location. Fictional stories as well as nonfictional stories tend to leave out the many safety and security solutions needed to be known in order to survive in a location. This information should be known if a traveler decides to visit a setting he or she learned of in a movie. This also goes for the other forms of popular culture where travelers will sometimes model the actions of an entertainer, politician, or other public figure.

Popular Culture Contributing to Safety and Security Affecting the Future of Travel

The main separation between popular culture and ways to travel safely can be found here. Travelers should know that once out in the real world, the main threat that faces them will be the weather and natural disasters. Manmade disasters are also a major threat. In addition to the disasters, there are many other security issues. A traveler needs to be able to travel under the current laws. These laws create specific procedures that need to be followed. If not followed this can make a trip short and prevent someone from being able to reach their destinations. If walking, driving, or being a passenger, a person's view and understanding of the difference between popular culture and reality is going to affect their survival and success.

When popular culture markets certain examples to sell products or to raise the public's awareness about certain issues that affect travel, there can be a significant impact on what travelers will do. The use of technology or description of technology in popular culture will also contribute to how the public travels. Popular culture can increase the popularity of certain technologies. Marketing and advertising to sell products also increase the development of technology. This can start to lead into the safety and security being influenced by popular culture. What is popular is what gets developed. For example users of electronic devices can probably name many applications for a smartphone related to entertainment, travel, and business. With all these factors being influenced by popular culture, these issues are sometimes mirrored in the popular culture. The issues of what was developed and marketed and then used by the public may become part of fiction and nonfiction stories. One example is Afghanistan. *National Geographic* used Afghanistan as a popular travel destination to write about in the beginning of the 20th century. This was also later written about by the author James Michener in his story *Caravans*. The popularity of using the country as a part of popular culture in the United States grew. Unfortunately, Afghanistan became a part of some security issues threatening the United States towards the end of the 20th century. The mirroring of the location in popular culture and then the U.S. government involvement to provide aid to the country influenced later security issues. The influence is very small in terms of an entire country, and the United States has embassies in many countries besides Afghanistan that also have security threats.

One more extreme example is the use of Afghanistan as a training camp by terrorist groups. Their ideology grew against the United States even though there have been counterinsurgency U.S. military missions ongoing to try to bring peace, democracy, and eradicate terrorists. This has been stated to be done to protect the United States as well as protect the local citizens in Afghanistan. It is possible that the popular culture only mirrored the location of Afghanistan partly and did not go deeper into explaining some of the security issues that may have created the past manmade terrorist threats against the United States.

Technology Affects the Future of Travel

GPS

With the importance in knowing how popular culture affects travel and technology, a traveler can look into the future. The simplest way to describe the future of technology is to look into the past and present. Some technologies that already exist are most likely to exist in the future. Technology changes though. It may increase in speed, be reduced in size, and collect more data.

One example is the Global Positioning System, GPS. Every form of public transportation currently has a GPS system for tracking, insurance, directions, timeliness, budgeting of fuel, and for additional security reasons. With the knowledge of how the GPS system is used by the government and public transportation systems there has also been an increase in its use by private companies and private individuals. The main point is that the future use of a GPS system is predicted to continue with the same function as it does now. One change is the increasing amount of data that these systems can add for the user's convenience.

For this reason a traveler should be aware of how this technology is going to affect the future. One main reason this will affect the future is that it provides an additional layer to the security of a trip. There are many layers that exist to include: driving safely, route security, vehicle maintenance, cyber security, and many other examples of areas that are needed to be secured for a safe trip.

A traveler can learn more about GPS through NASA at www.nasa.gov.

In Summary

Most people take their place and life for granted unless they have a close call with the weather or have been living or working in a hazardous area. Unfortunately, seeing the dangers of a disaster with a first person point of view is what usually starts the discussion about security. When witnessing this it can be considered too late and that more preparedness should have prevented more damage.

It is important to remember that if we are alive we are lucky for the time being. It is also important to know how to extend life and survival rates. There are options with having a government that is able to provide some lifesaving operations such and search and rescue. A traveler should do some additional research on what kind of personal locator devices are available for the type of trip they plan on taking whether on an airline, vessel, hiking, or another type of trip.

Another important piece of advice is to remember to check the weather ahead of time. Know of a good way to get weather information at every destination. Each location may vary when it comes to the best way to get news about the weather. So inquire as to what is the best news weather forecast for that area. Some remote destinations may surprise a traveler in that the weather is not a very important piece of information. When the public gets insight into the benefits of the DASS program and for the future of search and rescue it adds to the public's confidence in the U.S. government. This technology and report by www.nasa.gov is the future of search and rescue.

Crash Lane News Point of View on the Future of Search and Rescue

In the United States, there are many federal, state, and local laws. With the total amount of laws in the thousands for each state, there are some basic things forgotten such as the need to have a search and rescue plan. Many areas will state that they already do meaning the first responders but there can be more done to make search and rescue work more efficiently. With all the distractions preventing one from knowing about search and rescue it may be even more difficult to try to look into the future of what lies ahead for search and rescue. The future is limited as a result in the budget. There are also limits because of the priorities put in place at the state government side of managing public safety. This also goes for there being a limited effort to budget search and rescue by the federal government and the local city governments. There is always more that can be done but distractions tend to get the money due to the nature of politics, special interests groups, and an out-of-date government. With the expanse on disaster preparedness from manmade threats such as terrorism as a result of 9/11 and the creation of the current DHS, expanding and improving search and rescue operations should be a priority area to update and invest.

The reality is that search and rescue is not the first thing on the list for the Department of Defense, Department of Justice, and DHS. The reason comes from it not being a known priority and something the public wants the government to be involved in. Citizens need to use their voice and the democratic process of contacting and communicating with elected officials about the need to have more search and rescue planning and preparedness in their immediate area.

Many times the issue of search and rescue in popular culture is related to the weather being the contributing factor. With some public programs, the issues of search and rescue are not always the first topic of discussion for other areas in the United States. The average citizens who are educated about search and rescue do not have any direct communication or access to their local area's plan should someone go missing. There is no commonly known federal, state, or local area missing person plan. That is scary when thinking about it. What is scarier is that there is not much government transparency about search and rescue operations and missing persons in the United States. Compared to some government programs little is known and really available when it comes to being able to view from above which state is the safest in regard to missing persons reports. When it comes to search and rescue operations there might be such a high rate of failure missions the transparency is really proof of a failure to keep the public from harm. The news tries to show some of these issues, but it is so fragmented in single stories it is really hard to really know how many people are missing and in need of a rescue.

Currently, the United States culture could be described to have more of a focus on law enforcement, specifically traffic violations, than on search and rescue operations. This is reality. There are many missing persons that never get located. In some examples it is because of a lack of the locations failure to focus on search and rescue, while instead focusing on traffic management. Other factors of unsolved missing persons are the lack of search and rescue budgeting, government transparency of search and rescue, and search and rescue accountability. There are currently many areas within the United States to include some largely populated areas that do not attempt search and rescues. There are also many areas that do not have an office tracking missing persons in their area. Strangely, a few of these areas claim to have emergency management available to the public. Even more surprising, these same areas receive federal disaster relief from FEMA, and state disaster relief, yet the federal government does not hold these areas accountable when it comes to their search and rescue capabilities and their unsolved missing persons. As the United States public is accused of unsafe traffic violations, some other U.S. Citizens remain missing without an official search funded and managed by the U.S. government underway. With all the taxes the government makes off income and property taxes at the state level, and income taxes at the federal level, the public would think the government would search for them. Total government unaccountability is a reality when it comes to search and rescue. The suggested solution is to have a local area search and rescue plan for missing residents, and be accountable for those that go missing when they travel through their local area. The United States is a big country but with more local U.S. Citizens partnering together, things can really be made safer. No one wants to disappear or become a missing person, which is why U.S. citizens need to have more awareness. There can be more support for more government action to be developed and taken in that specific area.

Locally the closest thing to a search and rescue plan would be to contact a neighborhood watch group and file a missing persons report with a local police department. As a word of advice both those mentioned options may fall short of actually being able to locate and find someone. It is a scary reality that most people may not put much thought into until they find out someone they knew had disappeared and no one including law enforcement knew where they were.

Suggestions for Travelers

There are many good points about search and rescue improving in the above. However, there has also been the use of technology to search out someone where it may not be to be beneficial to them. For example, the instance someone uses a GPS device to stalk and harass someone wherever they go. With the developments and improvements of technology, the misuse of it can also be an area of increasing concern. A traveler should be aware of the misuse of devices in order to protect oneself from being turned into a victim of a GPS and transportation crime. The misuse of GPS is also not something that a company, a government agency, and a news agency is going to report about daily even though they are used frequently. Many businesses use them to help track their vehicles, vessels, and property, but there safety concerns like the intentional calling a driver's smartphone or cell phone when they know they are driving in a vehicle.

Aside from the issue of misuse, there are also other technologies separate from GPS that have been known to help search and rescue. There are also other tracking devices in that may transmit Wi-Fi, to cell phone towers, as well as through the radio spectrum. These have been misused when following someone and are considered a Fourth Amendment violation of an illegal search and seizure.

Some of the problems of the misuse of a tracking device for someone who travels a lot is that there would be a third party out there unknown to the traveler. This unknown individual would be able to know pretty much where a traveler is while that traveler is completely unaware of what is happening. In a more dangerous scenario where a traveler would not know they were, while being followed by someone that did know the area well, some things may be manipulated to cause the unaware traveler additional hardship, injury, property damage, information theft, and an accident. Because of this it is recommended to know what exactly a device is capable of doing and how it works in order to not get taken advantage of. The last thing someone needs on a trip is to have someone stalking them through an application on their smartphone, leading to a property crime or violent crime against its own user.

There is also the problem of a traveler having an unknown device transmitting one's location to an unknown third party. An unknown device planted on or inside their vehicle, in their bag, or inside their body. Not all devices are going to be able to run off a battery forever, which would require someone to replace it and or charge it up. Watch who has access to your property, vehicle, and yourself. Watch those with that access while they work on your property or around it.

The fact that someone has been followed to the point of someone placing a device inside them is much more serious and can result in serious injury to the internal organs. One example of this kind of device in the body was not for GPS but sending out a ping signal similar to the radio frequencies and the cell phone frequencies. They can also send audio.

An interesting point is that some healthcare workers are aware of such devices. Some will ask if the traveler had traveled to another country. This is a good tip that a device like this may be being put in someone if they have traveled to a foreign country. The reality is the technology is the highest in the United States, so that can be a diversion to the fact that your own next door neighbors are hearing your farts being born.

A traveler should also be aware that traveling to a foreign country may not be the only place where such a device would be placed inside of them but in any area where tourists are known to visit. They may be inserted where travelers on business are known to go. Once an unsuspecting traveler has a device in them there is no limit as to what the third party is able to know. Data collection has become more detailed by studying different things like transportation, and a device inside a body is possibly doing this as well.

Because of a device like this someone will know everything from bathroom breaks, office routines, where they are at during every moment at work, what they are doing at every moment, who they are with at every moment, and much more. That is all based on the device being able to give away their location or audio.

It can tend to sound like these devices do not exist but the proof that they exist is able to be witnessed by doing the simple research about the tracking of animals. The data collection about a species' movements is basically the same idea. For an unsuspecting human there is no radio collar that would be placed around their neck. There are tracking devices given to individuals in trouble with the courts. It is estimated that most people will have this inside their stomach in a plastic ball colored white, pink, red, or other colors. The colors could change with a person's health to disguise or camouflage it in their body.

Some business professionals that have access to sensitive information as well as access to sensitive areas in their company that are of high value to competitors have been targeted. Most people do not see a businessman as becoming someone followed like an animal but unfortunately it occurs. The reporting of such misconduct goes untold and is really an unknown even in 2014.

Traveling can get complicated with all that is mentioned here, and the public and travelers should know the practice and use of these devices have been out of the spotlight of news reports. The are many questions as to how many problems such as traffic accidents were caused as a result of a device like that. Someone following a signal will usually tend to have a crowd commonly occurring that would also be expected and could also be manipulated by misuse.

The tracking of devices on unknown transporters are usually in the shipping and logistics business. Most of these are on the vehicle, trailer, and in the freight. There are many shipments worth thousands of dollars so the product's manufacturer, warehouse workers, or the trucking company will have a tracking device on the package. A commercial carrier will have a tracking device that is GPS or something else on all their vehicles. This is considered legal since they are the owners of the property.

When the wrong people are using tracking devices and end up sneaking up on a driver when they are sleeping or following them on the road in a way to cause an accident, it should be considered an issue when it is normally not. Sneaking up on a driver is a safety concern if it is to stage an incident to where the driver is blamed for a theft or worse. The more well off companies in the trucking industry track their vehicles very closely. Many have that right to do so because it is their vehicle but the issue of how safe it is for the driver can get overlooked. When used to endanger their safety and security, the incident might also be concealed to look like it never occurred.

Theft is an issue. Theft is why a device like this is used as a deterrent. It may not always be to watch the driver but to watch if the driver gets hijacked, or something else happens like an accident. When something looks strange based off of a device's data along a driver's planned route where the driver is unable to communicate where he or she is, it can help in the recovery of a vehicle.

The estimated time this tracking technology has been used goes back to the tracking devices used in the military for aircraft and for tracking devices for airliners. The need to know where an aircraft is over the water can help in the search and rescue.

With that fact, more uses and strategies for such tracking to increase the security for a vehicle led it to being placed in someone. Also the issue of tagging wildlife led to the idea of tagging humans. There were different misuses that developed unreported. Some people think that the tracking of someone when they are unaware of it is legal. Some also believe that a device in someone is legal. The reality is the misuse of a device violates the U.S. Constitution in many areas to include the illegal search and seizure. It also violates many other rights of Americans regarding the freedom to live.

In summary of all the criticisms and misuse examples of a GPS or tracking device, the future use of devices requires more oversight. The benefits of it being used in a search and rescue are going to be as transparent as the U.S. government wants it to be, like with the NASA story. Those example uses appears to make GPS and tracking devices a valuable tool to use to save lives. The difficult thing is to find the right amount of budgeting in the government to develop useful and legal tracking devices while also providing search and rescue.

No American wants be followed around like he or she is being hunted as an animal to be slaughtered, which may lead to the need for additional privacy protections and the ability to know there is a way to check if your privacy is being protected. This also leads into the need for there to be more technologies that protect privacy and check for that. The solution is for the development of privacy and access controls checks.

13

Interview with the National Insurance Crime Bureau

The following is from an interview with the Public Affairs Director for The National Insurance Crime Bureau (NICB), www.nicb.org. The NCIB is a not-for-profit headed by a president/CEO with a Board of Governors overseeing all. The Board is insurance industry professionals nominated and appointed to serve a term. Investigating is a service that NICB provides to their member companies; no extra cost for it. The organization focuses on investigations for car accident reports that claim phony injuries. When the accident might be staged or appears to be perpetrated to collect money from phony injuries, NICB will investigate it. NICB also does vehicle theft investigations in foreign countries, but no accident investigations. When it comes to recommendations for travelers, the NICB believes that being informed about issues is every citizen's responsibility. There are many issues located on their website that can be of value to travelers trying to make improvements in areas they travel to and reside in.

NICB's website mentions its vision and mission, "The NICB partners with insurers and law enforcement agencies to facilitate the identification, detection and prosecution of insurance criminals. The vision of the NICB is to be the preeminent organization fighting insurance fraud and crime. The mission of the NICB is to lead a united effort of insurers, law enforcement agencies and representatives of the public to prevent and combat insurance fraud and crime through data analytics, investigations, training, legislative advocacy and public awareness." This description does go along with what they have in other areas throughout the website.

From an interview with the NICB, the most famous investigation NCIB worked on was the first World Trade Center bombing attack. NICB identified the vehicle used in the first attack on the World Trade Center in the state of New York, in 1993. NICB identified the vehicle from a partial serial number located on the axle.

The history of the organization started with auto theft investigations. From 1912 until 1992 it was solely focused on vehicle theft. NICB did not directly investigate other crimes like train robbers or bank robbers. Some of the same suspects investigated for insurance fraud or vehicle theft are involved in other crimes. The question of the NICB's involvement in investigations of other crimes that had occurred on high profile cases of the past was asked. The question about the infamous bank robberies of the 1930s was referred to since some suspected bank robbers may have stolen vehicles. But, the NICB did not take part in investigating the 1930s bank robberies.

NICB Current Focus Area

These days the emphasis is on medical fraud more so than vehicle theft. NICB does a significant amount of vehicle theft investigations but medical fraud is now the area with the most focus. The NICB website mentions, "Workers compensation and medical fraud criminals are more than just a pain to the insurance industry and the American public they are a menace threatening out nation's healthcare system. We all pay for their crimes, and that's a bitter pill for us to swallow. If you suspect workers' compensation claimant fraud and medical fraud activities, contact the National Insurance Crime Bureau in one of three easy ways: 1. Text "Fraud" and your tip to TIP411 (847411), 2. Call 1-800-TEL-NICB (1-800-835-6422), and lastly, 3. Submit the form on www.nicb.org.

As for where the NICB conducts its operations, the NICB has a presence in all states; there is no favorite. NICB's investigations count for one year can vary from several hundred to thousands. Some of the states have more investigations than others. Typically New York, Florida, Texas, and California are among the leading states with the most investigations.

National Insurance Crime Bureau NICB.org

NICB Helped Solve First World Trade Center Bombing

NICB Investigates Insurance Fraud the Most

States With Most Insurance Fraud

CALIFORNIA

NEW YORK

TEXAS

FLORIDA

Information is available to the public at NICB.org. Information here in interview is property of *Crash Lane News*. Map is property of *Crash Lane News*.

NICB participates in investigations that occasionally involve all levels of law enforcement and other government agencies. It depends on the circumstances for each. NICB has not worked with the White House, Senate, Congress, Supreme Court, or the Department of Defense on an investigation. They also do not investigate color of law violations which include excessive force, sexual assault, failure to keep from harm, planting of evidence. The reason is it is not the stated area they work on, and they are not law enforcement.

Many organizations now have a public affairs officer and NICB is open and helpful to the public. Their website mentions some good public information that the public can look up. When it comes to the NICB involvement in the media through feature films and books, their website is the best source. As for the NICB's involvement in the realm of politics there are no records of former employees later holding political office.

Auto Theft Questions

A citizen of a state that has a high statistic can sometimes be surprised if there is a negative high rate of something ongoing. Some residents are astonished that California has the highest auto theft rate out of all the other states. The map represents the high auto theft rankings for a few metropolitan statistical areas (MSA), cities in California. Each MSA has a ranking number next to its name. The Modesto MSA is number one. This is based on information from the NICB for the year of 2012.

2012
NATIONAL
AUTO THEFT RANKINGS
CALIFORNIA HAS THE #1
HIGHEST RANKED CITY
from NICB.org

#10 Redding

#34 Chico

31 Yuba City

8 Vallejo-Fairfield

78 Napa

6 San Francisco, Oakland, Hayward

#13 Sacramento

#4 Stockton

7 San Jose, Sunnyvale, Santa Clara

#1 Modesto

19 Madera

54 Santa Cruz

#2 Fresno

21 Salinas

16 Visalia, Porterville

217 San Luis Obispo, Paso Robles, Arroyo

3 Bakersfield

144 Santa Maria, Santa Barbara

121 Oxnard, Thousand Oaks, Ventura

23 Los Angeles

12 Riverside, San Bernardino, Ontario

35 El Centro

18 San Diego, Carlsbad

Property of *Crash Lane News*.

Auto theft is high in California according to NICB because of the size of the population in residence. When talking about the reasons behind vehicle theft in the nation's most populous state, California, one reason linked to the population size is that California has a lot of vehicles. The popular culture of travel in California is to travel by car. Car travel is used more than other available forms of transportation, which is also the reason there are more auto thefts. Whenever you have lots of people you tend to have all kinds, to include those that take part in crimes and auto theft. When a large group in the area's population is also driving many more vehicles compared to other states, there are more targets for the mentioned auto thieves. Marry that subset to the numerous targets for theft in the state and you have a good reason for why California always ranks at the top. Plus, a lot of the thefts are driven by a huge drug problem in California and drug problems always lead to more crimes, as junkies steal anything they can, supporting their drug habits.

The particular area or cause for auto theft have been thought up in order to know what happens and why. *Crash Lane News* also knows some say these crimes occur because of economic collapse in an area. They may also occur to fund terrorism, to fund illegal immigration, and occur as a result of color of law violations where a vehicle is stolen by law enforcement, or fabricated to be stolen, then later reported by the same law enforcement as a vehicle theft, giving themselves credit.

NICB responded, auto thefts are certainly not occurring to fund terrorism, although that is reported all the time, without good statistical reasoning. Vehicle theft is just a crime that occurs for all the reasons it always has—from joy riding to simple transportation to disguising and reselling for profit. The numbers could be doctored about auto theft. Yes, if no theft report is placed into the NCIC system, then the numbers can be skewed. There are several law enforcement agencies whose reporting has caused the FBI not to accept their crime stats. That tells you something. When dealing with numbers, perfection can be elusive. NICB has no clue on a margin for error; that's better asked at the FBI.

When a citizen witnesses auto thefts for themselves it can sometimes be a surprise that there is a high rate of unsolved investigations. There are thousands of stolen vehicles that are never recovered but unless it is part of a more significant crime (carjacking where a murder occurred) auto theft doesn't capture much attention anymore. Unsolved crime occurs involving auto theft.

In summary the NICB is going to be active in investigations that may end up affecting many that travel. The most obvious ones are for auto theft and it is recommended to take the precautions mentioned on the website at www.nicb.org. There is some information that may also be helpful regarding accident and fraud prevention, auto salvage fraud, boat theft prevention, disaster fraud, and towing fraud, along with the ways to avoid and protect you from being a victim of this. When on a trip and things go wrong it is good to know there are some organizations as NICB that can help.

14

Permission to use information from Truemileage.com given to *Crash Lane News* for book. This design is the Property of *Crash Lane News*.

About True Mileage from Truemileage.com

The following information is from an interview with True Mileage CEO Ryan Morrison, in November 2013. True Mileage does three main things. First, they help drivers save money on the cost of their vehicle. Second, they help drivers become safer. Third, a driver's privacy is respected. More details and specific information available about all of this is in the following report.

True Mileage will make it easy for drivers to collect driving information from an in-vehicle device and send that data to their insurance company in exchange for a larger discount. The device helps low mileage and low risk drivers, save money on their auto insurance. Many people that self-report low mileage are not really low mileage drivers so insurance companies can only offer minimal discounts without verified driving and/or mileage data.

There are predictions that as many as 50% of vehicles will have a device installed to collect driving information by 2020. Right now only 1 to 2% of vehicles have some kind of device recording driving information that can be use for insurance discounts.

Data Summary

The True Mileage device creates a summary of driving data including information on how many miles were driven late at night. Tracking late night driving is important because it is the most dangerous time to drive. This may help provide customers awareness of how much they are driving late at night, and hopefully encourage drivers to reduce late night driving.

The hard braking will also be shown in the summary report and hopefully encourage driving in a way that reduces hard braking over time, making their driving safer, and saving on fuel. A section on the miles driven and fuel efficiency will be shown in a way where the driver can try to improve fuel saving as well.

There will also be a section on error codes; those can have very valuable information for drivers when something is wrong with a vehicle. If someone is in their car and the check engine light comes on, they may want to know right away what caused it. With the True Mileage technology someone could get that information right away. A user with a smartphone can hold it against the device, and it will give them the vehicle driving summary including current error codes.

In summary, the driver will see their error codes, different risks they are exposed to based on their driving habits, and be able pass their low mileage and/or safe driving data along to get a larger discount on their insurance. Other benefits of the True Mileage devices are fuel efficiency tracking, mileage reporting for tax purposes, and mileage reporting for business trips.

Mileage Discount

True Mileage hopes numerous insurance companies will accept data from their devices and perhaps even use their recommendations when it comes to setting a mileage and/or driving discount.

True Mileage device data helps insurance companies know how many miles a vehicle is driven, and the company's Mileage Discount Analytics™ lets the insurer know how many miles typical rates cover. If a driver gets a new vehicle and drives less than 16,000 miles per year she or he might be deserving of a discount. If a driver has an older vehicle, those are typically driven 10,000 miles per year, so a discount would not be recommended unless they are driving less than that. True Mileage may also use driver age, state and other covariates to assist with the recommended mileage discount calculation.

Driving at Night Is a Greater Risk

Crash Lane News stated that there is more traffic density on the road during the day. The result is more accidents on the road during the day. At nighttime there are a lot fewer accidents, so few to the point it almost looks attractive to just drive at night, for the reason that no one is going to be out on the road. True Mileage stated, on a per mile driven basis, it is more risky to be on the roads at night. So if a driver was to take a 10 mile trip he or she would be a safer to take that trip during the day instead of at night. Nighttime driving is the more dangerous for a number of reasons. Darkness is the likely main issue because of the reduction in visibility. There are also issues with driving under the influence, and another factor is fatigue. As the day goes on people get more and more tired. Those factors combine to make nighttime driving much higher risk. A True Mileage study found it up to 5 times more dangerous for females to be driving late at night and up to 10 times more dangerous for males. True Mileage also provides recommendations to insurers on daytime driving discounts that account for the age and gender of drivers.

Hard Braking

Another interesting topic is how True Mileage is using sudden braking. True Mileage believes that braking in a given situation is a safe thing to do. If a driver is about to have a collision with another vehicle or object they should certainly hit the brakes, but if a driver is slamming on their brakes frequently over time that means the driver is consistently putting themselves in dangerous situations. Drivers that hard brake frequently are more likely to get into accidents. One form of un-safe driving that leads to hard braking is tailgating. This occurs when drivers do not leave enough space to the vehicle in front of them.

If a driver infrequently hard brakes he or she is a typically a safer driver, and an insurance company may increase his or her discount. If a driver is hard braking all the time and an insurance company is giving the driver a low mileage discount, the insurance company might want to reduce that discount.

There are other benefits to being aware of hard braking. Drivers that hit their brakes frequently are also likely to be accelerating too aggressively. Hard accelerations and hard brakes both influence fuel economy. Driving in a way to prevent hard braking is one of the ways people can increase their efficiency. On the maintenance side, drivers that hit their brakes all the time are hard on the car's braking system, increasing the maintenance on the brakes and other components.

The Device May Assist with Emissions Checks

The True Mileage device connects in the same place mechanics connect for smog checks and emissions testing. In the future True Mileage may do some intermediate smog or emissions testing. This could potentially reduce the amount of time and cost associated with going into a specialized shop.

True Mileage Uses Smartphone or Mail to Report Data

The True Mileage website states, "We have developed less expensive, more intelligent OBD devices that calculate all the elements needed for rating on the device including a comprehensive summary of all activity. This data set can be returned periodically through the user's smartphone at little cost to the insurer."

True Mileage suggests transmitting summary data at least once or twice per year for insurance discount purposes but drivers are welcome to tap their device and view their data whenever they like. Instead of having the transmission auto generated by the device, the data gets sent when the driver taps the True Mileage device with any NFC enabled smartphone. The information is easily passed along to the insurer or anyone else the driver wishes. True Mileage has a backup alternative option to NFC for drivers that just want a one-time data collection, they can simply mail their device in and a summary is emailed back.

Installation

The True Mileage device plugs in right below the steering wheel at the data outlet. It connects to the same place where mechanics plug in to check engine error codes and do smog checks. The technical term for it is the OBD, the onboard diagnostic port.

True Mileage can mail the device to a new customer, and the customer will self-install it. It usually takes 30 seconds to a minute to get under the steering wheel and find the data outlet and plug it in.

There are also plans to sell the device at auto parts stores, auto dealerships, auto repair shops, and possibly gas stations. At theses locations there may also be someone available to assist with installing the device and possibly even tap the device with an NFC enabled phone for them when they come back in.

NFC vs. Bluetooth

Some other data devices out there use a Bluetooth connection instead of NFC. True Mileage may re-consider using Bluetooth in the future as well, but it does have some downsides. Bluetooth technology sounds simple enough to use but there are frequent issues with pairing, an app download is required along with regular updates, the hardware is more expensive, it is less privacy sensitive, and Bluetooth takes a much large toll on battery usage. For all these reasons, and because nearly all modern smartphones have NFC, True Mileage is focused on their patent pending NFC approach.

Will Hacking Affect True Mileage?

For the reasons of white-collar crime such as hacking, the device will not have much personal information. The most sensitive information on the device is the VIN number, and this is not very sensitive since anyone can read it right off a parked car. There is no storing of any private information about the customer on the device. So there are not really any privacy concerns regarding the risk of having a device stolen. In terms of having the data intercepted, this is also considered low risk. There is just not much information available on the device that a hacker would later use in white-collar crime. The only thing someone would be able to get from the device is the VIN, how many miles someone has driven, the time of day when driving, the hard braking information, fuel efficiency, vehicles error codes, etc.

Warranty

Some vehicles have warranties that have rules preventing anything being added or modified. True Mileage devices are not expected to effect warranty for leases. The True Mileage device is a very passive, meaning it is not trying to go in and interact with the car's computer, it is really more for receiving information that is readily available and just summarizing it.

True Mileage and the Commercial Motor Vehicle

All the benefits for private passenger cars for reduced insurance rates could certainly apply to commercial drivers. For the private cars, the device is on the privacy sensitive side just sending a summary when the user taps. Some in the commercial industry might want more information including real-time location data. This sometimes leads that industry into buying more expensive devices to get all that extra information. That is not what True Mileage is developing currently, but if there are companies that want periodic summary level data, then True Mileage may be a really good solution for them at a much lower cost.

True Mileage Compared to OnStar's Device and Progressive's Device

Some customers paying for OnStar's service on General Motors' vehicles can opt in to have their OnStar reported mileage sent to their insurance company. As result, insurance companies are giving 50% to 55% maximum discounts. True Mileage devices are designed to be a solution for a wider variety of vehicles, at a lower cost. On top of mileage data, the True Mileage device will be able to provide insurance companies more information about what time of day people are driving and how much they are hard braking, which may lead to even larger discount for many drivers.

Progressive is the main insurance company working with this kind of driving data for insurance rating. About 1.5 million drivers have signed up for their program. The driver gets a device that plugs into their car and the data collected is used to calculate mileage, time of day, and hard braking counts. Progressive's technology is relatively expensive which means they can only afford to do six months of verification leading to max discounts of just 30% since they cannot be sure how people will drive in the future after that test period. Some customers are concerned about the Progressive devices because every day they transmit second-by-second speed data and can be used to triangulate a driver's location. The True Mileage devices do not send speed data and they will be about half the cost of the current Progressive devices over time which opens the door to on-going verification and the potential for discounts that are twice as big.

When do True Mileage Devices Come Out?

Numerous executives at major US personal auto insurance companies have requested and received prototype True Mileage devices to test out in their own vehicles to see how the ground breaking approach works. Once a list of insurance companies that accept True Mileage device data is available, the list will be released to the public. This will be available in a couple years when the insurer agreements are finalized, devices are fully tested, and high volume production and support are all in place.

15

Interview with HealthIT. gov, 16 December 2013

The future of healthcare can currently be described to be going in a completely new direction. One reason is the current Healthcare.gov website and Affordable Healthcare Act also known as Obamacare. President Barack Obama's vision and legacy may all come down to this one program. The Affordable Healthcare Act is still a work in progress.

The most positive point of view of the future possibilities of the Affordable Act is that it is the beginning of a new way the health insurance companies will be regulated. This new management of health insurance is estimated by the president to be better in the long run for the citizens of the United States.

www.whitehouse.gov. Public Domain.

One change in the new plan is modifying the previous system to provide more health insurance. Health insurance companies have been making more money off of prescriptions, medical fees, and insurance claims, than most businesses. At the same time there have been many claims denied, and the system has been repeatedly been proven to have a dark and self-destructive side. Claims were rejected, and as a result people died. The insurance companies that had claimed to be in charge of everyone's health were covertly able to cheat the citizens of the United States, failing to save lives. Health insurance did not get held accountable when they rejected a claim or denied coverage and someone died. Some people could have been saved with a single visit to a doctor in order to prescribe them prescription medicine for something like a heart condition that would thin the blood and reduce cholesterol. Heart conditions are the number one killer of citizens in the United States but the medicine requires a prescription through a doctor's authorization. Because of this the insurance company's time ran out. The insurance company's ability to find a solution to stay in business is now a reality.

The future of healthcare may be an increase in more healthcare technologies that can serve more patients in an affordable way for the insurance company and the patient. One direction that the technology has been used so far is to try to manage the record keeping process better. The ability to use computers to save data and also be able to access it can make the increase of patients for healthcare providers more manageable.

Another area of technology that has been mentioned in many news stories in the past few years is the use of the smartphone. The smartphone or medical devices that can transmit and communicate the status of one's health back and forth between doctors and patients could be the answer to many of the costs and expenses of running a hospital and health insurance company. The ability to find the right technology to monitor the different health conditions in a safe way can make the Affordable Healthcare Act a success. This is a positive and optimistic way to look at the current situation and there may be many unknowns that may arise to block and prevent this as being a solution.

At the same time, there have never been more people using smartphones and the demand for health insurance companies to change their ways of a heartless denial of coverage is now a reality. The health insurance companies that have run their business without the use of good ethics, where they would refuse some healthcare are now going to have to adapt by using some new technologies to lower costs. Or they can give up and file for bankruptcy, getting out of the business. The chance that they give up and leave one of the biggest industries in one of the biggest economies of the world is low. Therefore these changes will be occurring in each. In addition, once there have been improvements to the system on the insurance end on how to make a profit and follow the guidelines in providing healthcare, more improvements and investments can correct and fix all the details to become perfection.

There is also so much that a smartphone application about healthcare and a medical device can do. Health insurance companies are going to have a budget based on what this new healthcare law is going to allow. One of the main things they can do is to use the government's example of increasing the patient's ability to have more access to their records and use a different system to request and receive healthcare, through mobile applications, Internet, home visits, and other options. A doctor's examine or visit online can help reduce costs. This can be done with a user friendly website. Information and data can be uploaded to doctors and from the doctors to patients.

The elimination of a big bulky hospital, costing millions for taxes and utilities in order to get some flu medication or pain killers is a management option. There are many health issues that do not require that hospital room visit in person. If a medical device can take a person's vitals, for example his or her heart rate, transmitting data back to a doctor's office. There can be more reporting done this way and the closer monitoring of symptoms and data.

The vision of the elimination of waste while increasing the efficiency of health insurance and doctors is something the United States should hope is the outcome of the Affordable Healthcare Act. This hope is not that simple with the critics. There are also some issues with the transparency the program provides but hopefully things will get updated and improved over the next few months and years, making the healthcare system in the United States the cutting edge in the global world of health. The global outlook on this system then being shared and used worldwide can also be something to anticipate. When doctors are able to communicate and upload and send data that can eliminate a doctor's visit in person, patients and doctors can be separated by borders and even oceans. The Affordable Healthcare Act should use the smartphone's capabilities, remote healthcare devices that are wireless or able to transmit data online, and find a new way to manage in the United States as a model for the world.

One separate healthcare program that has possibly empowered some patients that rely on the federal government is the Office of Consumer eHealth. This office's program can be the hint that the public needs to know more about in order to see the possibility of the Affordable Healthcare Act. When there is more access from the patient's point of view and in a more mobile setting, healthcare will be more reliable and accessible. The following mentions the government's program to develop some areas of convenience and access but also includes the needed information about how this program will be safe for the user.

The Public Relations officer describes the office as "The Office of Consumer eHealth is one part of the HHS Office of the National Coordinator for Health Information Technology. Under our mission, we are working to help doctors and other healthcare providers adopt electronic health records that can help them improve and better coordinate the care they provide to their patients. As a federal agency we have regulatory authority to help ensure that those EHRs can help providers meet the federal requirements needed to get incentive payments and we create standards for those EHRs— including making sure they are able to be interoperable (which means that information can be shared between healthcare providers and then *used* by the receiver—the doctor or hospital, for example). When Congress created the Office of the National Coordinator for Health IT (ONC), it tasked us with the role of informing and educating the public (patients, caregivers, healthcare providers) about the use of health information technology more generally. We launched www.HealthIT.gov with that role in mind, and, working with the Veteran's Administration, we have been working to expand the use of the Blue Button."

The Blue Button initiative is a public-private initiative between the healthcare industry and the federal government to empower patients with their healthcare information in an electronic format. Blue Button was initially developed through collaboration between the VA and the Center for Medicare & Medicaid Services (CMS). In August 2010, President Obama announced that veterans would be able to download their personal health information from their My HealtheVet account. Today, over 1.5 million veterans and 50 million Medicaid and Medicare beneficiaries have access to their Blue Button enabled records. Over 500 private-sector companies have already supported the Blue Button initiative by participating in the Blue Button Pledge program. Under this program, companies and organizations voluntarily commit to advance efforts to increase patient access to their own health data to become more engaged and more actively participate in their health and healthcare.

Crash Lane News asked, what is the future of the Office of Consumer eHealth? Are there future programs or new technologies coming out that the public should know about not mentioned yet? Smartphone improvements?

One site mentioned by the HealthIT.gov public relations official stated to investigate upcoming trends at http://healthpopuli.com/. Jane Sarasohn-Kahn writes about new technologies through the lens of patients.

Crash Lane News asked, what is the most threatening type of issue from your office's point of view when using wireless medical devices? And what is the most threatening for travelers that use ehealth devices?

HealthIT states, consumers who use health IT need to protect their health information through encryption and other security tools. ONC has developed tools and information about security of mobile devices for healthcare providers, but much of this information can be used by consumers. That information can be found at http://www.healthit.gov/providers-professionals/your-mobile-device-and-health-information-privacy-and-security.

This website lists some suggestions that can start a plan to have more security when using devices that might have patients' information. This has been a big topic and healthit.gov states, "Physicians, healthcare providers and other healthcare professionals are using smartphones, laptops and tablets in their work. The U.S. Department of Health and Human Services has gathered these tips and information to help you protect and secure health information patients entrust to you when using mobile devices." This is a message to healthcare providers as well as the public introducing the webpage that mentions the government's point of view on how to increase security.

The Department of Health and Human Services also states that they had about thirty days of direct communication with the public about the concerns of the use of mobile devices.

HealthIT.gov also mentions the HIPAA Privacy Rule, "The HIPAA Privacy Rule establishes national standards for giving patients the right to access and request amendment of their protected health information (PHI) as well as requesting restrictions on the use or disclosure of such information. The HIPAA Security Rule establishes a national set of security standards for the confidentiality, integrity, and availability of electronic protected health information. The HIPAA Privacy and Security Rules apply to covered entities. Covered entities include healthcare providers and professionals such as doctors, nurses, psychologists, dentists, and chiropractors. Individuals and businesses that meet the definition of a covered entity and who transmit health information in electronic form in connection with certain transactions must comply with the Rules' requirements to protect the privacy and security of health information, even when using mobile devices."

There are some additional steps recommended that an individual and a healthcare organization should know and take to increase information security.

The website also mentions 11 ways to secure devices and the information. These include the commonly known ways someone can protect the device during use and also when it is connected to the Internet. HealthIT.gov states, "Take Steps to Protect and Secure Information When Using a Mobile Device Whether you use a personally owned mobile device or one provided to you by an entity such as a healthcare organization, system, or medical or private practice, you should understand how to protect health information. Follow these tips to help you secure the health information your patients entrust to you: 1. Install and enable encryption to protect health information stored or sent by mobile devices. 2. Use a password or other use authentication. 3. Install and activate wiping and/ or remote disabling to erase the data on your mobile device if it is lost or stolen. 4. Disable and do not install or use file sharing applications. 5. Install and enable a firewall to block unauthorized access. 6. Install and enable security software to protect against malicious applications, viruses, spyware, and malware-based attacks. 7. Keep your security software up to date. 8. Research mobile applications (apps) before downloading. 9. Maintain physical control of your mobile device. Know where it is at all times to limit the risk of unauthorized use. 10. Use adequate security to send or receive health information over public Wi-Fi networks. 11. Delete all stored health information on your mobile device before discarding it. Mobile Devices: Know the RISKS. Take the STEPS. PROTECT & SECURE Health Information. Find out more at HealthIT.gov/mobiledevices."

In Summary

The HealthIT.gov website is the beginning of a new trend in how healthcare information is accessible and secured by the government's point of view. This view of security is also ongoing in the private health insurance sector and other areas providing systems to collect and protect healthcare data. The future of healthcare has arrived with www.healthcare.gov led by President Barrack Obama. The government provides the information about how to secure and make affordable healthcare a reality. Private healthcare companies can take www.healthIT.gov examples and the information about security to better protect themselves and be able to follow all the privacy and security regulations.

Future patient care in the United States will use an increased amount of technology. This can bring a balance to the additional patients per existing healthcare providers. With the new system, the management needs to include plans for security and meet the requests by the public to raise the public's support. The future looks hopeful for a healthier United States. The additional medical devices that can connect a patient's information constantly or at their choosing from their homes or on a trip can also make healthcare more reliable. Streaming data can also make healthcare more precise. One yearly physical or appointment when suffering an injury or severe illness may not be enough to really track a patient's health. When it comes to moderating care to save lives through computerized devices, data can be used more, saving more lives.

16

AAA Interview with Cynthia Harris of San Francisco Regional Office

AAA offers many services and options for travelers to include: an application for a smartphone, car insurance, a membership package that includes road side service and discounts, and also serves as a travel agency.

One of the latest services is the AAA travel application available on smartphones. Travelers should keep up to date with applications, and this one is worth the membership fee required to unlock it once it is downloaded. The application includes maps, directions, roadside assistance, AAA member deals, car battery quotes, and hotel searches. Each point on the map is able to be clicked and opened for more detailed information to include the phone number, exact address, as well as having the diamond rating award system.

The map is one of the selling points of the application, as it includes useful points of interested for travelers. There is also a money symbol on each that gives customers an AAA discount. Some points of interest include: hotels, dining, entertainment, attractions, events, AAA offices, shopping, gas stations, health, automotive, travel, services, campgrounds, and electric vehicle charging stations. The map is easy to access and one of the more popular features of this application. This map is good to know of because it is marketed for travelers and has the mentioned listings easily available for the best customer experience.

As a travel agency AAA has trips available year round around the United States and the rest of the world. Their travel agency has a good reputation in the tourism industry and is using current technologies like the smartphone to keep their helpful services available to travelers.

Discounts and Benefits

Cynthia Harris mentioned members get AAA discounts for hotel fares. That helps to reduce a fare 10% to 15%. There are benefits for AAA members traveling on their own or with their families, including discounts for entertainment sites, museums, restaurants, and stores. Members have discounts guaranteed from participating vendors. Businesses offering the discounts have been approved by AAA for their quality and for their reliability. Members will also get the satisfaction that you visit a hotel that is approved by AAA. The Diamond rating system is continually being updated.

AAA has Sojours, which is a more specialized traveling experience. It is designed for a certain kind of traveler who wants more adventure, and it is off the beaten track of travel. It is a matter of members investigating what they want to do and the time of year they are going. Aside from the weather there is nothing that is going to be harmful when it comes to the trip itself. The trips do not place travelers in imminent danger.

Winter Traveling

There are things that travelers want to be aware of, such as weather conditions. When a member takes a winter trip, there are some additional things to know. Check the weather app for updates.

Precautions are definitely taken to maintain AAA member safety and security. One current example is the typhoon in the Philippines in November 2013. Big storms and other bad weather conditions happen, and members may need to modify their own travel plans. Travelers needs to know the options available about how to do this when on their own trip, and when traveling with AAA there is travel insurance available.

Travel insurance helps with rescheduling or issues with replacing luggage and is available for all AAA trips. If there is a cruise planned, for instance, and there are major storms in the sea and the crew sees it has to be postponed, then it is. Safety is the number one concern. Bad weather conditions occur all over the world. You may plan a trip, and maybe there is something that does not allow you to go on that trip. There is always a risk when you travel. There is always a risk when you drive through San

Francisco for work. There is always a risk when you go on a hike. Risk is inevitable, but finding the right conditions to do certain things can increase the overall safety.

Members have to be very informed. It is recommended to be prepared to make changes to a trip to stay safe. Normally there are travel seasons for different areas. Be smart about the way you travel and make smart decisions. Back yourself up with insurance. Talk to qualified people like AAA travel agents who can give background information.

Road Trip Suggestions

Everyone is advised to take their cell phones with them. Have contact phone numbers, emergency numbers, also GPS. If a member is traveling with their family on a road trip, AAA recommends you let people know exactly when you were planning on arriving at the next destination. Let someone know what time you left and what route you are taking. In the worst case scenario that a member does not arrive at the mentioned time, action can be taken. The people who know of the travel plans can immediately alert the authorities, if the travelers on the trip do not show up at their destination. This is a good backup plan to have in place.

Members should have a cell phone with them at all times during the trip. Have a charging device to recharge the cell phone. Be prepared when driving in the winter months. Have water, flashlights, flashers, and tools like a shovel. Some tools are very handy and a shovel can help dig a tire out of ice, snow, and mud holes.

We advise drivers and travelers to stay on the main roads. Do not take back roads off the beaten track to get away from traffic. You need to be safe when you travel. As an individual you need to be responsible for yourself, your vehicle, and your passengers. Driving is a privilege; it is not a right.

And be prepared. Have chains for your tires if you are driving in the snow. Travel with some additional emergency supplies such as food and blankets. For drivers the main thing is to maintain a full tank of gas. When you get down to half a tank, fill it up again. Make sure your phone is charged when making a stop at a gas station. Make sure everyone in your vehicle is safe. All these mentioned safety suggestions are what you need to do for a road trip.

AAA does advise people to have the AAA road service number on their cell phones so they can call immediately should they need road service. And listen to the radio for weather updates. If you are driving to Tahoe and there is a huge storm coming in, then it is probably best that you should wait for it to subside. Try not to drive at night, but wait for the early morning. Avoid heavy traffic if possible. Be cautious and watch the weather reports. If you need to delay your trip, so be it. Safety is the number one thing AAA wants drivers and travelers to be aware of.

Tour Group Accountability

On an AAA tour people and their belongings are safe. AAA tours are more controlled because members are traveling with a tour guide. The tour guide makes sure everyone on the tour knows exactly where they are staying. Tour members have itineraries and the trip is very efficient.

The itinerary helps in tracking the members if someone gets separated. Once on the tour the members get very specific information from the tour guide, who is responsible for making sure that everyone is very well informed, and knows exactly what the itinerary is. All members on the tour will have the needed information of where they are, what they are going to do, and where they are going to.

An article named "National Treasures" written by Bruce Newman was published in the *VIA* November/December 2013 edition. The website for AAA online about possible trips like this is available at www.aaa.com/via.

In conclusion Cynthia Harris at AAA mentioned that AAA has freelance writers who put these stories together regarding trips, and that Washington D.C. is a popular destination for travelers because it is the nation's capitol. This "National Treasures" story is a short list of places to go see in Washington D.C. including the following:

1. Abraham's Top Hat at the National Museum of American History (americanhistory.si.edu).
2. Preamble at the Smithsonian Art Museum (Americanart.si.edu).

3. Rosa Parks Statue at the Nation's Capitol (visitthecapitol.gov).
4. East Building, at the National Gallery of Art (nga.gov).
5. Native American Food, at the National Museum of the Native American Indian (mitsitamcafe.com).
6. Orchid Room, at the U.S. Botanic Garden (www.usbg.gov).
7. Chiseled Words, at the Martin Luther King Jr. Memorial (nps.gov/mlkm).

The seven places mentioned above include some history, art, and sightseeing at the national level. There are many more interesting stories mentioned.

17

About the Department of State and Federal Communications Commission Information for Travelers

(The information in the below report is public domain and available online)

The Department of State and Travel

There is a huge government resource about traveling available to the public. The information includes everything from traveling information in another country like a country's laws, passport information, and how to sign up and enroll in a program that lets the Department of State know you are going to another country. Most of the information the Department of the State makes available is available online at the link below.

The reality that there are global security issues related to travel that are mentioned in *Crash Lane News* makes knowing about the Department of State very important. It is also a free source of information online that can help travel safe provided by the government as opposed to buying something.

The following is available online at http://travel.state.gov.

Sign up for the Smart Traveler Enrollment Program so the State Department can better assist you in an emergency: Let us know your travel plans through the Smart Traveler Enrollment Program, a free online service at https://travelregistration.state.gov. This will help us contact you if there is a family emergency in the United States, or if there is a crisis where you are traveling. In accordance with the Privacy Act, information on your welfare and whereabouts will not be released to others without your express authorization.

Sign passport, and fill in the emergency information: Make sure you have a signed, valid passport and a visa if required, and fill in the emergency information page of your passport.

Leave copies of itinerary and passport data page: Leave copies of your itinerary, passport data page, and visas with family or friends, so you can be contacted in case of an emergency.

Check your overseas medical insurance coverage: Ask your medical insurance company if your policy applies overseas, and if it covers emergency expenses such as medical evacuation. If it does not, consider supplemental insurance.

Familiarize yourself with local conditions and laws: While in a foreign country, you are subject to its laws. The State Department web site at http:// travel.state.gov/travel/cis_pa_tw/cis/cis_1765.html has useful safety and other information about the countries you will visit.

Take precautions to avoid being a target of crime: To avoid being a target of crime, do not wear conspicuous clothing or jewelry and do not carry excessive amounts of money. Also, do not leave unattended luggage in public areas and do not accept packages from strangers.

Contact us in an emergency: Consular personnel at U.S. Embassies and Consulates abroad and in the United States are available 24 hours a day, 7 days a week, to provide emergency assistance to U.S. citizens. Contact information for U.S. Embassies and Consulates appears on the Bureau of Consular Affairs website at http://travel.state.gov. Also note that the Office of Overseas Citizen Services in the State Department's Bureau of Consular Affairs may be reached for assistance with emergencies at 1-888-407-4747, if calling from the United States or Canada, or 202-501-4444, if calling from overseas.

Required Travel Documents and Other Important Documentation

Passport Requirements and How to Apply for a Passport

A passport is an internationally recognized travel document that verifies the identity and nationality of the bearer. Only the U.S. Department of State and U.S. Embassies and Consulates have the authority to grant, issue or verify U.S. passports. For travel overseas and to facilitate reentry into the United States, a valid U.S. passport is the best documentation available.

A valid passport is required to enter and leave most foreign countries. Some countries may allow you to enter with only a birth certificate, or with a birth certificate and a driver's license. **Note, however, that rules established under the U.S. Intelligence Reform and Terrorism Prevention Act of 2004, require that all persons, including U.S. citizens, traveling by air, must present a valid passport to reenter the United States.**

If you are traveling by **land or sea**, make certain that you can return to the United States with the proof of citizenship that you take with you. U.S. regulations require that you document **both** your U.S. citizenship and your identity when you reenter the United States. For more information about U.S. passport requirements, see http://www.travel.state.gov/travel/cbpmc/cbpmc_2223.html.

Some countries require that a traveler's U.S. passport be valid at least six months or longer beyond the dates of the trip. In addition, with the number of international child custody cases on the rise, several countries have instituted passport requirements to help prevent child abductions. (Mexican law, for example, requires a child traveling alone, or with only one parent, or in someone else's custody, to carry written, notarized consent from the absent parent or parents if the child is not in possession of a U.S. passport.) Contact the embassy of the foreign destination for more information. A listing of foreign embassies and consulates in the U.S. is available on the Department of State's website at http://www.state.gov/s/cpr/rls/dpl/32122.htm. Foreign embassy and consulate contact information can also be found on the Country Specific Information for each country.

How to Apply for a U.S. Passport

Apply for your passport several months before your planned trip, and, if you will need visas from foreign embassies, allow even more time. Even if you don't have specific travel plans, but have family living abroad or are waiting to find a bargain trip, it is a good idea to apply as early as possible. Information about applying for a U.S. passport may be found at http://www.travel.state.gov/passport/passport_1738.html.

If You Need to Obtain a New Passport While Abroad

For information on obtaining a new passport if yours is lost or stolen abroad, see "How to Get Your Passport Replaced" below, under "Emergencies: Consular Assistance and Crises Abroad." Also visit the Department of State website at http://www.travel.state.gov/passport/lost/lost_848.html. Additional information is available at http://travel.state.gov/travel/tips/emergencies/emergencies_1197.html.

Federal Communications Commission

Travelers and the FCC Cyber Security Tips for International Travelers

The public should know about some of the government's suggestions about how to secure themselves when traveling overseas and to another country. One government agency that has put some suggestions together is the FCC. This is something to be aware of and can help a traveler be safer. Note checking a government's travel suggestions once a year could help keep what is out there currently. Things change every year and even the information available on the Internet and from the government is dated, so checking on updates can help also.

The below information is available at the link http://www.fcc.gov/guides/cybersecurity-tips-international-travelers.

Cybersecurity Tips for International Travelers

Be Aware

1. When traveling internationally, in addition to taking your passport, *take responsibility for your cybersecurity.*
2. Your information and communications—and the devices that contain and transmit them —are as much a part of you as the valuables in your suitcase. The more you do to protect yourself, the more secure your information and devices likely will be.
3. While in a foreign country, you are subject to its laws. Laws and policies regarding online security and privacy may be different in other countries than in the United States. If you would like to become familiar with other laws, the State Department website contains <u>safety information for every country</u> in the world, <u>information regarding treaties and policies</u>, and <u>general international travel tips</u>.
4. Protect yourself by leaving at home any electronic equipment you don't need during your travel.

Before You Go

5. If you take it, protect it:

   - Back up your electronic files
   - Remove sensitive data
   - Install strong passwords
   - Ensure antivirus software is up-to-date

While Traveling

6. Be vigilant about possession and use of your equipment and information. Don't assume it's safe. Culprits are visible and invisible.

- Keep your eyes on your electronics. Keep your devices with you in airports, hotels, and restaurants, etc.
- Be aware of your surroundings. *Other* eyes can take information from you by looking at your devices.
- Consider using a privacy screen on your laptop.

7. Your mobile phone and other electronic devices may be vulnerable to malware because they will connect with local networks abroad. They also may identify your personal location information to others.

8. Electronic communications, equipment, and services (*e.g.*, phones, computers and fax machines) in public places such as Internet cafes, coffee shops, book stores, travel agencies, clinics, libraries, airports, and hotels may be vulnerable. You may choose not to use these services at all, or avoid using them for sensitive communications.

9. Don't use the same passwords or PIN numbers abroad that you use in the United States. For example, if the hotel safety deposit box requires a PIN number, use a unique one.

Upon Return Home

10. Electronics and devices used or obtained abroad can be compromised. Consider safety measures such as changing passwords for your laptop or smartphone.

Additional Cybersecurity Resources

- Department of Homeland Security, Computer Emergency Readiness Team Tips
- FCC Privacy and Online Security Tips

For More Information

You can also contact the FCC's Consumer Center for more information about cybersecurity or other communications issues by calling 1-888-CALL-FCC

(1-888-225-5322) voice; 1-888-TELL-FCC (1-888-835-5322) TTY; 1-866-418-0232 fax; or writing to:

Federal Communications Commission
Consumer & Governmental Affairs Bureau
Consumer Inquiries and Complaints Division
445 12th Street, SW
Washington, D.C. 20554.

18

A Brief Look at James Michener's Popularity Affecting Travel

How Books of Fiction Affect Travel

This is a section about how fictional books can impact the safety of travel. This impact occurs as a result of someone not taking the book to be a work of fiction. Some people take fictional stories literally while going on a trip, expecting to see or be in an area that they had read about. There are many things that can occur as a result of someone trying to travel and live their life based on something that is considered not to be real, and some resulting issues can affect their safety. Because of a fictional story, the local area where they plan to take their trip can also become affected with an increase in tourism revenue or possibly other consequences of an increase of traffic in the area. For the most part, this is not a bad thing but there are also some critics of fictional books that may make the case that it negatively impacted an area. When something negative happens it is always unfortunate. But at the same time with all the negative things that can occur as the result of the weather and other disasters, an increase in tourism cannot pose that much of a risk. Much of Michener's work is also written in an American educator's point of view of the world. This can help explain the real intent of why he decided to write about the different exotic locations he had covered in the South Pacific, Asia, Europe, Israel, North America, South America, the Caribbean, and many other locations.

Also, the rate of tourism increasing as a result of someone reading a book could be low considering the reading public is a more sedentary part of the population, meaning that they might not be constantly traveling. This means that the reading public may not be the same kind of people going to travel based off of what they read. Most people who do travel at a high rate have not gone everywhere they read about. These travelers found a few places they liked for themselves or for business and just went more frequently, instead of randomly traveling the world based on everything they read. There is also a very small amount of the population that has tried to travel to everyplace. It can occur more as a result of the kind of person they are more than the kind of books they read. Note there are many reasons why there is tourism and a book can influence it, but there are many other variables which need to be remembered.

Also, some people were planning on a trip based on a piece of literature they read. Popular culture like literature, books, magazines, movies, television shows, sometimes motivated the public to go on a trip. These people were also already going somewhere and the fact there was something well known from a popular book guided them to that specific area. That example is possibly the most common way of how fictional writing may sometimes affect the rate of tourism in an area.

Some of Michener's books had been banned by some of the countries that they were about or took place in. This can affect travel for Americans when an American author's books had become unpopular for another country's government. When this occurs common sense should be used to try to avoid a trip there, or if there, to avoid praising an author where a work was banned. A few of Michener's books were banned by the governments where the books took place, including *Iberia, Poland, The Covenant*, and *The Caribbean*. The reversal of the banning of the books later occurred. This reauthorizing of the Michener books may have increased the author's popularity and America's popularity at that time. There may have also been more of his books that were banned as well, then later had the ban lifted.

Michener's book titled *Caravans* may have been banned in parts of Afghanistan with anti-U.S. hostilities, for example. That can be a serious thing for Americans that were there as a result of reading the book or having a copy of the book in their possession found by someone enforcing the ban.

Some current authors make references to Michener's work in their own writing. Some works of nonfiction have mentioned James Michener's work about *Caravan*s to include that of Retired U.S. Army General Stanley McChrystal's *My Share of the Task*, and published by Penguin in 2013. The fact that a general like McChrystal had read Michener, and knew of his work through his command of the U.S. Army in Iraq and then Afghanistan exists. Michener was well known and very influential to all who traveled then and even now. Michener brought some of the American storytelling to a place where travelers would go and where some in the military would live overseas. Even though his books were written decades before, they still were believed by some to be current to the present. Their style and information brought some Western logic to a chaotic situation that may occur in a foreign land. The result was that members in the U.S. military as high ranking as a general relied on fiction, read fiction, and hopefully did not make command decisions based on fiction. Some times a work of fiction has some truths to it, helping a reader later describe their own experience and life lessons about Afghanistan. *Caravans* may have this existing effect on those that travel to Afghanistan because it also is written in a more simplistic reality writing type of style. The simple writing of *Caravans* is able to let the reader fill in the blanks but while also mentioning some violent images and acts that have also been described as still occurring in the region. Compared to Michener's other books, *Caravans* is a faster and simpler story giving a fast-paced experience for the mind and eyes, which is timeless for a reader.

Many respect General McChrystal for his accomplishments while serving in the Armed Forces. Many real experiences are mentioned in his book and life story about his work in *My Share of the Task*. To this day he is considered and respected as one of the top leaders for the United States that fought in the Global War on Terrorism in a time of war, and as a Ranger and a Member of the Special Forces. He appears legendary to many enlisted soldiers and officers.

There is also always a critical side and view of the use of referring to some other books and pieces of literature to explain one's own life. The unfortunate thing is the meaning of when someone as high ranking as a general acknowledges a work of historical fiction. An out-of-date reference to *Caravans* used in real world decision making and describing a country like Afghanistan can also mislead a reader. The general does not mention that it affected his decision making, which is a good thing and a relief. The fact that a work of fiction is used to describe a place can mislead some audiences no matter who they are. Some readers are unable to understand the use of real experiences converted into entertainment. A more appealing version to entertain may not always include the full story of the people, way of life, and an entire country.

Caravans' romantic scenes and adventure sequences may have some truths to them, but the exaggeration of something to sell a book is sometimes forgotten about by the audience. Exaggeration is also forgotten to be mentioned by the general, but this is also possibly something he thought about and knew reasoning why he included it. *Caravans* does not have the typical happy Hollywood style ending, which is also why this book was used by McChrystal.

This can sometimes be worse than having someone that is unable to distinguish the difference between reality and a hallucination. It is a very complicated discussion, and mentioned by the general for that reason. A note for travelers is that a book about the life of a leader like a general is a good thing to add to one's existing knowledge. This also goes for the work of Michener in that there is some historical value, while remember Michener's writing were his career and money making enterprises. That style of writing is different from a memoir written from a military leader's point of view. The general's book has more reality and nonfiction than almost all of James Michener's books while readers may tend to believe and read Michener's books more. That is just how an audience is.

James Michener is summarized by the readers of his books to be a historical fiction writer, while some believe them to be the equivalent to a history or documentary. Fiction means the story did not occur exactly as written and things were added. This definition can be described as being a work of an author that writes about something that did not occur. It should also be known that the details and the history that are used to describe fiction include real events and real people, making the details more believable. With real details, fiction is not an attempt to be a real story. For that reason, the category of "historical fiction" has been used by some of Michener's audience to describe his work. The reason that Michener focused on historical fiction was that it can be easier for an author to make the needed edits and additions into a story, if considered fiction. Something convenient fiction tends to avoid is the issues of stolen ideas, or libel and slander. Fiction is still very popular in the United States as a result of influential authors like James Michener. At that time instead of Facebook, Twitter, LinkedIn, Gmail, Yahoo, email, or other online activities, people were reading. Some say that the Ebook has increased access to more books to more people than ever as well, but the other activities may have surpassed reading as the main escape and form of entertainment.

Because there was more reading he became famous as the result of the awards received for his first book, the *Tales of the South Pacific.* As an author, he focused on the development of the story in a different setting. The way he wrote was not to necessarily take the reader on a trip because each book was set in a different particular area. In that area, the story would be told and there could be some traveling in an area. As a writer, he tried to show some control as well to plot points into graphics that would summarize the different areas the story would take place. The reader would know what region and topic the book would take place in upfront for many of his stories. This helped advertise the book. Many of his books' titles were of the area the story occurred. The titles also include some of the subject matter that would be included in the book. Michener's books were not focused on how someone should travel. They are presented through the point of view of a fictional character. His style of writing allows the outside member of the audience to see what these characters see. Some places and events are a real part of history and the present, but it does not mean the entire book is meant to be read as happening. Michener seems like nonfiction and very real. But it is really fiction, and a recreation for entertainment.

It seems like his writing process begins based off the photos, videos, history, and newspaper stories, that one would obtain when living in an area for a certain amount of time. Living in different locations is what Michener did. The writing process could also be stated by the reader as the result of him taking vacations or being on a business trip to different locations, inspiring a fictional book. That is also exactly how some of his books developed and they ended up having the subject matter of some of the projects and jobs he had through his life placed inside his books. The first example of this is in *Tales of the South Pacific* where Michener was able to use his experience as an officer in the Navy to develop a story. It had turned out to be a popular book because of the timing of the book being released during World War II. This war affected the entire United States, so it had a huge audience for those that served overseas and for those that remained in the states.

The books by James Michener include: *Tales of the South Pacific, The Fires of Spring, Return to Paradise, The Voice of Asia, The Bridges of Toko-Ri, Sayonara, The Floating World, The Bridge at Andau, Hawaii, Report of the County Chairman, Caravans, Iberia, Presidential Lottery, The Quality of Life, Kent State: What Happened and Why, The Drifters, A Michener Miscellany:1950-1970, Centennial, Sports in America, Chesapeake, The Covenant, Space, Poland, Texas, Legacy, Alaska, Journey, Caribbean, The Eagle and the Raven, Pilgrimage, The Novel, The World Is My Home: A Memoir, James A. Michener's Writer's Handbook, Mexico, Creatures of the Kingdom, Recessional, Miracle in Seville, This Noble Land: My Vision for America, Rascals in Paradise,* and *Six Days in Havana.*

A reader who can read all the above books would be more knowledgeable about fictional stories for the most part. It is also said that they may be able to write a thesis at the college level about his work because it is so extensive and covers so much. Many readers also get so into the books they have taken them to be literal works of nonfiction, when there are only a few that are about literal subjects. One, for example, is his memoir that may include some nonfiction accounts of his life titled *The World Is My Home: A Memoir.* This is one of the few nonfiction works by James Michener, where most of his other books are in fact fiction. Overall his books of fiction and nonfiction have inspired many authors to write stories about far away destinations similar to his work. Some are better than others, but there seem to be some similarities seen in popular culture that can be a reminder of James Michener's influence.

The popularity of James Michener's books continues on. Many of his books are still present where new print editions of his books are sold. *Hawaii* seems to be one of the most commonly advertised books. There are also some names borrowed from his books that are used in businesses. For example, Bali Hai, was also used in his book *Space* as the bar /hotel where the astronauts met and resided in Florida, when there were launches and training. Unrelated to the use of the name Bali Hai, in *Space* one of the lead characters who was an astronaut died in a car accident. The choice to title the book *Space* and not *Crash* is obvious in readers' appeal. The popular culture is known and reused about the Michener's books and their contents. Bali Hai is also the name of a popular golf course in Las Vegas, next to the *Welcome to Las Vegas* sign; on Las Vegas Blvd. Michener's real life experiences were transformed into fiction and are still used by businesses to this day to help advertise. The golf course's appearance has a Pacific Island look and style on the outside and in. The owner of this golf club is a famous icon of Nevada named Billy Walters. Everyone knows him through his businesses in Nevada.

The different settings of Michener's stories and the chosen exotic locations combined together to the build on the popularity of the author and the contents of his work. There are many authors who may have some more current information about exotic destinations in faraway lands, but James Michener can be considered the twentieth century's most famous author regarding historical fiction books.

Some advice for those who enjoy the work of fiction and later travel based on it in an attempt to live out the destination, try to be sensible. Check the news, government warnings, and always know about the weather. With all the fantasies and the excitement that popular destinations may offer, be cautious to what may be a risk and threat. It is important to have fun traveling and have a good time. With that, understand the entire cycle of how tourism works to best protect yourself on the trip.

Special Thanks

Thank you to those that helped support this book's inspiration, namely, the U.S. citizens and the U.S. government. The college degree was paid in part by the Montgomery GI Bill and for that reason a special thanks goes to the USA and the U.S. military. With the challenges facing the members in the military some of the more random and less memorable lower ranking personnel have some amazing stories of survival. Many of these individuals stories are never mentioned in any form of public news reaching the U.S. public, due to the U.S. military personnel's location in remote location during a weather event overseas. All events are preventable but most go unreported. These lead to other problems of internal management, leaving these same soldiers behind once again until the system decides to end their service with honorable discharges, medical discharges, and the unfortunate other than honorable discharges. Thank you to all who helped, whether you're good, bad, or ugly.

A special thanks goes to the University of Phoenix online, making education more accessible and being able to accept the GI Bill. Not all trade schools, craft schools, and even some colleges allow the GI Bill to be easily applied. Without the GI Bill and the University of Phoenix, the degree used as the outline of content would not be as developed as it was. Educators are real heroes that do go unnoticed many times in the news and in public. Their places in the United States have not been seen as being the ones that can help start others search for the solution to preventable problems.

Thanks for the material provided from U.S. citizens and their real-life experiences. These experiences were used as an example of what security solutions can be in the future. Thank you to the readers that believe there is a need for change, starting the process to make travel more secure. Thanks to those who see this as a self-help book and use it to be safe travelers, positively affecting travel in the United States.

A special thanks for the editing by Author House, *Crash Lane News Editing Department,* and the Editorial Freelancers Association at the-efa.org.

Thank you to those who helped with publishing at Author House, authorhouse.com, and *Crash Lane News Publishing*.

A special thanks for the advertising to the *Crash Lane News Public Relations Office*, www.*CrashLaneNews*.com, GODADDY.com, Google Adwords, Twitter, Facebook, LinkedIn, and the Book Expo of America, www.bookexpoamerica.com, Author Hub table #15, and the BookCon. An additional thanks goes to VistaPrint.com for low prices on promotional items such as pens and business cards.

My last thanks goes to those that gave an interview in exchange for free advertising. Thank you to the AAA; the Auto Club; the National Weather Service in Massachusetts, North Carolina, Georgia, Louisiana, Kansas; NOAA, the National Oceanic Atmospheric Administration; Truemileage. com; CTIA-The Wireless Association; HealthIT.gov; and NASA.gov. These interviews helped accumulate the need to have weather awareness more than ever stated before. It also added into the repeated points about the need for weather preparedness solutions for travelers. Many more challenges exist and these interviews lay a plan to correct the preventable problems. They added the information needed to create a comprehensive travel plan that included weather information. Hopefully these interviews can be a good example to the mentioned aimless areas of security that still exist in the United States now and foreseen to exist in the future.

Psalm 139 verse 12

Indeed, the darkness shall not hide from YOU, but the night shines as the day; the darkness and the light are both alike to YOU.

Index